Luminos is the Open Access monograph publishing program
from UC Press. Luminos provides a framework for preserving and
reinvigorating monograph publishing for the future and increases
the reach and visibility of important scholarly work. Titles published
in the UC Press Luminos model are published with the same high
standards for selection, peer review, production, and marketing as
those in our traditional program. www.luminosoa.org

Dangerous Love

Dangerous Love

*Sex Work, Drug Use, and the Pursuit of Intimacy
in Tijuana, Mexico*

Jennifer Leigh Syvertsen

UNIVERSITY OF CALIFORNIA PRESS

University of California Press
Oakland, California

Suggested citation: Syvertsen, J. L. *Dangerous Love: Sex Work, Drug Use,
and the Pursuit of Intimacy in Tijuana, Mexico*. Oakland: University of
California Press, 2022. DOI: https://doi.org/10.1525/luminos.133

Library of Congress Cataloging-in-Publication Data

Names: Syvertsen, Jennifer Leigh, 1974- author.
Title: Dangerous love : sex work, drug use, and the pursuit of intimacy in
    Tijuana, Mexico / Jennifer Leigh Syvertsen.
Description: Oakland, California : University of California Press, [2022] |
    Includes bibliographical references and index. | This work is licensed
    under a Creative Commons CC BY-NC-ND license. To view a copy of
    the license, visit https://creativecommons.org/licenses/by-nc-nd/4.0/.
Identifiers: LCCN 2022012650 (print) | LCCN 2022012651 (ebook) |
    ISBN 9780520384392 (paperback) | ISBN 9780520384408 (ebook)
Subjects: LCSH: Prostitutes—Mexico—Tijuana (Baja California)—Social
    conditions.
Classification: LCC HQ151.T54 S98 2022 (print) | LCC HQ151.T54 (ebook) |
    DDC 306.740972/23—dc23/eng/20220425
LC record available at https://lccn.loc.gov/2022012650
LC ebook record available at https://lccn.loc.gov/2022012651

31 30 29 28 27 26 25 24 23 22
10 9 8 7 6 5 4 3 2 1

CONTENTS

LIST OF FIGURES

Writing a book is never a solo endeavor, even when only one person's name is on the cover. I have many people to thank who have helped me over the years to complete this project, some of whom I mention by name here. Thank you goes to the late Jim Inciardi for introducing me to the world of drug research; my most enduring friends and colleagues, including Chrissy Spadola, Janelle Christensen, Carylanna Taylor, and Shana Hughes; my supportive dissertation committee for my degree program at the University of South Florida, including Nancy Romero-Daza, David Himmlegreen, Elizabeth Bird, Bryan Page, and Robin Pollini; the inspiring scholars I met while affiliated with the University of California, San Diego, including Angela Robertson Bazzi and María Lusia Mittal, who accompanied me on fieldwork in Tijuana, and Alicia Vera, Larry Palinkas, Daniel Hernandez, Gustavo Martinez, Gudelia Rangel, Monica Ulibarri, Patricia González-Zúñiga, Jaime Arredondo, Daniela Abramovitz, Irina Artamcnova, Peter Davidson, and Karla Wagner; Steffanie Strathdee for giving me the incredible opportunity to work on Parejas; the staff in the Hillcrest and Tijuana offices who made the work possible; and all the *parejas* who shared their lives with us. Without their trust and friendship, none of this work would have been possible. I have also been inspired by many colleagues and students in my faculty positions at Ohio State University and the University of California, Riverside. At UCR I am especially grateful to João Costa Vargas and the Faculty Commons Health Inequities group, including Juliet McMullin, Kim Yi Dionne, Tanya Nieri, and Dana Simmons, for their advice and feedback. The regular writing groups on campus and virtually and writing retreats at Lake Arrowhead and Indio, California, helped me advance the work. Subsequent writing retreats with Carylanna Taylor in Los Osos, Solana Beach, and San

Clemente, California, helped me finish. Thank you goes to Jane Jones and Tamara Nopper for their editing skills and encouragement. At UC Press I am so grateful to Kate Marshall, Enrique Ochoa-Kaup, and the anonymous reviewers who pushed my work further. Finally, a heartfelt thank you and sincere love and appreciation go to my family: Mom and Dad, Allison, Tom, Katrina, and Nolan, including my chosen family of Ron Chavez, Charlie, Kitty, Chula, Blue, Bonita, Loco, and Freeway, who have brought love and meaning to my life every day.

Sources of support for this project include the University of South Florida Presidential Doctoral Fellowship, funding from the National Institute on Drug Abuse (R01DA027772 and T32DA023356), and the University of California Regents Faculty Development Award.

Given the scope of the Parejas project and the interdisciplinary, collaborative nature of the work, more than thirty publications have come out of the study. This book draws from and adapts a portion of that work in which I led the conceptualization, analysis, and writing. A small part of the introduction about Cindy's death is adapted from Jennifer L. Syvertsen, 2019, "Death Poems for Cindy," *Medicine Anthropology Theory: An Open-Access Journal in the Anthropology of Health, Illness, and Medicine* 6 (2): 120–32. The last section of chapter 1 about couples' conceptions of love is based on Jennifer L. Syvertsen, Angela M. Robertson, Lawrence A. Palinkas, Gudelia M. Rangel, Gustavo Martinez, and Steffanie A. Strathdee, 2013, "Where Sex Ends and Emotions Begin: Love and HIV Risk among Female Sex Workers and Their Non-commercial Partners along the Mexico-U.S. Border," *Culture, Health and Sexuality* 15 (5): 540–54. Portions of chapter 3 were developed from Jennifer L. Syvertsen, Angela Robertson Bazzi, and María Luisa Mittal, 2017, "Hope amidst Horror: Documenting the Effects of the 'War on Drugs' among Female Sex Workers and Their Intimate Partners in Tijuana, Mexico," in "Crafting Synergies between Medical and Visual Anthropologies," special issue, *Medical Anthropology* 36 (6): 566–83. Finally, chapter 4 is a revised and extended version of Jennifer L. Syvertsen and Angela M. Robertson Bazzi, 2015, "Sex Work, Heroin Injection, and HIV Risk in Tijuana: A Love Story," in "The Ethnography of Affect," special issue, *Anthropology of Consciousness* 26 (2): 191–206; the revised vignette that opens the book is also based off this article.

Introduction

Dangerous Safe Havens

It was early in the morning, but Cindy and Beto had already been waiting on the street corner to "connect," or score heroin, for what seemed like hours. They woke up really sick, so Cindy sold her cell phone to get money for the couple's "cure." Referring to both the dose of drugs and act of injecting, curing relieves individuals from the debilitating pain of heroin withdrawal. Both partners felt anxious, achy, and nauseous and sweated profusely from these withdrawal symptoms, locally known as *la malilla*.

The connect involved waiting for a dealer to drive a designated route through their Tijuana neighborhood. For their morning cure Cindy and Beto needed a hundred pesos' worth of black tar heroin (eight to ten US dollars at the time). Once the driver passed by, and they whistled for him to pull over, the couple hurried back inside the fenced family compound where they lived and disappeared into their room. Their single-room structure was a modest but intimate and comfortable space that Beto built himself. His admiration of Cindy was evidenced in the magic-marker messages scrawled all over the walls, including "te amo y te amare por siempre mi flackis" (I love you and I'll always love you) and "Solo tú yo por siempre" (Only you and me forever).

Beto stirred the black tar heroin and water with the butt of a syringe in his makeshift cooker. The sticky consistency of black tar heroin requires heating it into an injectable form. Beto prepped the drugs on the floor in the light of the single window; without electricity and even in the daytime it was difficult to see, and the task required precision. Beto equally divided the liquid into two syringes, one for Cindy and one for himself. The daily ritual began. Cindy sat on the floor and intently searched for a viable vein. Just like Beto, her long-term injecting had left scarring all over her body, and she frequently struggled to cure. Unable to locate a vein, she resorted to injecting herself in her upper left arm. While not as instantaneous as intravenous methods, it provided her with needed relief.

Meanwhile, Beto attempted his own injection. As he struggled, Cindy gasped, "*¡cuídate!*" It was too late. He missed the vein but already injected some drops, which created a burning sensation. He tried again and the same thing happened, but this time it was worse. His arm started to swell, and his skin was besieged with bright red hives. His arm, face, and chest turned red and glistened with sweat. His hand swelled to nearly twice its normal size. This painful *mano de* Popeye (Popeye hand, after the cartoon character) sometimes happened when he missed injections, and the unpleasant symptoms can take hours to subside.

Attentive to his discomfort, Cindy tried to help him inject. Her first attempts caused him to grimace in pain. She apologized for hurting him but persisted because she didn't want to see him suffer. She calmly instructed him to stand still as she carefully scanned his body, eventually settling on his right calf. She kneeled down to tie a tourniquet at his knee, loudly slapped his calf to fully engorge the vein, and then gently and patiently injected the contents of his syringe. Once they were finished, she stood up, and they embraced and kissed. The process was complete. They were cured.

*   *   *

I first met Cindy in the project office of a global public health research study that I helped coordinate in Tijuana's famous Red Light District. Cindy appeared at the door, looking badass with impossibly long, thick black hair and multiple tattoos. She sported dark sunglasses even inside the dimly lit hallway. She had recently qualified for our study of HIV and other sexually transmitted infections among female sex workers and their intimate, noncommercial male partners. She showed up without an appointment and demanded to be interviewed by our project coordinator, who was out of the office. I offered to conduct Cindy's qualitative interview in what turned out to be the first of our many interactions.

Through multiple structured interviews for the project and less formal interactions, I learned that Cindy was far from the tough exterior of her first impression. Her life was complex beyond the category of "female sex worker" or "FSW," the classification many public health studies, including our own, would assigned her.[1] Over time I came to know Cindy as insightful, artistic, and funny, as well as a survivor of sexual abuse and multiple traumas, a high school dropout who loved literature, a nurturer who had always wanted children, a deportee with an arrest record, a sex worker addicted to heroin, and a caring partner deeply in love with Beto.

Her partner of nearly two years, Beto was soft-spoken at first but gradually opened up about what he called the "emotional disease" of addiction that he attributed to his own childhood trauma and hardships. The couple met one day while waiting to connect, and, soon after, Cindy and her dog Paloma moved in with Beto. Although Beto was not fond of living with dogs, he made the exception for Cindy. After all, they finally found in each other a partner who had similar experiences and understood, did not judge, and provided critical forms of emotional and material support. Their relationship was different. Cindy described Beto as the "one she was looking for." Beto said she was "everything" to him.

Although their relationship provided emotional security, physical risk was omnipresent. As the opening vignette illustrates, drug use was a central feature of their relationship. In their mutual addictions they purchased drugs by pooling financial resources through sex work and other illicit means, shared all of their injection equipment, and helped each other through the act of injecting. While intravenous drug use was a form of bodily harm, it was also a shared pratice imbued in love and intimacy, as Cindy and Beto helped each other alleviate suffering during periods of withdrawl. Similarly, Beto knew that Cindy engaged in sex work, but they chose not to use condoms with each other because of their mutual love and trust.

On the outside Cindy and Beto's relationship appears to be full of contradiction as they navigate multiple types of physical harm and social suffering together on a daily basis. On the inside their relationship represents an anchoring presence, providing both partners with a sense of safety and mutual support in conditions of material scarcity and social exclusion. How do couples like Cindy and Beto judge and account for competing risks in ways that maintain their health and make sense for their relationship? And why should those of us working to promote global health equity pay attention to these dynamics of love and risk?

While couples like Cindy and Beto are typically viewed through a clinical gaze focusing on risk and disease avoidance, *Dangerous Love: Sex Work, Drug Use, and the Pursuit of Intimacy in Tijuana, Mexico* posits that a more loving view acknowledging the importance of intimate relationships will better address the ongoing HIV epidemic and its related forms of interlocking oppressions. Linking the political economy of inequalities along the Mexico-US border with emotional lived experience, this book centers on a framework of love to rethink how intimate relationships between female sex workers who inject drugs and their noncommercial male partners fundamentally shape both partner's health and well-being. I conceptualize sex workers' relationships as "dangerous safe havens" in which HIV-risk behaviors, such as unprotected sex and syringe sharing, represent meaningful forms of love and care despite their potential for real physical harm.[2] Attending to the emotional experiences of socially marginalized couples has implications for how we understand the embodied effects of structural oppression and interpret "risk." Furthermore, rethinking sex workers' intimate relationships urges us to reimagine love as a pathway to health equity.

DANGEROUS LOVE

This book is about how individuals struggle to find love and meaning in lives marked by structural violence, social disadvantage, drug addiction, and HIV/AIDS. The relationships between female sex workers and their steady, noncommercial male partners are often assumed to be coercive, anchored in risk, or dismissed as "pimp-prostitute" arrangements by scholarly and lay audiences alike, if these relationships are even acknowledged at all. However, such stereotypes unjustly erase the complexity of lives we imagine to be consumed by social suffering. *Dangerous Love* explores the underappreciated importance of intimacy, care, and love in the relationships of sex workers and their primary partners.

Theoretically, my analysis situates the experiences of sex workers and their intimate partners at the intersection of critical and meaning-centered approaches in medical anthropology to articulate a dynamic, multifaceted conception of love. Critical medical anthropology is concerned with how power relations configure access to material, economic, and social well-being.[3] A core focus is how systems of political and economic organization disproportionately concentrate ill-health among disadvantaged populations while constraining their access to vital health and social services. Critical approaches also critique taken-for-granted power structures as naturalized, instead acknowledging how systems are designed to perpetuate forms of structural violence by limiting life chances and entrenching health inequities.[4] As a complement to these materialist approaches, meaning-centered anthropology is a deeply humanistic practice that focuses on individuals' personal experiences and how they make sense of their world.[5]

In integrating these structural and sentient frameworks, I draw on foundational work in medical anthropology on the "mindful body," in which Nancy Scheper-Hughes and Margaret Lock (1987) call for a theorization of emotions as "an important 'missing link' capable of bridging mind and body, individual, society, and body politic." Conceptualizing love as a "missing link" allows for its examination as an embodied emotional experience shaped by the broader social, material, and political conditions that structure our opportunities. This opens up a space to break down distinctions between personal and political practices of love and put anthropology into conversation with visionary scholars such as bell hooks, Chela Sandoval, Gloria Anzaldúa, June Jordan, and others whose critical feminisms and decolonizing social theories envision the socially transformative power of love to reshape future possibilities.[6]

A foundational contribution of this book is to center on intimate relationships as a way to shift narratives of risk and reimagine global public health research and practice. Much of our knowledge base about sex work and drug use is informed by epidemiological studies, which by design do not have the ability to assess how interpersonal dynamics influence our risk and overall health. As a quantitative science, epidemiology is incredibly useful in identifying statistical health trends at a population level, including the risk factors associated with diseases and health outcomes. With its concern for lived experience, ethnography drills down into the grounded practices of our individual daily lives, including how love, intimacy, and care not only shape our health behaviors but make our lives worth living. Putting these perspectives together lends a powerful mixed-methods approach to better understand and address health concerns. However, global public health campaigns, especially for "high risk" groups such as sex workers and people who use drugs, all too often remain grounded in medicalized notions of risk that fail to attend to the emotional dynamics of loving, intimate relationships. By analyzing epidemiological data in tandem with ethnographic perspectives, my project constructs a fuller picture of what is at stake for socially vulnerable couples, which can better inform our efforts toward achieving health equity.

Dangerous Love thus develops a twofold intervention to consider interpersonal and political forms of love. First and foremost, it focuses on interpersonal love as a way to better understand sex workers' relationships as commitments to collective solidarity and survival in contexts of oppression. I argue that when the state oppresses and society stigmatizes individuals, forging a loving relationship with an intimate partner represents a source of resistance and refuge from an unjust world. Drawing from these couples' experiences, a second intervention of this book urges us to reimagine a political role for love in transforming conditions of injustice in the first place. Reading sex workers' relationships as dangerous safe havens acknowledges the critically important subjective sense of emotional intimacy, love, and care that these relationships engender without glossing over the destructive uncertainties of couples' life circumstances.

Indeed, my invocation of *dangerous safe havens* is intentionally contradictory and jarring to compel us to rethink notions of danger, safety, and love. In public health, danger is sometimes synonymous with risk, but the latter term has become foundational in discourse and practice. *Risk* in the epidemiological sense refers to the probability of a harmful event occurring; this is often assumed to be a scientifically neutral and value-free calculation of an outcome occurring among groups of people. Epidemiological studies consistently demonstrate that sex workers and people who inject drugs are at heightened risk for multiple health and social harms, including HIV/AIDS, hepatitis C virus (HCV), sexually transmitted infections (STIs), fatal drug overdose, violence victimization, stigma and discrimination, and other forms of social death.[7] Importantly, however, risk is also a politically and ideologically loaded construct. Harmful outcomes are not equally distributed among populations, but, rather, political economic factors bear directly on how and among whom risk is circulated to cluster along gendered, racial, and class lines of disadvantage. Ideologically, risk can signal blame and the need for surveillance of those assigned to "risk groups," particularly those who in the individualism of our neoliberal society "fail" to take accountability for their own health. The problem is that not everyone conceptualizes, prioritizes, and weighs risk in the same way or even has the ability to fully control their risk for harmful outcomes.[8] My invocation of *danger* in relation to couples' relationships acknowledges the real potential for harmful outcomes but gestures to a sense of subjectivity in the perception of risk.

In contrast, *safe havens* are socially constructed spaces that support individuals' need for comfort, safety, care, and protection in light of widespread risk. Safe havens help individuals contend with the stress and uncertainty of life, imparting physical and mental health benefits. Couples who engage in sex work and drug use must constantly navigate multiple, competing forms of physical, social, and emotional risk that shape their individual well-being and the stability of their relationship. As the narratives in this book reveal, disadvantaged couples often negotiate a situated rationality favoring the immediate socioemotional security of their relationship over a logically rational avoidance of disease or other physical health threats. The desire for emotional intimacy and social safety that drives the formation of these safe havens is a fundamental but underappreciated part of the human experience that gets erased in wholly negative constructions of risk. Rather than reading these relationships through a lens of "dysfunction" and "codependency," a core argument of this book suggests that we rethink *love* as a creative response to *risk*. Dangerous safe havens allow us to analyze the concrete yet contradictory ways that female sex workers and their noncommercial male partners support, care for, struggle, fail, and love each other in the pursuit of intimacy.

As we will see, Cindy and Beto's everyday lived experience of love and risk is one of structural vulnerability in the margins of Tijuana. This vulnerable positioning in society imposes physical and emotional forms of suffering that become internalized into couples' subjective lived experience. The narratives in this book reveal how couples are impoverished and excluded from educational opportunities and suffer from cumulative trauma and violence victimization. They grew up in loveless families, had early exposure to drugs and alcohol, and contend with social stigma, exclusion, police surveillance, incarceration, and deportation. Given their experiences and limited prospects, they are often forced into informal and illegal activities to survive, including sex work and the informal drug economy. In a symbolic violence of blaming themselves for their situations, their drug use often escalates to cope with extraordinary hardships, which in turn reinforces their vulnerability.

In finding a partner who has suffered similar adversities, dangerous safe havens offer a critical source of love and emotional solidarity. In an otherwise loveless world, forging an intimate bond with a partner offers meaning, hope, and security. To hold onto this hope, "risk behaviors" such as unprotected sex, drug use, syringe sharing, and even sex work are transformed into practices of caretaking that prioritize relationships rather than the physical health threats typically targeted by global public health campaigns. Dangerous safe havens thus protect partners in some ways while simultaneously recasting their exposure to harm in others. As a social construct with public health implications, dangerous safe havens help us to rewrite risk and draw deeper connections between love and health equity.

But a question remains—why *love?* Traditionally, love has been a fringe topic of academic scholarship. Even anthropology, tasked with studying all of the human condition, has a fraught history with the concept of love. Anthropologists have studied and understood love in multiple ways, from theoretical debates about its utility as a concept, to cross-cultural surveys looking for evidence of love across the world, and even to brain scans to examine the biobehavioral and neural underpinnings of love.[9]

I acknowledge a cynicism surrounding love that, if ill-defined, it can mean everything, nothing at all, or even something counterproductive. Many of us in the Western world have been indoctrinated to equate love with romance and a singular, monogamous experience that compels individuals to surrender any sense of rationality toward a pursuit of the elusive "happily ever after." My favorite critique of this view originates from novelist Toni Morrison, who writes that romantic love is one of "the most destructive ideas in the history of human thought" ([1970] 2007, 122). To Morrison idealized versions of romantic love begins in envy and insecurity, leading to a disillusioned fantasy that substitutes romance for genuine acts of love.

Dangerous Love follows in challenging conventional ideas, urging us to think beyond stereotypes to critically evaluate how love can transform relations in contexts of social disadvantage. As a multilayered construct, love is relational: it is a transformative experience, a form of solidarity, and a way of being in the world that has the potential to resist conditions of violence and dispossession. At its core love is imbued with emotional qualities that transform and inspire individuals toward concrete efforts that are greater than the self. The late Black feminist scholar bell hooks conceived of love as a mix of "ingredients" that includes "care, affection, recognition, respect, commitment, and trust, as well as honest and open communication" (2001, 5). Many of these very same ingredients align with couples' own descriptions of love in their relationships, as further elaborated in chapter 1. Accordingly, love is also a verb: it is an active force that can be studied through emotional expressions and concrete actions in relation to the broader sociopolitical conditions that shape its lived experience. As this books shows, love can coexist in conditions of oppression and inequality; such conditions may in fact heighten our awareness of and need for love.

Thus, a second major intervention of this book urges us to reimagine a political role for love in carving a pathway to health equity. A political love could inform our approaches to address the violence, drug use, disease risk, social and economic disadvantages, and related harms that couples navigate on a daily basis. Political love, just like interpersonal love, is relational and affective, oriented toward taking care of our communities by promoting health and well-being for *all* people. Black feminist theologian Keri Day notes that political love brings people together, forging relations among physical bodies into a body politic, as it is "in and through *the body* and its emotions that love and subsequent commitments associated with love become possible" (2016, 110). Such an articulation of love reflects Scheper-Hughes and Lock's (1987) concept of the "mindful body" and call for a theory of emotions linking individual, societal, and political bodies. This conceptual mapping of love can help explain why and how inequalities are produced and mitigated and motivate us to create positive change. In this sense love holds the potential to inform new political agendas, transform programming and policy, and reorder our research priorities toward transformative social and health justice. Put another way, the same principles that shape the possibilities for interpersonal love to improve individual lives can also guide our collective actions to improve the human condition on a broader scale.

Within this conceptual framework, the central questions driving *Dangerous Love* are concerned with how the political creation of social and health inequities along the Mexico-US border profoundly shapes the intimate emotional experiences of sex workers and their partners. Its goal is to explore what it means to love and care in contexts of sex work and drug use and how we might envision new pathways to address health inequities. In the chapters that follow, I ask, Under what sociopolitical conditions do sex workers form intimate relationships? How do couples navigate their relationships when one partner's job is to have sex with other people? How are love and emotional intimacy experienced and enacted by both partners in contexts of disadvantage? How does love shape partners' health "risk" behaviors? And, finally, what can a study of interpersonal love in conditions of oppression teach us about the transformative power of love to break through these very systems of oppression?

PROYECTO PAREJAS

My exploration of love emerges from a somewhat unconventional anthropological academic pathway. This book is based on my experience as a research assistant and postdoctoral fellow as part of a National Institutes of Health (NIH)–funded global public health project from 2009 to 2013 called Proyecto Parejas (the "Couples Project" in Spanish and simply "Parejas" from here forward). As the largest study of its kind anywhere in the world, Parejas was a longitudinal, mixed-methods study of HIV/STI risk among female sex workers and their noncommercial male partners in Tijuana and Ciudad Juárez, Mexico. We followed 214 couples over a two-year time span: every six months couples completed surveys and HIV/STI testing, while a subset of couples at each site also participated in qualitative interviews at enrollment and one year later to contextualize the quantitative and biological data. Collecting multiple forms of data over time and documenting the experiences of *both* partners in these understudied relationships are extraordinarily unique features of this study and thus of my book.

I was involved in all aspects of Parejas from the very first project meeting, including culling together survey questions, drafting protocols, passing documents through multiple regulatory boards, pilot-testing instruments, training staff, acting as a liaison between staff in Mexico and California, and collecting, analyzing, and writing up data. During the project I lived in San Diego and became part of the estimated force of more than eighty thousand daily commuters along the San Ysidro–Tijuana crossing, the busiest of all ports of entry in northern Mexico. This is part of a normal rhythm of life in this region of the world that reflects the intensely interconnected economies of two neighboring countries. I regularly commuted back and forth from the University of California, San Diego, campus in La Jolla, where I was based, to the data-management office in the neighborhood of Hillcrest and to the main Tijuana office and health clinic in the Red Light District for project activities, fieldwork, and team meetings. As such, my fieldwork was a layered experience of traversing geographic, cultural, social, and disciplinary borders, in which I came to appreciate how varying priorities and interests shape the process of knowledge production. My own affective experience of fieldwork in Tijuana inspired my theorizing about *dangerous love*, the emotional effects of living amid extreme inequalities, and how we might differently address conditions of oppression.

In Tijuana my fieldwork took place within the Parejas office to experience the production of data, outside of it to develop a sense of the broader social context, and later within couples' homes to gain insight into their personal lives. I also frequently ventured out with the field team to visit different locations around Tijuana, including health-care settings, drug treatment centers, an AIDS hospice, rural health clinics, and scattered communities throughout the city, usually to locate participants for studies (and sometimes just to eat incredible food out of a truck or small cart). I also helped lead tours of our research sites for visiting researchers and prospective students and their parents before it became "too risky" and we suspended the program due to concerns of violence. Almost daily I witnessed busloads of deportees dropped off at the border with practically nothing.[10] I also frequently visited the squalid Tijuana River Canal, where some of those deportees, as well as migrants and other precariously housed individuals, pass the time. I often witnessed injection drug use there out in the open. Whenever we had supplies, we ran a mobile harm reduction program in the canal to reach those in need of sterile injection equipment. All these experiences provide critical contextual insight into a specific slice of this diverse and culturally rich metropolis of approximately 1.7 million people.

However, I spent the majority of my time in the project office in the middle of the Red Light District. It is located within walking distance or a short cab ride from the border, so within a matter of minutes one is transported to the middle of a concentrated hub of strip clubs, bars, hotels, eateries, street vendors, and streets lined with *paraditas*, or the diverse group of women who carve out their sidewalk space to solicit sex work clients. It is mostly a loud, chaotic sensory overload nearly twenty-four hours a day. It is also the perfect place to host a health clinic and research office for sex workers. The project office was housed on a second floor, which required entrance through a nondescript stairwell door behind a popular *taquero* on the street whose constant chant of *ta-co, ta-CO* is permanently etched in my mind. This corner office had multiple windows overlooking the constant bustle of the street below. It was often unbearably hot in the summer months and so cold in the winter that a few times I observed staff wearing gloves inside. From this vantage point I could see, hear, smell, and sense the frenzy of activities of everyday people on the street below going about their lives, including the sex workers and their partners who traversed this daily reality and enrolled in the Parejas project.

The office represented an important centralized and trusted space for participants from multiple projects to drop by. It was a central point to meet with other researchers and a base point for outreach activities. By spending time in the office both formally and informally collecting data, I had many valuable and often unexpected interactions that fostered significant insight into the social lives of the participants and the project itself. This is where I first met Cindy and conducted her first qualitative interview as part of Parejas to learn about her life experiences and relationship with Beto.

When the couple failed to show up for their Parejas surveys, I accompanied the field team to their home in a nearby neighborhood to bring them into the office. Cindy and Beto were inside their house injecting heroin, so it took a really, really long time for them to get ready to go. At that point I had not yet been inside their house to fully understand what was happening, but I had a sense that one day I would be invited in. Indeed, building my relationship with them through the Parejas project over time proved a valuable anthropological method of gaining trust, which can help produce deeply humanistic data.

Back in the office that day, I administered Cindy's survey. Our epidemiological interaction took nearly four hours because she frequently elaborated on her answers that did not fit neatly into predetermined answer choices. She also needed to take multiple cigarette breaks. Like many public health surveys, ours contained an extensive number of detailed questions, including sociodemographic characteristics, sexual behaviors, drug use, sex work, and measures of relationship quality and conflict. However, I was most struck by what we *did not* capture in the instrument. One of the more positive relationship questions asked, "On a scale of 1–10, how much do you trust your partner?" Without hesitation Cindy answered, "13." During one of our breaks, Cindy contextualized this sentiment by admitting that she and Beto shared syringes. Although this is a public health "risk behavior," for Cindy it symbolized "trusting your life" to another person.

My interactions with Cindy and experience working on the Parejas project inspired my focus on love and emotional intimacy within sex workers' relationships. In Parejas we asked a question about love in the initial qualitative interviews that elicited rich responses (discussed in chapter 1) and a question about trust in the survey, which obviously failed to capture the magnitude of its importance for Cindy. The questions in Parejas were pathbreaking, but clearly there was more to know.

I conducted independent research on love and emotional intimacy among female sex workers and their noncommercial partners in 2011 as part of my broader field experience with Parejas. Altogether *Dangerous Love* focuses on seven couples sampled from the larger Parejas study, with whom I conducted serial in-depth interviews, participant observation fieldwork, and a photovoice project, in which I gave partners cameras to document their lives, their relationships, and the things they deemed important. I designed the study to complement the office-based modes of data collection in Parejas and unearth the emotional lived experience of couples' day-to-day lives.

When my earlier sense of being invited into Cindy's home came true, it provided a different kind of opportunity to observe her social interactions with Beto and experience the material conditions of their everyday world. My visits to their home and that of several other couples also provided my first opportunities to witness injection drug use and begin to better understand the exigencies of addiction. My ethnographic approach to studying drug use builds on a long tradition of anthropologists, including Bryan Page, Merrill Singer, Mike Agar, and Philippe Bourgois, whose fieldwork has offered seminal insights into the political economy of addiction and how drug use forges social relations even while heightening risk for infectious disease. I am inspired by the pioneering work of women, including Nancy Romero-Daza, Claire Sterk, Lisa Maher, Angela Garcia, and Kelly Knight, whose ethnographic research has centralized the unique experiences of women who use drugs through caring and attentive analyses that humanize, rather than revictimize, women who use drugs. Although, worldwide, women probably use drugs less often compared to men and have been a less frequent focus of ethnographic study, intersecting factors including gender, race, class, migration status, and reproductive histories intensify their experiences of drug-related stigma and social vulnerability. Importantly, these and other ethnographers reveal the structural production of gendered vulnerabilities while also showing that women do not always fit into neatly predetermined roles in the drug economy, nor do they get enough credit for their agency.[11]

My work offers a unique contribution in accounting for the relational dynamics of drug use among women who engage in sex work and their intimate partners. These couples in many ways defy so-called traditional gender roles, and drug use is no exception. I attend to the social contexts of drug use, and I observed couples together when invited and it was appropriate to do so. The project accounts for both partners' perspectives on drug use, including how trust, care, cooperation, suffering, and conflict shape drug use practices and configure conceptions of safety and danger. The choices that we make in representing drug use are never straightforward, which extends from the "moral ambiguity" of conducting fieldwork involving potentially harmful and illegal behaviors (Page and Singer 2010, 126). While I consciously try to avoid unnecessary and lurid details of drug use, I also refuse to gloss over the urgent role it plays in couples' lives that underscore the need for harm reduction approaches (discussed in the conclusion).

In addition to ethnography beyond the clinic, this book's portrayal of dangerous safe havens is uniquely enhanced by the use of the photovoice project, in which partners were provided with cameras to take photographs of their lives. The images were then discussed in open-ended interviews to elicit deeper insight into the things that they considered to be important. I used the method as an experimental means to give participants greater input into the research process. I also wanted to test if the visual material could evoke more emotional responses than conversation alone, thus cutting to the core of my humanistic research interest in emotional intimacy within couples' relationships. This book reflects on that process through the couples' stories and curates a deliberate space for the couples to reveal the world as they experience it. While a significant number of photos revealed personal identities and many depicted graphic scenes of drug use, speaking to the centrality of addiction in couples' lives, I mostly avoid such content. The limited number of photographs that appear here intentionally protects confidentiality and avoids a voyeurism into suffering, while aiming to reveal another layer of humanity in these couples' complex lives.[12]

INTIMATE RELATIONSHIPS AND HEALTH

Although still rare in studies of sex work and drug use, love has increasingly come into vogue in the social sciences and public health scholarship, offering a foundation on which to build an understanding of dangerous safe havens. Perhaps our renewed interest in love is a response to our underacknowledged societal needs for affirmation, hope, and change within a broader climate of neoliberalism that has supported capitalist expansion and consolidated global wealth. Anthropologists have written about how forms of interpersonal love have emerged as a global response to the alienation of these modern conditions that have left so many of us feeling lost, disconnected, and disillusioned. Modern forms of "companionate love" are about finding a partner in life to trust, share emotional and physical intimacy, and rely on for companionship and care to try to build a meaningful life.[13] This work shows us that, despite the inequalities unleashed through global political conditions, the possibilities for love and care persist, coexist, and even strengthen amid oppression.

Intimate heterosexual relationships are also a site in which to understand how such political processes and cultural changes shape personal health and well-being. Key scholarship has challenged rational models of "risk taking" by revealing how protection, trust, intimacy, and care are crafted within relationships as responses to broader conditions of uncertainty. Anthropologist Elisa

Janine Sobo's (1995) pioneering research among low-income women in relationships reveals how condom use is a socially complex negotiation, and decisions are not based in biomedical models of risk. For vulnerable women, not using condoms demonstrates closeness and partner fidelity—or at least the illusion of fidelity—and helps maintain the critical economic, material, and emotional support that these relationships provide. Even among HIV serodiscordant partners and other "high risk" couples who may have multiple sex partners, emotional meanings signified by unprotected sex can outweigh partners' concern with viral exposure to disease.[14] Jennifer Hirsch and colleagues' (2009) comparative ethnographic research on love and HIV in the context of marriage is notable for its approach to extramarital sex as a reflection of globalized, shifting sociopolitical conditions that often encourage infidelity but do not necessarily diminish the emotional intimacy within marital relationships. This work also shows how social risks are weighed against health-related risks in ways that have reshaped HIV-transmission dynamics to put married women at a high risk of infection in some locations. These studies and others point to the importance of understanding personal relationships as shaped by global processes; in other words, love is personal and political.

Global political economic and cultural shifts also call attention to the complex linkages between economics and intimacy.[15] Sex work subverts ideas about gender roles and power relations while also reflecting broader societal anxieties and desires for pleasure, sociality, love, and intimacy. For many women sex work offers a way to gain autonomy in patriarchal societies through economic independence from their work. Although this autonomy may be considered paradoxical in that it does not change the broader structures of power that entrap women in the first place, neither does sex work destroy women's own emotional desires and ability to forge meaningful relationships.[16] Among a growing chorus of researchers, psychologists Catalina Betancur and Andrés Cortéz (2011, 47) point out that women can separate the physical, economic, and emotional dimensions of sexual exchange, as sex can be a means to an end to improve their lives and care for their families, but "love cannot be bought" *(amor no puede ser comprador)*.

For other women sex work offers an opportunity to blur boundaries with clients and shift the emotional currencies of monetized sexual relationships. Particularly in lower- and middle-income countries characterized by intense socioeconomic inequalities and sexual tourism, women may leverage sex work to intentionally develop relationships with (often Western, white, and wealthy) clients for not only financial gain but intimacy and hope for a better life, including prospects for marriage and migration.[17] Men may also look to sex workers for more than physical acts of sex, but to counter loneliness and build social status amid changing economic and cultural expectations.[18] To simplify a complex topic, sex work means many things, including some kind of transactional exchange, but emotional intimacy may or may not be one of them. The women themselves often decide.[19]

Importantly, emotional intimacy in different kinds of paying and nonpaying sexual partnerships carries public health significance. Studies have consistently found that female sex workers are less likely to use condoms with intimate, noncommercial partners compared to clients.[20] Just like we see in other intimate relationships, sex workers can find condoms to be a physical and emotional barrier to trust, intimacy, and pleasure; for sex workers in noncommercial relationships, it is particularly important to demarcate the physical and emotional boundaries of their personal lives. Still, in-depth studies of female sex workers' intimate, noncommercial relationships remain rare, and studies are not typically dyadic in design to include their male partners' perspectives. The extant work is insightful in documenting the complex negotiations and tensions in maintaining emotional intimacy in the context of transactional sex, including how jealousy and conflict shape relationship quality. Overall, however, these intimate relationships are meaningful and important to partners and offer a critical socioemotional space for women to feel accepted and loved despite the stigma associated with their involvement in sex work.[21]

Drug use is even less frequently viewed through a lens of relationships and emotional intimacy, even as drug use often overlaps with sex work for women, and sexual partners often use drugs together and influence each other's behaviors. Trust, intimacy, and care within the context of relationships significantly shape drug-related practices, including syringe sharing, which places partners at heightened risk of HIV/HCV.[22] Medical sociologist Tim Rhodes and his colleagues have made significant contributions to rethinking how relational dynamics affect both sexual and drug-related behaviors. This work reveals how couples negotiate the pragmatics and emotions of addiction that complicate intimate relationships. Couples can insulate each other from social stigma and other harms through provisions of care and social protection, but these strategies do not objectively protect them from drug-related risks or fundamentally change the social structures around them enacting harm.[23] Other recent scholarship corroborates how trust, cooperation, intimacy, and power commingle to shape injection practices among drug-using couples, which may shift over time and require specific attention in health programming.[24] I read these currents in scholarship toward the relational and emotional dimensions of drug use as a significant discursive and political move to cast a more humanizing understanding of addiction and offer a revision to punitive programming and policies, a goal to which this book also aspires.

*　*　*

Love is foundational to our shared human experience and an important, if traditionally underappreciated, topic of scholarly inquiry. Intimate, loving relationships also bear critical implications for health and well-being. A growing body of scholarship is challenging prevailing stereotypes that female sex workers do not have steady, noncommercial partners, nor share the same desires for intimacy and love as anyone else. This work further suggests that the social and emotional dimensions of sex workers' relationships are often prioritized over more distal pathogenic risks such as HIV. However, even as our academic interest in love grows, applied attention to love in sex workers' intimate relationships and the ways that trust, care, and emotional intimacy shape health outcomes remains largely marginalized in health programming, particularly in terms of addressing injection drug-related risks. Moreover, the emotional experiences of sex workers' male partners remain largely excluded from the dialogue. After decades of research we still know virtually nothing about these male partners with whom sex workers fall in love.

Building on scholarship centering on love and care, this is the first full-length ethnography to offer insight into sex workers' intimate relationships through a lens of love while accounting for *both* partners' perspectives. It interweaves strands of often disparate scholarship in sex work, drug use, and health and emotions to construct an ethnographic account focusing on intimacy within sex workers' long-term, established relationships rather than their broader search for intimacy. In building a conception of love, it grants attention to not only how partners describe love but how the multifaceted components of love are embodied and enacted within sociopolitical contexts of inequity and disadvantage. Reading these relationships as dangerous safe havens offers conceptual insight into how couples navigate very real epidemiological risk but prioritize the subjective emotional comfort of their relationships as a collective means for survival. Not only do the forthcoming narratives reveal love, care, trust, and cooperation among partners, but we see the spaces of violence, conflict, risk, and abandonment in couples' lives where love has been lacking, generating the need to build dangerous safe havens in the first place. Thus, the couples' stories also create a springboard for a broader political discussion of the role of love in transforming health programming, policy, and research ethics and practice.

LOVE AS A PATHWAY TO HEALTH EQUITY

Years after completing my project and thousands of miles from Tijuana, I absentmindedly checked my email on my iPhone one day to learn terrible news: Cindy had passed away. As indicated by her appearance throughout this chapter, Cindy was not an ordinary "research subject" to me. She was an inspiration for my project. More than that, I had become friends with her and Beto in the blurry sense of friendship formed through anthropological fieldwork. She couldn't have been but thirty-five years old at the time of her death. I was devastated.

Cindy had been periodically ill throughout my fieldwork with undetermined flu-like symptoms, but I was unaware of the seriousness of her condition. She once told me she felt like she was "going to die" during one of these bouts. How could I not know how foreboding that statement would be? In trying to reconcile my personal and emotional reaction to her early death with the intellectual sensemaking that I've tried to craft of her life, I revisited her interview transcripts and photos in remembrance and looked to creative methods for healing.[25] Of course, many researchers before me have confronted death in their fieldwork, sometimes on a much more massive scale. However, we do not always openly reflect on and write about these deaths. But death and mourning jar us out of the mundane demands of our work, taking us back to a core value in anthropology: the fundamental importance of forging meaningful human relationships. As I reflected on Cindy's death, new forms of meaning arose from her life, inspiring me to write this book against sanitized and dispassionate scholarly depictions of sex work, drug use, and HIV risk. Both her life and her death make clear that, even amid conditions of inequality and social suffering, individuals can find meaning through emotionally intimate relationships. More broadly, Cindy pushed me to reflect on my role as a scholar, including all the inequities that plague our research and can make it feel futile. For me Cindy's death opened up critical questions about the purpose of our work and led to me wonder, Is there a bigger role for love in our research? Going further, is there a role for love in developing equitable health programming and policies?

Cindy's dangerous safe haven with Beto could not protect her from an untimely death. But her life matters: in its own right, in relation to Beto, and for the many other sex workers worldwide who also find themselves trying to survive difficult circumstances. We have much to learn from the experiences of socially vulnerable couples that can help us transform research, policies, and practices into coconstructed processes that aspire to social change and health equity. If love is a strategy to resist oppression even in a life cut short like Cindy's, then organizing for a broader political love can help us dismantle those systems of oppression in the first place. Put another way, I want to explore how love can help us carve a pathway to health equity.

Here I return to the second major intervention of this book: the critical power of love as a force of sociopolitical change and health justice. I don't want to only document love as such; I use love as a heuristic to think through our collective actions to address health inequities. I find inspiration in *Methodology of the Oppressed*, postcolonial feminist scholar Chela Sandoval's work that draws on a long line of revolutionary thinkers to understand love as capable of producing a different consciousness in which we can break through oppression to create "understanding and community." According to Sandoval, "Writers who theorize social change understand 'love' as a hermeneutic, as a set of practices and procedures that can transit all citizen-subjects, regardless of social class, toward a differential mode of consciousness and its accompanying technologies of method and social movement" (2000, 139). In this sense "falling in love" is not romantic mirage but a metaphor for transforming ourselves into a new state of social awareness. In this state of being, individuals develop new subjectivities about the self and others and recognize the need to transform repressive structures of knowledge and power. This revolutionary potential of love lies at the center of anti-oppressive liberation movements, including Brazilian educator Paulo Freire's ([1970] 2018) transformative pedagogies to raise consciousness to enact broader social transformation.

Anthropologists have also used love as a lens through which to think more deeply about questions of morals, politics, and ethics. In this sense, as anthropologist Jarrett Zigon (2013) notes, "love" is like the "good" that has recently seeped into anthropology's more typically "dark" focus on the misery and social suffering of our neoliberal global order. Focusing on the good doesn't erase suffering, but it opens up a counternarrative to locate the cracks and gaps in our current order to reveal how people build meaningful lives despite bleak circumstances.[26] Likewise, I document the struggles of sex workers and their partners not as voyeurism into darkness but to adjust the theoretical aperture and shed light on the changes we need to grapple with as a society if we are to address health inequities.

Developing a political love could enable us to move toward health equity in new ways. Following bell hooks (2001a), drawing on the principles and values ("ingredients") of love to inform policy means coming together to map out justice-focused programs that would affect the good for *everyone*, not just the privileged few. According to Keri Day, such a political project not only needs reasonable and sound (i.e., evidence-based) policy making but broad emotional support and societal buy-in. With such support, Day imagines that "love can birth new moral worlds in response to the pathologies of neoliberal societies" (2016, 105). In contrast to the self-interest and materialism of the neoliberal political order, an affective political love cultivates empathy, compassion, and collective motivation to rise against injustice. In other words, if we better understand and empathize with the plight of the most vulnerable—in the case of this book, drug-using sex workers and their partners—we are more apt to speak out, act up, and work hard for social and health justice.

The narratives in this book offer a means to think about incorporating love not only into policy but into our own research as a way to enact change. Love can be integrated from project conceptualization to dissemination, including inviting love into our scholarly writing. As anthropologist Virginia Dominguez (2000) points out, academics are professionalized into particular forms of scripted writing to specifically excise the love out of our work. But Cindy taught me that applying love to our anthropological writing can reveal our own love and respect for the people with whom we work while opening up a space to reflect on our political commitments. Importantly, this does not mean presenting only positive portrayals of participants, avoiding violence and conflict, or tiptoeing around our privileged positionality. Rather, writing with love is itself a political project. Our politics of representation can build compassion and support toward more humane policies addressing sex work and drug use that resist moralizing discourses of blame and punishment.

I write this book with a loving lens to prioritize a humanistic representation of couples whose lives are marginalized, pathologized, and socially forgotten. These couples have something important to tell us about the revolutionary forms of social change needed to effectively address the lifelong social and health harms related to sex work, drug use, trauma, violence, and poverty. The dangerous safe havens that couples construct are paradoxical spaces that sometimes protect but sometimes cannot shelter partners from harm and early death, as in the case of Cindy. However, examining sex workers' relationships through a lens of love gives due attention to couples' creative resiliency while also revealing the larger societal deficiencies that need to be addressed if we are to achieve health equity.

Bringing a political love into our research resets our research priorities to center on transformative health justice and equity. This means incorporating a multidimensional understanding of love into a research ethics that privileges relationships with participants and their needs, while critically examining our own role in systemic oppression. This also means that academic documentation alone is not good enough, but that active participation toward change is needed. Love in this broader political sense can carve new pathways through the transformation of our research questions and methodologies, which in turn can iteratively inform more humanistic global public health programming and policies. These points are further taken up in the conclusion in recommendations to move forward. In thinking through the overwhelming amount of work to be done to achieve health equity, I find solace in the words of bell hooks, who reminds us that "the transformative power of love is the foundation for all meaningful change."[27]

LOVE STORIES

The stories in this book are not your typical love stories. They offer a counternarrative to stereotypical images of sex workers' lives and intimate relationships. They portray the more private side of sex work and drug use that coexists with the public sex industries and violent drug markets in globalized cities like Tijuana. The chapters provide ethnographic case studies contextualized with epidemiologic and qualitative data from the larger Parejas study to offer insight into couples' lives. Careful analysis of dangerous safe havens lends insight into the various ways that love is embodied, expressed, practiced, and lived out in sickness and health. Each chapter explores a different dimension of dangerous safe havens to reveal their complexity, meaning, and importance in both partners' lives. In doing so, the chapters also build toward concrete suggestions about how to better address the social and health inequities that couples in Tijuana—and elsewhere globally—will continue to face unless we harness the revolutionary potential of love in our work.

Chapter 1 takes readers into the Red Light District of Tijuana to understand the sociopolitical context of sex work and multiple risks that sex workers and their partners navigate on a daily basis. A historical background of sex work and

Tijuana's centrality as a node in a major global drug-trafficking route concretizes some of the structural factors shaping women's work environments and survival strategies. Within this context the chapter tells the story of how Proyecto Parejas, the NIH-funded study that inspired this book, came into being to address an unacknowledged but critically important dimension of sex workers' lives: their intimate, noncommercial relationships. The chapter concludes by examining qualitative data from the larger Parejas study to begin sketching out how couples describe and enact love, care, and commitment within their relationships. These descriptions simultaneously begin to answer and ask new questions about love, which situates the rest of the book's in-depth focus on seven sex workers' intimate relationships.

Chapter 2 delves deeper into how couples cultivate sexual intimacy in the context of sex work. Through the creative-writing device of "composite couples" to protect confidentiality around a sensitive topic, this chapter explores the paradox of how couples can be emotionally close and love each other but have sex with other people and lie about it. These stories demonstrate how multiple meanings of sex, especially *outside* of the primary relationship, reveal the importance of intimacy *within* the primary relationship. For these couples sexual risk and deception in the context of patriarchal norms, shifting masculinities, and changing gender expectations shape the possibilities for love, but what do outside sexual partnerships actually accomplish? What is preserved and what is lost in negotiations of deception and how does this inform our rethinking of sexual and social forms of risk?

Against the backdrop of the drug war in Tijuana, chapter 3 explores the stories of Celia and Lazarus and Mildred and Ronaldo, whose relationships are embedded within extended family networks and social relations ordered around drug use. Their stories illustrate how drug use demands analytical attention not only for health risks but also for how the violent institutions of the drug war reshape social relationships. These couples offered their homes as *picaderos* (shooting galleries), which functioned as safe spaces where friends and family could inject drugs. In this sense the couples' homes became extensions of their dangerous safe havens that absorbed kin and other trusted social relations. The communities of care that emerge in the wake of war push back against depictions of people who use drugs as always selfish and illustrate how couples, families, and friends entangled in addiction navigate their complex relations in terms of love and collective survival.

Returning to Cindy and Beto's relationship, chapter 4 explores the couples' experiences through a lens of love as both feeling and embodied practice. Their dangerous safe haven represents the embodiment of shared histories of trauma that brought them together and illustrates how health risk behaviors that could enact physical harm also express solidarity and emotional commitment. While I attend to how the extraordinary risks of injection drug use and sex work shape their relationship, I also draw attention to the more quotidian aspects of their daily life together. The couple shared an emotionally close relationship, and its transformative power was constantly revealed in small ways and endured in bigger ways until its tragic end. What does their relationship tell us about the transformative power of love even in a life cut short?

Chapter 5 examines the complexities of love in two women's lives as a way to also think through bigger questions about research methodology. I focus on the stories of Maria and Gwen, both US women with long histories of drug use and sex work in Mexico and relationships with Mexican men. Both women's stories offer ethnographic insight into the epidemiologic concept of "lost to follow-up," when researchers cannot retain participants in studies, and they are therefore "dropped" from longitudinal analyses. In other words, neither woman was able to finish their participation in Parejas, nor my own project for that matter. Telling Maria's and Gwen's stories through their limited involvement in a research study shows the complexity of women's experiences that are only ever partially captured in a research project. What happened to these women, and what does this tell us about the stability and precarity of dangerous safe havens? Furthermore, how do their stories challenge us as researchers to develop methodologies grounded in love?

Given the health and social harms described throughout this book, the concluding chapter explores love as a pathway to health equity. This chapter uses a lens of political love and harm reduction to make recommendations for programs and policies to improve the health of drug-using sex workers and their partners. As a movement for social justice and pragmatic but compassionate approach to health care, harm reduction articulates with a framing of love as social analysis and political practice that can reorient our priorities to concrete action. Furthermore, we as scholars have a significant role to play in creating change. I conclude the book with a reflexive articulation of lessons learned through this research and how love could transform our work.

Ultimately, love does not necessarily bring an end to suffering, nor can it entirely erase the risk for negative health outcomes and early death. However, as the forthcoming narratives reveal, what love *can* offer is a form of solidarity and resistance, a bigger meaning in life, a way to feel safe and secure, and the ingredients to help us counter an unjust world of disadvantage. *Dangerous Love* urges us all to consider new pathways forward and represents a small contribution toward a broader project centering on the transformative power of love.

Parejas

Early one Monday morning, on my way to the Parejas office with a colleague, I observed a scenario that encapsulates the inequities and contradictions of working in the Red Light District of Tijuana. On the left side of the street was the usual spot where very young *paraditas* (street-based sex workers who stand along the sidewalks) adorned in schoolgirl outfits lined up to sell sex. On the right side a disheveled older woman was lying in the sidewalk, her blackened bare feet hanging into the street. We stopped the car, fearing she was dead, but it turned out that she was sleeping. My colleague commented, "The girls on the left side of the street never think they'll turn into the woman on the right side of the street."

As I worked on the Parejas study, I grew to understand how the concentrated spaces of exclusion and disadvantage along the Mexico-US border configured life opportunities, which in turn profoundly shaped the interior emotional experiences of the sex workers we studied and their strategies for survival. Multiple study participants told me stories of being out on the streets alone, experiencing hardships, and even almost dying before they found their partner. I started to realize how the multiple forms of support that partners provided each other were critical on so many levels. When the stakes of intimate relationships are so high, the situated rationality of dangerous safe havens that to outsiders seem "risky" begin to make sense as strategies for ensuring collective survival.

This chapter takes readers into the Red Light District of Tijuana to explore the historical economic, social, and structural contexts of sex work and drug use in a world-renown tourist district just minutes from the US border. I then discuss how a series of studies about sex work here gave rise to new research questions, including those driving the development of Proyecto Parejas, the inspiration of my book. To date Parejas remains the largest study of HIV/STI risk among female sex workers and their intimate, noncommercial partners. Based on my long-term engagement in this project and regular fieldwork in Tijuana, I developed my own study's focus on love and emotional intimacy among sex workers and their partners and sampled a small number of couples from Parejas who make up the focus of this book.

Within this broader historical and research framework, the final section of this chapter provides a brief overview of the couples who participated in the groundbreaking Parejas study. It begins sketching out the material and emotional grounds on which couples formed intimate relationships amid the risks of sex work and drug use. I explore some of the key dimensions of sex workers' intimate relationships as a way to situate their emotional importance, including how couples define love within their relationships. This sketch sets the stage for forthcoming chapters that raise additional empirical questions and offer theoretical considerations about what it means to love and care in contexts of inequality.

WELCOME TO TIJUANA

The modern-day Mexico-US border is drawn on land stolen from indigenous populations and stands as a legacy of US colonial expansion and imperialism asserted during the Mexican-American War of 1846–48. Today the Mexico-US border traverses eighty *municipios* (municipalities) in six Mexican states and forty-eight counties in four US states. With a population of about five million people, the San Diego–Tijuana corridor makes up about 40 percent of the total border population, representing the most heavily populated as well as economically polarized region of the 1,993-mile-long border (Loucky and Alper 2008, 23).

But borders are not only geographic spaces; they are social spaces of deep symbolism. Chicana feminist scholar Gloria Anzaldúa calls the Mexico-US border *"una herida abierta* [an open wound] where the Third World grates against the first and bleeds" ([1987] 2012, 3). But in this grating, Anzaldúa also notes that new spaces for contradictions and contestations emerge, with the potential to generate new forms of consciousness. Likewise, anthropologist Josiah Heyman (1994) notes that the border is a distinctive space characterized by inequality, extraction, ingenuity, creativity, marginalization, and resistance, all of which shape interior emotional experiences and generate new social possibilities. The sociopolitical complexity of the border region serves as a critical backdrop through which to understand couples' experiences, opportunities, and search for intimacy and emotional security.

Tijuana often evokes a strong collective imagination of sin, curiosity, and fear that is perpetuated by the popular media. Although Tijuana is a cosmopolitan metropolis home to more than 1.7 million residents and boasts vibrant cultural, culinary, and arts scenes, its seedier reputation for sex, drugs, and violence often supersede its virtues. To be clear, such stereotypes exaggerate but a small slice of life in this dynamic and complex border city. Furthermore, by no means is it "natural" that Tijuana developed industries of vice and garnered a notable reputation; it did so because of a specific historical political economy that is deeply intertwined with the United States.

Tijuana's geopolitical location has profoundly shaped its history from that of a small cattle-ranching village in the 1880s to the busiest land border crossing in the Western Hemisphere, where more than thirty million residents, visitors, family members, schoolchildren, tourists, sex work clients, researchers, and many others cross the border northbound into the San Ysidro port of entry annually.[1] Much of Tijuana's growth and development in the early 1900s is linked to its famous leisure economy, in which bars, liquor stores, and night clubs catered to Americans. By 1919 Tijuana was linked by railway to Southern California, where the US Volstead Act federally established alcohol Prohibition. The 1920s saw the city as a destination for indulgence and a "Satan's Playground" for movie stars, celebrities, and other tourists (Vanderwood 2009). Around this time gambling and racetracks became principal tourist draws, and Avenida Revolución developed into a concentrated street of bars and dance clubs that continues to function as a central tourist attraction. The establishment of new military bases in Southern California in the 1940s also provided a significant population of young men who crossed into Tijuana to take part in leisure pursuits.

Given its location as a gateway between northern Mexico and Southern California, migration and mobility have always played a key role in Tijuana's history. Significant social and economic disparities between southern and northern Mexico have been key drivers of migration to the urban centers and industrial zones along the northern border, which promised new opportunities and proximity to the United States. During the 1940s–60s Mexican migrants also passed through Tijuana to work in the agricultural sector in the United States, thanks to the bracero program and guest-worker visas that opened the border. Mexico's increasing integration into the world economy has continued to push migrants northward for employment opportunities both within the country and into the United States, particularly in times of economic precarity.

Although from the 1940s through the 1970s, policy makers in Mexico prioritized strategies to support local industry and domestic growth, a major economic crisis in the 1980s ushered in significant political changes, including the reorganization of labor markets and reduction in public sector employment, food subsidies, and public expenditure (Middlebrook and Zepeda 2003). The urban poor were hit particularly hard by shrinking wages, increasing unemployment, stagnant job opportunities, and decreased public spending on social services and subsidies for basic goods that provided a safety net (Latapi and González de la Rocha 1995). The financial crisis devastated families and necessitated households to economically and socially reorganize themselves to survive, including contributing to growing informal economies. In the 1990s the Mexican government devalued the peso as consumer prices and unemployment soared. During this time

Mexico agreed to a series of structural-adjustment policies and market reforms authored by the International Monetary Fund and the World Bank that liberalized trade policies, deregulated financial institutions, and privatized Mexico's state-owned enterprises (Middlebrook and Zepeda 2003). The well-known 1994 North American Free Trade Agreement (NAFTA) eliminated barriers to free trade between the three nations of North America and opened the flow of capital across borders while clamping down on the flow of laborers and labor rights. These policies have carried a range of consequences, including decimating local agricultural markets in the interior of Mexico while facilitating maquiladora (factory) expansion along the northern border, drawing poor migrants from all over Mexico for economic opportunities. The factories only exacerbated inequalities through exploiting a migrant workforce, particularly women, with low wages, weak labor protections, exposure to toxic substances, and vulnerabilities to social harms like sexual harassment and violence (Bucardo et al. 2004; Katsulis 2009).

In 2020 NAFTA was replaced by the United States–Mexico-Canada Agreement, a complex revision of policies ostensibly designed to open economic markets while better safeguarding labor, environmental, and intellectual property rights. Although it is still early in its implementation, some scholars forecast that the agreement will actually further entrench economic and health inequities (Labonté et al. 2019, 2020). Taken together, ongoing historical relations with the United States and promises of neoliberal reform have largely failed to promote equitable and sustainable development in Mexico, which has a tangible impact on the lives of border residents.

Amid shifting political conditions individuals continue to migrate to Tijuana for a variety of reasons. Some end up settling there unexpectedly if they are unable to cross into the United States or if they get deported. According to the 2010 Mexican Census, over half of Tijuana's residents (52.4 percent) were born in another Mexican state or country (INEGI 2010). Limited opportunities for economic mobility have left many people without formal employment, seeking survival in the growing informal economy. Research has suggested that informal jobs in Tijuana represent 25–40 percent of the city's employment alongside a growing sector of related criminal activity (Koff 2015, 478). Anthropologist Mercedes Gonzáles de la Rocha, who has studied gender and shifting household dynamics among the urban poor, has characterized the precarity of Mexican cities as a "social and cultural context of *radical exclusion*" (2006, 69). In other words, multiple forms of economic hardship and social exclusion shape the individual lived experience of those who have been cast to the edges. Individuals pushed into informal activities like sex work and the street-level drug economy become only further excluded from development initiatives and social opportunities.

The Zona Norte, or northern area of Tijuana, remains a destination of concentrated bars, dance clubs, strip clubs, hotels, and restaurants (including the one that invented the Caesar salad), where active economies of sex work and drug use flourish. During my fieldwork heightened concern over drug-related violence had slowed (but never stopped) tourism, even if the news media and university system expressed concern over the safety of Americans. However, toward the end of my project and in the years immediately afterward, in the wake of the drop in tourism, yet another reinvention of this resilient city occurred, with art galleries, craft-beer bars, and an incredible culinary scene sprouting in place of kitschy tourist bars.[2]

SEX WORK AND THE CITY

In Mexico no federal laws regulate sex work, though local jurisdictions may legislate its practice. In total, thirteen of the nation's thirty-two states have such regulations where sex work is typically designated in *zonas de tolerancia* (tolerance zones, or Red Light Districts). Along the Mexico-US border these zones began to emerge during a period of economic insecurity at the end of nineteenth century. Border cities attempted to fill economic gaps by appealing to US markets, which helped transform the local economic and tourist landscapes during US Prohibition. In Tijuana sex work is woven into the city's history and deeply shaped by the city's ties with the United States, patterns of migration, border policies (e.g., militarization and deportation), and its location on a major drug-trafficking route, which has simultaneously influenced the development of local drug markets, drug tourism, and drug-related violence.

Most famously, Tijuana's Red Light District is located just across the US border, where sex can be purchased from a diverse group of women in any number of clubs or on the streets. As a practice, sex work in Tijuana is quite diverse and differentially configures the types of risk that individuals must navigate. One limitation of my book is that I interacted only with women engaged in sex work who were involved in intimate, heterosexual relationships. But a diversity of male and transgender sex workers who may or may not be in heterosexual or same-sex intimate relationships are also a key part of Tijuana's sex industry and face unique risks that merit social and health support (Bringas Rábago and Gaxiola Aldama 2012; Katsulis 2009; Salas-Espinoza et al. 2017).

Nonetheless, the most iconic image of sex work in Tijuana—that of the carefully sculpted women who appear on billboards in and around the city—are those women working in the sex clubs in the Red Light District. These women are considered venue-based sex workers. Outside such venues on the Calle Coahuila and surrounding streets are the highly visible and diverse group of *paraditas* who line the sidewalks to solicit clients. There are also other areas outside of the city center with clubs where sex work occurs. While these are the most visible forms of sex work, many other types of commercial exchanges take place in Tijuana outside of such formalized work spaces as forms of small scale, self-organized, and informal sex work. Such "freelance" sex workers operate outside of state regulation and may have a considerable amount of agency in terms of their labor.

Prior research in Tijuana suggests that women who engage in sex work are a diverse group who experience a range of social and health-related effects depending on the context of their work (Burgueño et al. 1992; Castillo et al. 1999; Choudhury 2010; Katsulis et al. 2010). Women span a wide age range and work for periods from a few weeks to many years, and many engage in sex work out of economic necessity as the primary supporters of their families (Bucardo et al. 2004; Castillo et al. 1999; Ojeda et al. 2009). In her ethnography of sex work and geographies of occupational risk in Tijuana, anthropologist Yasmina Katsulis (2009) notes that many of these women work for "milk money," or provisions for their families, which may include sending money to relatives to support children. Other women may use sex work as a way to attain social mobility, while others support their drug use. Sex work may be monetarily driven but may also involve negotiations of housing, clothes, school fees for children, other material goods, and drugs or money to directly support drug use.

Reflecting broader historical trends of migration to the northern border of Mexico, a substantial number of female sex workers in Tijuana are not originally from this city. Many of these women are migrants from southern or central Mexico who come to Tijuana looking for new opportunities. They may vacillate between sex work and other options in response to economic need, family caretaking responsibilities, or the intolerable working conditions in the maquiladoras. Lack of skilled employment opportunities, high living expenses, and financial obligations often constrain sex workers' options for geographic, economic, and social mobility to secure other positions (Katsulis 2009). Most recently, women who have been deported from the United States are joining this diverse group of women practicing sex work, as many find themselves with few economic opportunities other than the informal economy (Robertson et al. 2012).

As is the case globally, women involved in sex work in Tijuana tend not to be viewed for their complexity as individuals but rather for their potential to spread disease. Local regulation of sex work is focused on disease surveillance and prevention. On the surface this seems like a reasonable public health strategy, but the benefits of the registration system to the sex workers themselves are arguable. As anthropologist Patty Kelly (2008) details in her ethnography of the Red Light District in Tuxtla, Mexico, public health–based registration systems have sociopolitical implications. Kelly documents how the state's system links public health measures with ideals of modernity, while stigmatizing poor women who are not intended to be included in projects of modern development and progress.

Similarly, in Tijuana the effects of registration are uneven at best and may further marginalize the women most vulnerable to HIV/STIs. The registration system requires that women have regular medical checkups to obtain health cards to work. Sex work registration in Tijuana costs hundreds of dollars per year and requires regular HIV/STI testing. Women registering as sex workers who test positive for an STI are treated with antibiotics according to federal guidelines, and, if they test positive for HIV, their cards are revoked, and they are referred to specialty care in the city HIV clinics. However, enforcement of sex work registration is difficult, and the penalties of noncompliance often fall disproportionately on women rather than the owners of businesses where these women work. Women with infections cannot work, but the bars that employ them can remain open.

As such, the regulation of sex work may actually contribute to health and social inequities. Women who are not registered often cannot afford the regular check-ups or may be migrants without proper documentation who do not want to be included in the system. In a study of 410 female sex workers in Tijuana, just 44 percent were registered with the health department. Registration was less likely among women who engaged in street-based sex work, used stimulants, and were born outside of the state of Baja California. Registration did not independently predict lower rates of HIV/STIs compared to women who were unregistered (Sirotin et al. 2010a). In practice the registration system largely fails to serve the health needs of street-based sex workers who use drugs and are at the highest risk for HIV/STIs (Sirotin et al. 2010b).

The women in this book are largely freelance sex workers who use drugs and operate under the radar of the state surveillance. These women occupy the bottom of what has been called the "whorearchy," or the ranked ordering system that assigns certain sex workers less worth than others. These rankings are driven by stigma and judgment that even come from within sex worker communities.[3] The rankings relegate sex work driven by drug addiction to be among the least respectable and even outright reprehensible reasons to engage in the job. Ethnographies of sex work in the Mexico-US border region have shown that the overlap between sex work and drug use is highly stigmatized by other sex workers who engage in the work to fulfill their social and moral obligations to their children and families (Katsulis 2009; Luna 2020). Common discourses individualize blame against these "selfish" women for their drug use without taking into account their life circumstances and the pervasive drug economies that create and sustain the conditions of women's addiction in the first place.

WARS ON DRUGS

Tijuana's economies of sex work are intertwined with its location on a strategic global drug-trafficking route. In the early twentieth century, much of the original drug trafficking in the Western Hemisphere was concentrated in the western border cities of Tijuana and Mexicali. More recently, the border has been caught in the crosshairs of two ongoing "drug wars."[4] The first is former president Richard Nixon's War on Drugs, a now multidecade, multibillion-dollar offensive that has essentially had no significant effect on drug demand, consumption, or importation of drugs into the United States (Campbell 2010; Lusk, Staudt, and Moya 2012a). Even before the official 1971 declaration of war, Mexico was singled out as a key source of drugs entering the United States and targeted for increased surveillance. In 1969 Operation Intercept demanded thorough car inspections for drugs at the Mexico-US border, causing major transportation disruptions. This likely signaled the beginning of local consumption markets due to the "spillover" of drugs that did not make it across the border.

The second major offensive is the drug war in Mexico, launched in 2006 by former president Felipe Calderón, which was waged among competing cartels, gangs, federal and municipal police, and the army, who have all vied to control drug-smuggling operations into the United States (Lusk, Staudt, and Moya 2012a). These efforts have resulted in periods of horrific and highly publicized violence, much of which remains tied to US demand for drugs even as vast numbers of US weapons travel southbound to arm cartels (Boullosa and Wallace 2015). Overall, Calderón's offensive resulted in more than 121,669 homicides, which breaks down to an average of more than 20,000 people per year (Heinle, Ferreira, and Shirk 2014). Between 2007 and 2011 alone, Mexico's homicide rate tripled from 8.1 to 23.5 homicides per 100,000, reaching what the World Health Organization considers "epidemic" levels (Heinle, Molzahn, and Shirk 2015). Political scientist Héctor Bezares Buenrostro (2019) has argued that constructions of Tijuana as a violent and dangerous city in the global drug trade have only enabled further acts of violence to be perpetrated by state and private agents against people who use drugs, thus exacerbating conditions of fear and precarity along the border.

In the context of drug-related violence and growing rates of drug use across the country, Mexico started experimenting with public health–informed approaches to drug policy. In 2009, when the Parejas research first began, the government set forth legislation offering alternatives for drug treatment rather than incarceration for drug-related offenses (Robertson et al. 2014a). By 2010 Baja California enacted these *"narcomenudeo"* reforms, which decriminalized possession of small amounts of drugs for personal use (Beletsky et al. 2016). When apprehended by police, individuals with amounts below the tolerated drug thresholds are not to be charged with a crime but reported to the health authorities and released. On the third "strike" individuals are incarcerated or mandated to drug treatment. However, drug treatment in Mexico often means deplorable conditions that enact further violence.

Harm reduction efforts have also been variously implemented across Mexico as a public health strategy to reduce disease transmission and other harms related to drug use. Harm reduction is a philosophy that provides an alternative to punishment and aims to build autonomy and dignity among people who use drugs by providing the tools to make drug users safer. This can include safer drug use supplies (e.g., syringes, smoking supplies); linkages to HIV and hepatitis C virus testing and care; wound care (for injection-related abscesses); education and access to naloxone (an opioid overdose reversal medication); and referrals to drug treatment, among a host of other services. Although harm reduction provides a promising alternative to the drug wars, programming has been inconsistent and inadequately funded to meet the demand in Tijuana. Furthermore, while federal law does not criminalize syringe possession or over-the-counter pharmacy sales of syringes, decisions around nonprescription pharmacy sales of syringes can be arbitrary and frequently denied to people who "look like" a person who uses drugs (Pollini et al. 2010, 2011).

Yet local drug markets in Tijuana have proliferated and offer opportunities to sell and purchase heroin, methamphetamine (meth), cocaine, cannabis, and more. According to government survey data, the northwestern border region of Mexico has the highest rates of drug consumption in the country, as 2.8 percent of the general population twelve to sixty-five years old reported past-year drug use, compared to 1.5 percent of the national average (INPRFM 2011, 33). However, household surveys miss the most vulnerable populations and may underestimate drug use. A recent review of studies in Mexico suggests much higher rates of drug use among female sex workers, with lifetime estimates of drug use among this group ranging from 52.5 to 61.0 percent, rates of any recent drug use ranging from 10.6 to 38.2 percent, and rates of recent injection drug use ranging from 10.3 to 23.6 percent (Iversen et al. 2021, 101).

High rates of drug use among sex workers also intersect with concerns about policing, and during my fieldwork I heard a lot of stories from couples (and others) subjected to constant police harassment and violence. A recent study in Tijuana reflects these concerns, as 68 percent of a sample of 584 sex workers who inject drugs reported experiencing some form of police violence (West et al. 2020, 10). The forthcoming chapters illustrate not only the constant harm enacted by arbitrary and violent policing on couples' daily lives but how the urgency of drug addiction can be mutually reinforcing in women's sex work. The violence of the drug wars provides a critical backdrop to couples' stories, all of whom navigated the health and social risks of local drug markets as their drug use also shaped their notions of intimacy and care.

WHO IS MISSING FROM SEX WORK RESEARCH?

The growing visibility of the sex trade, emerging local drug markets, and public health concern for cross-border infectious disease transmission has drawn increased attention over the years by researchers and policy makers alike. Tijuana is now a robust research site with investigators and cadres of students who have invested their energies into addressing the HIV epidemic and related health concerns. While there is a longer history of local research with sex workers (e.g., Burgueño et al. 1992; Castillo et al. 1999), here I focus on the genealogy of a collaborative research program that began between investigators from the University of California, San Diego (UCSD) and a team of Mexican collaborators from a nongovernmental organization called Prevencasa (the Prevention House).

This partnership began with a small qualitative study with sex workers to learn about their HIV risk behaviors but has blossomed into a well-funded portfolio of significant public health interventions.

The original qualitative work suggested that sex workers along the border were at high risk of HIV infection due to their sexual behaviors in the context of sex work, yet access to information and health services was limited (Bucardo et al. 2004). Driven by these findings, this team developed the first public health intervention trial in the region to focus on HIV risk among sex workers. *Mujer Segura* (Safe Woman) was a National Institutes of Health (NIH)–supported behavioral intervention that investigators developed based on the intervention literature and formative qualitative work. Mujer Segura used motivational interviewing and theory-based techniques of behavioral change to increase condom use and reduce the number of new HIV/STI infections among sex workers and their clients in Tijuana and Ciudad Juárez (Patterson et al. 2006). The results were promising: the intervention group showed a 40 percent reduction in HIV/STI incidence, or new cases of infection, over the study period (Patterson et al. 2008).

However, it turns out that this intervention did not work equally well among all sex workers, particularly women who injected drugs. At enrollment into the study, the women who injected drugs were more likely to have an STI (HIV, syphilis, chlamydia, or gonorrhea) and HIV prevalence was 12.3 percent among sex workers who injected compared to 5.1 percent among those who did not. In a multivariate statistical analysis, a number of factors were independently associated with injection drug use, including identifying as a street-based worker, speaking English, being married or in a common-law relationship, engaging in sex work and living in the study location for longer periods, and associating with fellow sex workers who also injected drugs. These epidemiologic data reflect the social history of the border region, including its deep and ongoing connections with the United States, how the drug market and economic precarity in Tijuana can shape individual behavior, and the importance of social relationships for women who inject in the context of sexual HIV/STI risk (Strathdee et al. 2008b). Compared to the women who had never injected drugs, those who injected showed less improvement in sexual risk reduction, and their drug-related risks such as needle sharing did not change (Strathdee et al. 2009). Essentially, the women who injected were at higher risk for poor health outcomes, but they did not benefit from the intervention because it was not tailored to address drug use. The risks associated with injection drug use carry clear global health implications for dynamic, cross-border infectious disease epidemics and merit attention. These findings inspired *Mujer Mas Segura* (Safer Woman), an NIH-funded intervention study addressing *both* injection and sexual risk behaviors among sex workers who inject drugs (Strathdee et al. 2013; Vera et al. 2012).

During a project meeting one winter day in Tijuana, Steffanie Strathdee, the principal investigator of Mujer Mas Segura, began to realize that another critically important factor in female sex workers' lives was being neglected: the role of their intimate male partners. In this meeting women complained to Strathdee that the project's intention to create a "woman-only space" in the office meant that the sex workers' male partners were left out. One sex worker in particular, who had been a health-care worker in the United States, was impassioned and convincing that excluding intimate partners overlooked a critical part of women's lived experience, including their health and well-being.

Back in San Diego, Strathdee asked a statistician to check the percentage of women in the study who reported having a common-law or steady partner and found that it reached 50 percent. "I was so struck by this that I thought it warranted a new study to see if the couple could be a target for an intervention rather than the individual," she told me.[5] A subsequent analysis of the Mujer Segura data also confirmed that the original sexual risk–reduction intervention had no effect on condom use with intimate partners, with whom women were more than twice as likely to have unprotected sex with compared to clients (Ulibarri et al. 2012).

Taken together the evidence suggested both the epidemiological and social importance of sex workers' intimate male partners. From an epidemiological perspective the lack of condom use with intimate male partners who may engage in their own risk behaviors could intensify an already concentrated HIV epidemic along the border. The efficiency of injection drug use to spread disease could further compound forms of sexual risk. From an anthropological perspective the lack of condom use could also signal the social meanings embedded in noncommercial relationships, calling for new approaches to health interventions. However, we knew virtually nothing about these male partners or how they shaped their female partner's health and well-being. Thus, a new NIH-funded study was born: Proyecto Parejas, or the "Couples Project." I started a fellowship at UCSD three days before the very first team project meeting, which I attended by invitation. The rest of this chapter, and indeed *Dangerous Love*, is an outgrowth of my serendipitous involvement in this pathbreaking project.

A FIRST OF ITS KIND

Parejas was the first prospective, mixed-methods study of the social context and epidemiology of HIV/STIs among female sex workers and their primary, noncommercial male partners. In total 214 female sex workers and their male partners in Tijuana and Ciudad Juárez participated in quantitative surveys and HIV/STI testing (106 couples in Tijuana and 108 couples in Ciudad Juárez; total individual n = 428). The mixed-methods study design included a quantitative survey and biological testing every six months over a twenty-four-month period. At each visit nurses drew blood to test for HIV and syphilis and collected urine samples to test for chlamydia and gonorrhea, for which all positive cases received free treatment. A subset of couples at each site participated in qualitative interviews at their first (baseline) visit (n = 46) and one-year follow-up (n = 29) to contextualize the survey data and provide additional insight into the social dynamics of these relationships over time.[6]

The specific aims of Parejas were to examine the social context and sexual and drug use behaviors among female sex workers and their noncommercial partners; determine the prevalence (existing cases) of HIV/STIs and their correlates at the individual and partner levels among couples; identify predictors of HIV/STI incidence (new cases) at the individual and partner level; and assess the feasibility of conducting a behavioral intervention either individually or as a couple. Reflecting NIH priorities, the aims focused on generating public health data to inform health interventions. While I offer insights on the study's public health significance throughout the book, and many of my recommendations are focused on such efforts, I also want to note that the mixed-methods study design opened opportunities to ask complementary, open-ended questions about the lived experience and meaning of sex workers' relationships. This is just as the sex workers had demanded.

To give readers a sense of the sociodemographic characteristics of the overall Parejas sample, men were significantly older than women (median age thirty-seven vs. thirty-three years, respectively), and participants completed a median of seven years of education, with an interquartile range of six to nine years (IQR is a statistical measure of dispersion between the twenty-fifth and seventy-fifth percentile). Economic insecurity was prevalent, as 43 percent of couples earned less than US$200 per month. Less than half (47 percent) of the sample reported being born in the city study site, indicating high levels of migration and deportation, and 60 percent reported being arrested in their lifetime. In terms of health risk behaviors, the majority of couples reported never using condoms together. Recent drug use was common, with 63 percent of participants using heroin, 31 percent using meth, 20 percent using cocaine, 14 percent using crack, and 60 percent recently injecting drugs.

Couples had to be in a stable relationship for at least six months to qualify for the Parejas study, but we found that many were in longer-term unions. The median relationship duration was three years (IQR: two to six years). However, there were outliers to this range, and some of the most durable relationships persisted over decades. Quantitative measures of relationship satisfaction (median score of 15 out of 20) and trust (median score of 9 out of 10) were high among couples. However, conflict and violence were also prevalent across our sample, as 49 percent of partners reported perpetrating some type of interpersonal violence, and 47 percent experienced interpersonal violence in the past year (Ulibarri et al. 2019, 556). While high scores measuring both positive relationship aspects and violence may seem antithetical, anthropologists have pointed out that love and violence commonly co-occur in contexts of extreme inequality and duress (Garcia 2010; Luna 2020).

Taken together the survey data indicate that couples come largely from disadvantaged backgrounds and live in economic precarity. Their relationships are not just short-term arrangements; many are enduring, trusting relationships satisfying to both partners. Even though men were aware of women's sex work, not using condoms within the primary relationship was the norm. High levels of drug use, and particularly injection drug use, introduced additional health concerns. While these survey data give us a general description and indication of how common particular behaviors are across the sample, qualitative data allow us to explore the social context of behavior, including how life circumstances shape decision making and configure opportunities to build meaningful lives.

LOVE AND RISK

At the intersection of historical political economy, social vulnerability, and emotional lived experience, possibilities for love emerged in the intimate relationships of couples enrolled in Parejas. Similar to Sarah Luna's (2020) approach to studying love and obligation among sex workers in the border city of Reynosa, I also draw on a set of emic (insider) concepts to develop an ethnographically-grounded analysis of love. However, rather than the obligation *(obligar)* that shaped the various social relationships of the sex workers Luna studied, the couples in Parejas used a different set of concepts to describe the love in their intimate relationships. The following passages begin to tease out the caring, complex, and often contradictory meanings of love in contexts of sex work and drug use based on the perspectives of the couples themselves.

I start by exploring baseline qualitative interview data from the Parejas study to ground our understanding of these understudied relationships while opening up further questions to be addressed throughout the rest of this book.[7] The forty-six couples in Parejas who participated in these interviews were asked questions about their relationships, including how they met, their economic and household situation, how (if at all) they discussed and managed sex work, and their drug use patterns, sexual risk behaviors, and drug-treatment experiences. The interviews opened by asking if they considered themselves to be in love with their partner.

In the Spanish language "love" is a more nuanced construct compared to its usage in English, and it can be expressed with multiple words to convey different strengths of emotion. Partners described the meaning and emotional intensity of their love along a continuum. The verb *querer* typically signifies a warm, friendly love, while *amar* and *enamorarse* typically imply a strong, passionate love, akin to being "in love" with an intimate partner. Nearly every couple said that love was foundational to their intimate bond, even if its intensity varied. Moreover, reflecting a multifaceted and active definition of love as a "mix of ingredients," partners drew on several other common words to describe their relationships, including trust *(confianza)*, respect *(respeto)*, feelings *(sentimientos)*, understanding *(comprensión)*, support *(apoyo)*, gratitude *(agradecimiento)*, affection *(cariño)*, friendship *(compañerismo)*, protection *(protección)*, and happiness *(felicidad)*, in the good times and the bad times *(en las buenas y las malas)*.

About half of the forty-six couples subjectively assessed their relationship as loving and caring. These couples may not have been *in* love *(enamorarse)* or have felt *strong* love *(amar)*, but they expressed love *(querer)* for each other in a caring sense. Another quarter of these couples considered themselves to be *in* love. These couples were unequivocal in their deep emotional connection with their partners, and these relationships were often described as transformative in partners' lives. The remaining quarter of the sample considered their unions less based on love as such and more oriented to mutual care, feeling "comfortable" or "accustomed" to each other, and offering forms of "support," including raising their children together. Importantly, other ingredients of love such as understanding, respect, and standing by each other in the good times and the bad times were interwoven across descriptions of all relationship types. A fine-grained reading of the data reveals that these relationships transcend westernized imaginations of romantic love. The couples embodied common experiences of emotional intimacy that were invariably and uniquely shaped by the broader sociopolitical context of their precarious lives, including women's economic need to engage in sex work.

Some relationships started out based on not love but a desire for companionship and support amid challenging life circumstances. Over time this often grew into love. These couples' experiences lend insight into how structural violence shapes interior emotional experiences and compels individuals to look for hope. Speaking to the transformative potential of these relationships, several couples reflected on how much they struggled prior to meeting their partner and how their partner made a fundamental difference to their well-being:

> *I'll be honest with you. When I met him I never thought that I was in love with him* [estaba enamorada]. *When I decided to be with him, it was because I was feeling very lonely and stressed, and I felt I needed someone by my side. But slowly I came to realize that I love him* [lo quiero y lo amo] *as a partner, husband, father of my son, and as a person. He has respected me as a person, and I respect him.*
>
> —MONA, TWENTY-EIGHT

> *I met her, and then I started to change my life; then I wasn't just hanging out anymore. Everything changed. I think that if I hadn't met her maybe I would even be dead now. . . . For me she is the most beautiful thing I've had in my life. . . . She is my light; she is my star; she is the path to my happiness.*
>
> —FRANCISCO, FORTY-TWO

Many couples described the emotional importance of their relationships amid their challenges related to economic insecurity and the social exclusion they experienced due to their involvement in sex work and drug use. Raphael, forty-two, and Martina, thirty-four, were in a relationship for nearly two years. Martina said that she "needs him emotionally" and loves him. In the following passage she describes what she values about their relationship: "His maturity that he has and the way that he thinks of doing things, that it is not a game, that he has shown me that it is not to get money from me, that it is not just to have sex with me and to leave. . . . He supports me in many ways, and, like I tell you, his maturity more than anything. 'In love,' I can't say that, but I do love him a lot *[enamorado, no te puedo decir, pero si lo quiero mucho]*."

Likewise, Raphael explained that their relationship remained strong and that he feels "affection and gratitude" toward her. He acknowledged that outsiders often dehumanize and mistreat sex workers, but he saw another side of her: "Most people judge people like her [sex workers] like trash, you know? Like something that has no worth. We don't see if they have feelings, or if it's someone who is worthy. But she is making an effort. There are men as well as women that don't fight to make it, to survive. She has done whatever she has to. I think that it is difficult for a woman to make a decision like that [engaging in sex work], and it is difficult to find someone that will support them, someone that values them, you know?" Through their shared struggles, they cared for and valued each other. Raphael said they were together not out of self-interest but for emotional connection: "We have gone through tough times, and we are still together because there is something there, right? Because we *feel something*."

Similarly, Karla, forty-three, and Miguel, forty-nine, have been together for nearly fourteen years, including struggling with economic insecurity and their limited options in which her sex work is about the couples' survival and provision for their child. Karla loves her partner and described the comfort of their relationship as "more than anything I find support, protection. I can count on him because before I just counted on myself. . . . In the good times and in the bad times, in sickness and happiness, together, morally as well as economically, we complement each other." Karla describes some other sex workers as not understanding their relationship, some of whom have accused her of having a "pimp." She tells them to "go to hell." Across our sample, both quantitatively and qualitatively, couples denied that male partners were "pimps" and explained that their relationships were meaningful and distinct apart from sex work (Mittal et al. 2018).

Typical of other male partners in our study, Miguel loved Karla and expressed the meaning of their relationship as emotionally distinct from her job. However, he acknowledged the emotional turmoil that he has had to negotiate in the context of Karla's sex work: "I mean, she is my wife. Yes, I love her *[la quiero]* and to know that she was having sex with another person would make my head go crazy. How is it possible? But I had to go through some rough times to be able to accept there is no other option, and she is my wife and I think that even then she still loves me. I mean she keeps loving me and she has been taking her job like a job, without mixing her feelings." Miguel's experience was common in terms of what he and other male partners like him go through in reconciling the intimacy of their relationship with their partner's work. The distinction of women not "mixing feelings" with their job represented an important form of boundary making that distinguished intimate partners from pimps and helped both partners cope with their situation.

Juan Carlos, age fifty-two, offered one of the most provocative and clear explanations of the emotional importance of sex workers' relationships amid the myriad challenges that couples faced. In discussing his six-year relationship with his wife, Paz, forty, he eloquently delineated the difference between physical and emotional relationship boundaries:

> In a relationship like mine [with a sex worker], you need to define where sex ends and emotions begin. I think it is the same for my partner, because it is more of an emotional need that I need to give her because of her work, and in that sense I don't think there is someone out there who loves her like I do *[vaya a haber alguien que la vaya a querer a ella como yo la quiero]*. I also don't think that there is another woman who will love me like she does *[como ella me quiere]*. I don't feel that there is a threat, so there is no reason for me to be jealous, because the physical is just physical, and the emotional is a whole other thing. That is why I said that you need to define your relationship.

These brief sketches begin to materialize a key theme of this book: the emotional importance of sex workers' relationships emerges from and must be understood in relation to the broader circumstances of disadvantage and vulnerability that underpin their work. These circumstances put women into situations in which they—and their male partners—rely on sex work amid few other options. Sex work creates challenges to their pursuit of intimacy and necessitates adopting strategies of emotional boundary making.

As elaborated in the composite stories of Lucia and Jaime and Julieta and Mateo in chapter 2, sex work also shifts gender roles, complicates notions of masculinity, and introduces social and health-related risks through concurrent sexual relationships that threaten to create conflict and emotional injury to partners. In response couples strategically negotiate their competing risks to uphold their emotional fidelity to each other and prioritize their dangerous safe havens. As I argue throughout the upcoming narratives, it is critically important to understand how couples emotionally demarcate their relationships, which allows us to redraw the boundaries of "love" and "risk."

* * *

Further complicating these relationships, sex work is often intertwined with drug use. For many couples, addiction reinforced women's need to engage in sex work to help support the couple. Couples who use drugs have daily physiological needs to cure, including people who use heroin who often need to inject anywhere from three to five times per day to stave off debilitating withdrawal symptoms. For couples like Jazmine, forty-six, and Eduardo, thirty, who both injected heroin, "drugs don't have a role" in their relationship—drugs are *"our reality,"* as Jazmine put it. How does a shared reality of drug addiction shape these intimate relationships?

Per eligibility criteria, all women enrolled in Parejas reported recent drug use, as this is an epidemiological indicator of risk for HIV and other health harms. While their male partners did not have to report drug use to enroll, the majority of these men also used drugs. Couples talked about their drug use and its role in their relationship in a range of ways, from it being the glue in the relationship because that is all they had ever known together, to something the couple shared that did not diminish their love for each other.

While there is a growing literature centering on the emotional dimensions of drug use among couples (e.g., Morris et al. 2019; Rhodes et al. 2017), some social theorists have remained skeptical. In writing about drug use, bell hooks (2001a) acknowledges that individuals who have suffered pain and hardship in their lives may turn to drugs to experience the pleasure and comfort that they have been unable to find elsewhere. In the process of developing an addiction, individuals become cut off from other people and focused on drug use, which, she asserts, keeps people from being able to love. But does drug use really erase any potential for love and care?

The couples in the forthcoming chapters all experienced chaotic drug use, and, as we will see, the answers are not always so clear-cut. While plenty has been written about drug use in terms of health risks, conflict, the vulnerability of women, exploitative relationships, and other negative angles, I am more interested in writing about drug use with love (Dominguez 2000). This doesn't mean glossing over the ugliness of addiction, but it does entail digging beneath dominant narratives to explore the emotional side. It also demands an empathetic attention to the context of the border region, where saturated drug markets, drug-related violence, and the lack of evidence-based and humane drug treatment options for couples enact even further violence if partners want to seek help.

Some partners, like Jazmine, seem to have internalized dominant ideas about how drug use makes love a condition of impossibility: "They say an addict doesn't love, 'since they love themselves they can't love any other person,'" she repeated from an unknown source. When not using drugs, "you get your feelings out and you're more aware," she admitted. But Jazmine and Eduardo have been together for two years, and she said she loves him *(lo quiero)*. She wouldn't want to leave him even if they stopped using drugs, and she might even appreciate him more if he were "normal" (not using drugs). Eduardo had a similarly complicated view of their relationship, as he explained: "With drugs I'm not romantic," but "there are feelings" in the relationship, and he described them as "good partners." Neither of them knew if they would ever stop using drugs, and, if they did, what that might mean for their relationship.

Addiction is a complex physiological, social, and emotional condition, and it is perhaps unsurprising that couples often shared ambivalence around quitting and worried what that could mean for their relationships. This was further complicated when partners had different desires and motivations for quitting or in cases in which both partners used drugs but had different patterns of use that did not align with each other (e.g., injecting heroin vs. smoking meth, with their different physiological responses). However, in all cases, drug use, quitting, and relapse are not individual actions but embedded within broader sets of social relationships. These themes are further explored in chapter 3 in the stories of Celia and Lazarus and Mildred and Ronaldo.

In fact, many couples admitted that while drug use was a shared "reality" that created hardships and health risks, they contested that drugs were the *only* reality of their relationships. In some cases couples in Parejas met each other because of drugs; in these examples each partner already lived through hardships and trauma that pushed them toward drug use, and finding another partner who had similarly suffered and soothed their pain with drugs fomented a shared understanding. Many of these couples insisted on defining themselves as more than their drugs use:

> *The truth is, I am a person, and, above all, I am with her, and I am with her because I have feelings for her, right? But yes, everything started with drugs. If I remained with her when I started giving her drugs, it was with one thing in mind. . . . That's how our relationship started, and, I don't know, I imagine it was the same for her, right? If she remained with me, it was for drugs too, right? But now, there's feelings from her to me, and from me to her, more than anything.*
>
> —ESTEBAN, AGE TWENTY-TWO

> *My relationship with her is not based on drugs now; it's based on feelings* [sentimiento] *that I have for her. I am in love with her* [estoy enamorado de ella], *and I love her* [la quiero] *the same way with drugs or without drugs. I have told her, the day that I want to leave drugs because of boredom or because of medical necessity, to say it that way, I will continue to love her the same, and I need her more than I need the drugs. And the same if she wishes tomorrow to stop using drugs, she has all my support. . . . My relationship with her doesn't just revolve around a syringe.*
>
> —GUILLERMO, AGE FORTY-FOUR

Can couples have loving relationships while using drugs? Is this only talk, or could it be that shared addictions refashion the possibilities for care, support, and understanding that people who use drugs otherwise fail to find in society? Chapter 4 explores these questions through the story of Cindy and Beto. Their relationship challenges common notions like that of Jazmine's, who internalized the idea that "an addict doesn't love" because of preoccupation with drug use. Chapter 5 further complicates these questions, as drug use is interwoven into the life histories of Maria and Gwen but leads to different health outcomes that shaped their intimate relationships. Without romanticizing the experience of drug-using couples or ignoring the real health harms of drug use, abjectly dismissing possibilities for love in these relationships contributes to the dehumanization of people who use drugs and enacts further harm to partners. Attention to drug use not only for its production of health-related harms but for its deep entanglements in social and sexual relations can open up new ways of thinking about what it means to love and care in contexts of disadvantage.

*　*　*

For sex workers and their intimate partners in the Mexico-US border region, lifetimes of trauma, drug addiction, and forms of social and economic exclusion converge to shape couples' emotional well-being and collective survival strategies. In the border context, economies with deep histories of sex work and sexualized geographies connected to the United States offer women an option for economic independence and survival. While many studies of sex work focus on health risks, violence, and hardships—and I don't gloss over that—other dimensions of sex workers' lives are equally important in understanding their well-being. This chapter provides a historical overview of Tijuana, focusing on its economies of sex and drugs, while paying homage to an evolution of research studies that began to push beyond the usual foci in sex work scholarship. Building on these histories, this book prioritizes a space for sex workers' relationships and the possibilities of love, just as sex workers have demanded.

This chapter also offers a basic description of the Parejas study, from which the couples in this book were sampled. Drawing on data from the larger study offers insight into experiences of love and care among sex workers and their non-commercial partners. It positions the experiences of couples in the forthcoming chapters not as outliers but as illustrative of the major themes we identified across our data sources in Parejas. While the strength of the emotional bonds, the kinds of love shared, and forms of support varied across the couples in Parejas, these relationships were foundationally important. What is significant is how little attention we have paid to this critical aspect of sex workers' experiences in research and global health policy.

Certainly, key questions remain. Of course love is more complex than a description; if love is a verb, then it also needs to be understood in terms of practice. How do couples demonstrate love and care, particularly in challenging social contexts? What can ethnographic case studies help us see beneath the epidemiologic indicators of risk? Some of the creative means that couples use to define their relationships and prioritize their emotional well-being in the context of concurrent sexual relationships and sex work are taken up in greater detail in the next chapter.

Where Sex Ends and Emotions Begin

Jaime first saw Lucia in the Red Light District of Tijuana shortly after he was discharged from a drug rehabilitation center. He was enamored but initially too shy to speak to her. After he relapsed he got up the nerve to approach her when he saw her again. Lucia also used meth and injected heroin, and the two quickly formed a relationship. Within a few months they moved into a hotel room together. They used condoms in the beginning of the relationship but stopped after they established themselves as a couple because they loved and trusted each other. However, Lucia engaged in sex work, and Jaime pursued casual sexual partnerships apart from Lucia. Lucia's sex work was motivated by financial and material support, but Jaime sought outside sexual partners for pleasure. On the surface the sexual activity of both Jaime and Lucia complicates—and perhaps even contradicts—the notions of love and commitment that each of them proclaimed. How do we make sense of this?

Overlapping sexual relationships are often understood in terms of "sexual concurrency" in global public health research. Concurrency refers to overlapping sexual relationships that can facilitate transmission of HIV/STIs due to the shortened periods between multiple sexual contacts, in which inconsistent condom use among partners can exacerbate disease transmission and acquisition (Morris and Kretzschmar 1997). While diseases are clearly a concern, as explored later in this chapter, there is less scholarship theorizing the structural, social, and emotional contexts surrounding sexual concurrency. As a result, the voices of couples themselves often get lost in narratives of epidemiological risk and infection.

This chapter explores emotional intimacy within sex workers' primary relationships by reinterpreting patterns of sexual concurrency. Drawing on the stories of Lucia and Jaime and Julieta and Mateo, it shifts the narrative beyond individual, risk-based explanatory models of sexual behavior to a broader conceptualization bridging sociopolitical contexts with emotional lived experience. Through Lucia's relationship with Jaime, we learn that even while clients and outside sexual partners are shrouded in secret, these partners have a different symbolic meaning than the primary relationship. As shown in Julieta's relationship with Mateo, the secrecy of such outside partnerships introduces real worries about health risks. This opens up questions about the weight of disclosing these risks, including HIV/STIs, given that couples try to preserve their collective emotional well-being amid ongoing physical health threats. Put another way, both couples' stories illustrate how the multiple meanings of sex, especially *outside* of the primary relationship, say something important about emotional intimacy *within* the primary relationship.

Importantly, studying sexual behavior lends itself to a unique set of challenges in research. Sex is a sensitive topic, and it is difficult, if not impossible, to validate self-reported information about sexual practices in standard data collection methods. I draw on fieldwork, multiple interviews, and photovoice projects with Lucia and Jaime and Julieta and Mateo, while contextualizing their stories within other findings from the Parejas study to show the commonality of their experiences. Integrating multiple sources of data lends rich, even if still incomplete, insight into the practice and social meaning of concurrent sexual relationships.

Of further note, working with couples on questions of sexual behavior and the potential consequences of testing positive for HIV/STIs introduces ethical questions around confidentiality and the sensitivity of data. For participant protection the couples presented here are "composite couples," meaning that all the experiences and direct quotes are grounded in data, but I obscured some of the potentially identifying partner characteristics and spliced together details from multiple couples to construct the stories.[1] As an example of an ethical quandary, Lucia and Jaime participated in my photovoice project. Like I did for all couples, I asked about their preferences for where they wanted to meet for the photo interviews and if they wanted to be interviewed together. I asked Lucia about how she wished to conduct our interviews, but she deferred to Jaime. When I asked him about his preference, he wanted to do individual interviews in the office in the Red Light District and apart from Lucia because "there are secrets."

LUCIA AND JAIME

At twenty-five, Lucia was one of the youngest women in the entire Parejas study. She always wore flowery dresses, and her long, dark hair was streaked with fuchsia and purple highlights. Her enviably clear skin and wide, light eyes exuded a youthful appearance. Lucia was from central Mexico, but her mother moved the family to Tijuana when she married an American man. Her mom had documentation to cross the border to the United States, but Lucia and her five sisters did not. When her stepfather died, her mother moved the family back south, but Lucia stayed behind. Although all of her family lived in their hometown, Lucia said she had

FIGURE 1. Inside Lucia and Jaime's dangerous safe haven, a decorated hotel room in the middle of the Red Light District of Tijuana. Photo by Lucia.

more autonomy in Tijuana. She called her lifestyle "fun and free," whereas in her hometown people were "discreet" about engaging in socially stigmatized behaviors such as drug use.

Also a migrant, Jaime, thirty, grew up in a small city in western Mexico. He had been living in Tijuana since he was deported from the United States on drug charges several years ago. He spent nearly a decade in Los Angeles, where he loved the anonymity of the big city and the freedom to live his life as he wanted rather than conforming to familial expectations. Jaime said that where he grew up, people "worked all the time" and that people who used drugs were judged. After Jaime was deported he settled in Tijuana, where he met other deportees who helped him navigate his way in a new city. Although he spoke about wanting to be open about his life, he also portrayed a carefully managed image. Jaime always presented for his interviews impeccably dressed in a crisp button-down shirt neatly tucked into jeans, with his long hair shiny and greased back into a ponytail.

Lucia and Jaime lived in a hotel room in the middle of the Red Light District. They recently moved there after their previous residence was broken into and nearly all of their belongings were stolen. They felt more secure in this new location, which had staff working the front desk twenty-four hours a day. It was a small space, but they liked spending time there. Juxtaposed to the noisy chaos and frequent violence outside of their walls, their room had a whimsical feel, almost like a child's bedroom or a college dorm room. Lucia had a significant hand

FIGURE 2. A poster of Minnie Mouse that Lucia colored herself. This was one of Lucia's favorite photos. Photo by Lucia.

in decorating it with all types of accoutrements like stuffed animals, dolls, and flowers. The Virgin of Guadalupe on the wall was an important cultural symbol of their religious beliefs, except that Jaime refused to attend mass, which worried Lucia that the devil will torment him. Other than this, their walls were adorned with secular items, such as colorful construction paper, a poster of Tinkerbell, and Lucia's drawings. One of Lucia's favorites was a poster of Minnie Mouse that she had hand-colored with crayons and wrote, "Te Amo" (I Love You). Jaime and Lucia spent most of their time alone together in the dangerous safe haven that they had cocreated. As migrants apart from their families in the city, they provided comfort, support, and care for each other in the physical and emotional safety of their dangerous safe haven.

Like many couples in Parejas, Lucia and Jaime loved each other. "I have a heart for her," Jaime told me, "and I love her *[la quiero]*." When I asked him what he considered to be most important to him in an intimate relationship, he said "respect" and "love" were key and defining characteristics of what they shared as a couple: "Respect is the most important thing . . . and love, right? Because where there is love and there is respect, the couple can move on. But if there is disrespect and bad words, then it is as if it were a toy. I would just play with her . . . but there has always been respect and love between us." Here Jaime signaled the commitment in his relationship; she was not a "toy" but rather a partner with whom to build a life. Even in having outside sexual partners, in his mind, he was not "playing" with Lucia in this relationship.

Prior to Lucia, Jaime never had a long-term relationship, nor a relationship serious enough to let his family know. Even in their shared drug use, Lucia was different:

> The other partners I have had have been a maximum of four months, but I have now been with her for two and a half years. We understand each other well, and I know when she wants something, and she also knows when I want something, and we try to give that to each other. We have a good time. With the other partners, I've only been accustomed to them and that's it, but not with her; with her it is different. In other words, despite the fact that we use drugs, she is a different person than the other partners that I have had. She talks to my family on the phone, and we talk with her family; we have communication between the families. But my family does not use drugs, and neither does her family. What we try to do [is] to lead another normal life, as they do, but for two and a half years, we haven't stopped using drugs.

For Jaime and Lucia, their "fun and free" life in Tijuana had to be managed in relation with "another normal life" that would be accepted by their families. However, "it is the life that one lives here in Tijuana," Jaime said, explaining that they passed much of their time injecting heroin and smoking meth together in their hotel room. Within the perceived safety of their dangerous safe haven, they had always used drugs together. In their ambivalence and difficulties in cutting down or stopping their drug use, they found ways to navigate their shared addictions and cultivate a socially acceptable script of their relationship to outsiders.

Despite the centrality of drugs to their relationship, Lucia and Jaime were the only couple in the photovoice project who did not take any photographs of drug use. Lucia did not want to risk her family members finding any drug photos when they came to visit. Jaime did not take any photos of his drug use either, which he claimed was out of respect for Lucia's wishes. Related to Jaime's concerns with respect and image management, the couple took a whole series of photos of him well-dressed in button-down shirts, with the intent to share these "respectable" photos with his family. But he also posed for a series of photos wearing Los Angeles Dodgers gear and throwing gang signs; one photo depicts him opening his jacket to reveal the sizeable tattoo across his stomach in homage to his former gang life in Los Angeles.

By capturing and avoiding certain images on film, Jaime curated a specific personal image he wanted to project in real life. While both of them may have felt young and free in Tijuana to do as they pleased, they were also still careful to manage their reputations back home.[2] Thus far at least, they had been able to manage their drug use without breaking their familial relationships. In the same way, they were just as careful to manage their outside sexual partnerships without spoiling their own relationship and the image of the good partner that they projected to each other.

SEX WORK AND SECRETS

Lucia supported the couple primarily through sex work. Although Jaime contributed as he could, she had more flexibility and earning power than he did. While the couple had learned to navigate the complex and potentially volatile dynamics of the arrangement, this does not mean it was easy for either partner. Each deployed a set of strategic practices in relation to sex work to ensure their emotional well-being. I start by contextualizing Lucia's sex work strategies within the larger Parejas study to show the commonality and meaning of these practices.

Lucia, like other women in Parejas, had to negotiate her work without it interfering in her intimate relationship. As one key strategy, women exerted considerable autonomy and agency in their work that they kept separate from their partners. Lucia and most of the other women enrolled in Parejas could be considered in the category of "freelance" sex workers. In our larger study just 10 out of 212 women surveyed reported having a "manager, administrator, or pimp" *(supervisor, administrador, o padrote)*, 5 of whom said it was their intimate partner with whom they were enrolled in the Parejas study. Most women reported sharing their earnings from sex work with their steady male partner and exerted substantial individual control over everyday decisions, including when to work, how much to charge, what type of sex acts they were willing to engage in, and negotiations around condom use. We asked these survey questions separately of women and men, and their answers speaking to women's autonomy matched remarkably well (Mittal et al. 2018). For Lucia and others, her decisions in her sex working life were her own, and it was important that she maintain a separation between her clients and Jaime.

Within the autonomy of sex work, client selection is another important strategy for women to both provide financially and maintain their health and relationships. The women in Parejas described different types of clients whom they assessed as posing both health and social risks. On a scale of least to most desirable clients, "one-time" clients posed the greatest potential harm through their unknown health status and threats of violence, while regular, steady clients women had known for some time were considered the safest (and all the better if these were wealthy men from the United States). However, women had to balance the physical safety and financial security that regular clients provided while preempting the social risks of these clients "falling in love" with them. Crossing such emotional borders could render client condom negotiation difficult and jeopardize their primary relationship (Robertson et al. 2014b). Overwhelmingly, women like Lucia considered their clients to be sources of income and not pursuits of love or intimacy, but any illusion as such to women's intimate partners could create emotional harm and jealousy within their relationship.

Lucia's youth and beauty attracted a range of clients, particularly much older men. Lucia's three regular clients were important sources of steady income. One older American client had erectile dysfunction and paid her US$50 in cash per hour for her to take off her clothes. Another regular is a Mexican man who paid 400 pesos (about US$33 at the time) for forty minutes, and they always used condoms. Her final regular client was most lucrative—and problematic—from the standpoint of managing emotions. This fifty-year-old American crossed the border every Friday night to have sex with her at least three times over the weekend, for which he paid $US100 in cash per interaction. He insisted that they not use condoms, and Lucia relented not because she had feelings for him but because such consistent and relatively well-paying arrangements were difficult to come by. However, she had to balance her negotiations with him to let him know that she did not love him without threatening the business arrangement. As she reflected, "I guess sometimes having regulars is good because you know it is there and it is for sure, but at the same time I am like, 'No, no, no, I have a partner that I love. I don't love anybody else apart from him. I am not trying to make you love me.'"

Lucia also sometimes engaged in two to four transactions per day with one-time clients to supplement her income, but she insisted on using condoms in these circumstances because the men were unfamiliar to her. The most annoying clients in this category were those who used meth. They had a hard time "finishing" and wanted additional time beyond the standard fifteen minutes. "But I can't be taking care of them as long as they want," she explained. For Lucia sex with clients was strictly a business transaction, while sex with Jaime was "different" because there was "*feeling* in it."

Although it was strictly a job to Lucia, and Jaime knew about her sex work, they rarely discussed it directly. Tactics of avoidance, telling little lies, and glossing over sex work were common among couples in Parejas, and consistent with larger and pervasive forms of "sexual silence" in many parts of Latin America (Carrillo 2002; Padilla 2007). Sexual silence refers to the complicated set of strategies that individuals employ to avoid speaking directly about sex, while simultaneously maintaining a thinly guised communication about it. Silence creates an illusion of fidelity, preserves the emotional integrity of the relationship, and diffuses any questions that might shatter this mirage. It upholds ideals of culturally acceptable social and sexual identities in contexts in which "normal" sexual behavior is narrowly defined. In this sense couples' unspoken acceptance of sex work is based on a "mutual pretense," or a social permission for certain sexual behaviors to coexist, so long as it was not discussed openly (Padilla 2007, 50). Essentially, sexual silence is a strategic tactic employed by socially marginalized individuals to avoid certain kinds of sexual disclosure. As we will see, in addition to sex work, these forms of silence also apply to the pursuit of outside sexual partners for pleasure and HIV/STI disclosure within relationships.

Jaime found out about Lucia's sex work a few weeks into their relationship, right after being released from a short stint in the *pinta* (jail). While they were handwashing their clothes one day, Lucia confessed that she had been with clients to earn money while he was gone. At first Jaime was furious and impulsively threw the bucket of cold, dirty laundry water at her. But as Lucia reminded him, "I'm going with clients not because I love them. . . . Would you rather sell meth and go to jail?"

Given his clean-cut appearance and basic English proficiency, Jaime sometimes sold drugs to US tourists who crossed the border to wander around the Red Light District looking for a good time. However, this put Jaime at constant risk of police surveillance, and he had been arrested multiple times but always released for lack of evidence. He also worked odd jobs, including earning money from working at a "swap meet" (an adopted English name for informal places that sell a variety of used and recycled items, akin to a flea market). However, his informal and unsteady employment was not enough to support their expenses of rent, food, drugs, and other basic needs. Lucia's job brought in steady income and created less risk from law enforcement, reducing the chance they would be separated through incarceration. The one time Lucia was stopped by the police trying to sell things in the border-crossing area without a permit, she sobbed and pleaded with the authorities not to be taken to jail. She and Jaime made a pact not to leave each other if one were jailed.

From Jaime's perspective, sex work was something to reluctantly accept as part of their relationship. Although he wanted to cultivate "another kind of life for her to get out of prostituting," he had to become accustomed to Lucia's sex work because they needed the money and selling drugs was risky. Although he learned to tolerate it, that doesn't mean that he felt good about it:

> Well, like my wife, she has relationships with other people, right? Because for money or drugs. And then one, as a man, has to put up with that, right? I have also had relationships only with women, but never in exchange for drugs or in exchange for nothing, just always for pleasure. But, well, it is a bit difficult for your partner to be with another man—that is, one feels bad, but then one cannot do anything. If one wants to do something, then he has to have to work to be able to give her a house or give her comforts.

All at once Jaime remained frustrated that he couldn't provide more, internalized the blame for his inadequate provision, and tacitly justified his own acting out in pursuit of other pleasures because of the difficulty of the situation. While he never outright admitted he was jealous of Lucia's clients, Lucia confirmed it: "It's true—he's super jealous," she said, which is why she never talked about her work with him. It upset him and in turn further damaged his self-perceptions of worth. In grappling with the fears and anxieties embedded in jealousy and love, French philosopher Roland Barthes writes, "As a jealous man, I suffer four times over: because I am jealous, because I blame myself for being so, because I fear that my jealousy will wound the other, because I allow myself to be subject to a banality: I suffer from being excluded, from being aggressive, from being crazy, and from being common" (1977, 146). In other words, jealousy is not just about the act of sex; it is embedded in multiple forms of social and emotional injury. As Jaime internalized his defeat in accepting Lucia's sex work, he struggled with his relationship and his life circumstances and found other outlets to reconcile his jealousy and restore some sense of his masculinity.

Unbeknown to Lucia, Jaime had three other sexual partners during the course of their relationship. He claimed he always used condoms with these other women because he did not love them nor have the same trust in them as he shared with Lucia. With these partners he indulged in sex only for pleasure in the context of drug use. Indeed, the "secrets" Jaime alluded to as part of his photovoice project turned out to be a series of photographs of one of his outside partners. This partner was an American woman living in Tijuana, who dated a much older American man who smoked meth and often became violent with her. They had a particularly nasty fight that day, so she went to Jaime's room to seek condolence and smoke meth with him. Although they did not have sex on that occasion, they did several months prior in an open hotel room down the hall from Jaime's room. Jaime said he would do it again if the opportunity presented itself, but he spent so much time with Lucia that it had not been feasible.

Jaime explained that he engaged in these outside sexual pursuits to satisfy his appetite for sexual variety and adventure: "And with the others, it's like for pleasure, right? It's like feeling, oh, like a man, good! *[Laughs.]* Right? With Lucia, I only do it for love, and with the other ones I don't. I'm like a bull, right? One does different things. . . . I'm not as forward with my wife as I am with them. With them, if you want, you can do it like this, or this, and this, or that, but with Lucia, it's only like this, and that's it." Jaime emphasized that there were distinctions between his casual sex partners and Lucia. His outside partners were purely for sexual pleasure. Jaime framed his discussion of sex with Lucia as typical sex, whereas outside partners allowed him to feel masculine and indulge, experiment, and enjoy a variety of activities incongruent with a stereotypical image of the good wife, even if the wife herself led another sexual life (Castañeda and Ortiz 1996; Hirsch et al. 2002).

Lucia did not know about the American woman or any of the other outside partners that Jaime had been with. However, further complicating their story, she was suspicious that he had other sexual relationships with men. She had seen him talking to men on the street, which Jaime had claimed to be in relation to his small-scale drug dealing, but Lucia was unsure: "If I ask him, 'Are you gay, or what?' ¡Nombre, chale! [Oh God, wow! (implying a feeling of simultaneous surprise and disappointment)]. I ask him, 'Why do these men come to look for you? No one just gives you free money.' Then I stop asking questions because that's how we start arguing." Just like Jaime, Lucia's own approach to sexual concurrency was to resort to silence to avoid arguments and keep herself from getting hurt. "I don't keep on about it because I know it's the drugs," she later rationalized. "Everybody who uses drugs at some point or another exchanges sex for drugs."

Jaime claimed to sell meth to several gay men who called him to meet at a hotel downtown, but he never told me about any outside male sexual partners. Although Lucia read beyond his script, she did not have any concrete evidence of his outside sexual conduct. If neither partner asked or offered details, the secrets and little lies kept each other socially and emotionally safe in their relationship.

As bell hooks (2001a) notes, men's lies are often forgiven, which is part of the power, privilege, and demand of patriarchal societies in which being a "real man" means being above the law, whether that be an actual political framework or the rules of intimate relationships. Further, hooks notes that it is not an accident that a greater cultural acceptance of lying coincides with women gaining greater social equality; as women's earning power increases, and we become more economically self-sufficient, men often deploy subtler strategies to retain a sense of masculinity and some level of social control.

Read within the broader sociopolitical and cultural context, it thus "makes sense" for Jaime to pursue outside sexual encounters and lie about it. His behavior is rooted in oppression, poverty, feelings of inferiority, and a loss of dignity and self-worth, which can trigger men to act out in harmful ways (Anzaldúa [1987] 2012). He truly felt bad he couldn't give Lucia more, and her sex work tormented him. Outside sexual partners enabled him to recapture some semblance of his masculinity and control, while the little lies and silence around such pursuits didn't risk what he had with Lucia.

Lucia and Jaime's story also speaks to the methodological and ethical difficulties of conducting sexual research: Whose version of these events is "true"? If lies are told with good intentions, are they necessarily harmful? If Jaime was concerned about his image, did he hide sexual transactions with men and take photos of an American female sex partner to curate a specific heterosexual image for me, an American female researcher probing into his sex life? Regardless, Jaime's photo project revealed something important about the meaning of dangerous safe havens. In contrast to his secrets, Jaime took a series of photos of Lucia, which he looked at in a very different light. There are photos of her goofing off in the hotel room, eating ice cream, and making faces at him. He deeply belly laughed several times throughout his interview at a selfie of them lying in bed together. She wore a wide-eyed, surprised expression on her face that appeared so childlike and innocent even though she was high on meth. When I asked him if there were any differences between the American woman and Lucia, he looked deeply at Lucia's photo, clenched his fist to his heart, and said that she was the one he really loved. The other woman was just sex. But Lucia represented an emotional connection: "She is my life."

JULIETA AND MATEO

The story of Julieta, thirty, and Mateo, thirty-six, further illustrates the complexity of outside sexual partnerships in terms of how we assess risk. I met the couple when they returned to the project office to retrieve their HIV/STI test results as part of their participation in Parejas. Julieta later admitted to me that she was terrified to receive her results but had to play it cool in front of her partner. Their story reveals how physical health threats and conditions of chronic illness become entangled in the silences of concurrent sexual relationships.

Julieta had a tattoo of three tiny dots in a triangular formation to signify *la vida loca*. She was tall and slim, with expressive hazel eyes and an animated style of communicating. Mateo was the more reserved partner of the pair; he had a slight build and slender face that often wore a serious expression. Mateo had lived in the United States, and most of his family was still there, but he was convicted of murder (which he claimed he was framed for), spent eight years in prison, and eventually was deported to Tijuana.

Julieta and Mateo first met in a drug rehabilitation center in Tijuana several years ago. At the time Mateo was "tired" of his heroin use and wanted a change. On the other hand, Julieta was forced into rehab after family tragedy: when her young son died in a motorcycle accident, she fell into a profound depression, began to drink heavily and use drugs, and lost her will to live. Her family forced her to enter an inpatient rehabilitation program, as is permitted by Mexican law. But Julieta was not particularly interested in rehab, and she described horrible, abusive living conditions and tactics of humiliation as part of her "treatment," which has been reported in facilities across Mexico.[3] The experience did not help her. She marked her child's death as a turning point in her life and said she has never been the same.

After she was released from rehab, she went back to her hometown in western Mexico. Mateo was released soon after and promptly followed her there. He spent nearly two years searching for her before they reconnected and eventually became a couple. After living there for five years, they recently moved back to Tijuana. After a brief stay in a rat-infested apartment in the Zona Norte where Julieta witnessed someone get shot in the street, they moved to a modest apartment in the quieter outskirts of the city.

A major reason for the couple moving back to Tijuana was Mateo's chronic illness. Mateo said he had advanced cirrhosis. Every day he took up to twelve pills and vitamins to treat his condition and related health issues, but he still often vomited blood and had bloody bowel movements. He required blood transfusions and recently almost died during a lengthy period of hospitalization. They wanted to be closer to advanced medical care and his family for support, but in reality they did not see them very often. Mateo's family sent money to help with rent, and his sister lived near them, so they could often rely on her for material support. But the rest of his family was on the other side of the border; since he could not cross into the United States, he had to wait until they came to Tijuana to visit.

Their collective traumatic experiences intensified their relationship on many levels, as they increasingly came to count on each other. Mateo acknowledged the role of love in their relationship and explained how their emotional bond strengthened over time: "Love is very important because if there was no love we would not be together. And then if the only thing that keeps us together is because of money—but we do not have money, right? In other words, she is not with me for anything but for love, right? Over time I think I love her more *[la quiero más]*. I take care for her more. When we started together, we were okay for a while, but today I think I take more care of her, and I appreciate her more." Reflecting on the role of illness in their relationship, he continued, "I love her a lot *[la quiero mucho]*; she has supported me a lot through my illness, in everything. I count only on her; she's for me. I can now say that she's everything for me. I don't have anyone else, in my mind and everywhere it's only her."

Separately, Julieta described a similar evolution of her feelings over time. Early on in the relationship, he was the pursuer. She cared for him, but she was not as serious about him as he felt for her. However, over time she came to love him, which intensified in the course of his illness: "I've changed with him—that is, now I feel like I have more responsibility because he is very good to me. Now since he is sick I feel that I love him more *[lo quiero más]*. His disease has brought us closer together."

Mateo's health condition dramatically shaped their relationship, both emotionally and materially. Due to his illness, he could no longer work as an electrician. Julieta took on the role as the primary financial provider, which made Mateo upset. According to Julieta, "He wants to be well because he wants to go back to work. He gets depressed, he feels bad that I work and he does not work. He thinks that I'm going to get angry and that I'm going to go away and I'm going to leave him here. And he gets sad about it because he can't work and help me."

But Julieta was not angry. In fact, she too often felt sad because she thought "he is going to die." She accepted the need to be a provider and had no plans to leave. Instead, their situation shifted their roles and the forms of care and support they provided for each other. Mateo stayed home and cooked (Julieta hated to cook), while Julieta became the primary breadwinner. In turn, they joked that he was a *mandilón*—connoting a man who does as he is told by his female partner and takes on "traditional" gender roles often reserved for women.

The complexity of shifting gender roles and notions of masculinity interwoven into both couples' stories in this chapter represent emergent themes across the stories of couples enrolled in Parejas. Like other couples, Julieta and Mateo's relationship pushes back against a reification of masculinity. Their story highlights the need for historicized understandings of gender relations in local contexts.[4] Matthew Gutmann (1996) offers one such example in his work on masculinity in Mexico City, in which he deconstructs the social complexity underlying categories used to describe men, including *mandilón*, which is often thought of in diminutive and disparaging ways. But Julieta and Mateo reclaimed this term.

Even though Mateo was sick, Julieta said that she would always take care of him "no matter what." To Julieta "*Somos uno, no somos dos, somos uno* [We are one, not two, we are one]." As Gutmann notes, ideas about masculinity "make sense only in relation to other identities" (1996, 238). Julieta and Mateo's relationship worked because they were "one" in relation to each other and against a world where they lacked social support and sufficient material means to attend to his serious medical condition. The couple loved each other and met each other's needs, even if it defied "traditional" understandings of masculinity. These gendered dynamics played out in several ways, including their shared heroin use and concurrent sexual relationships.

As it turns out, part of the "no matter what" that Julieta committed to in the relationship was their mutual relapse into heroin use. It was much easier for the couple to remain abstinent when they lived farther from the border because the heroin market was not well developed there compared to Tijuana, where drugs were "everywhere." They turned back to injecting heroin shortly after they arrived in Tijuana because of easy availability and the temptation to soothe their struggles with depression and illness. Now Julieta's new role as the main provider included both earning money and purchasing heroin for the couple, a traditional male role among drug-using couples.

My colleague and I caught a glimpse of the gendered dynamics of their drug use when visiting their home nestled in the crackled hillsides outside of the city. From the office downtown we rode in a communal van along the narrow and steep roads snaking underneath homes perched precariously on cliffs. When we reached a corner market, we disembarked and Julieta headed to a *connecta*, a nondescript house, where some young males milled about outside. A man wearing a San Diego Padres jacket rode up on a bike and stopped in while she was inside. She emerged and we piled into a taxi and took off up another impossibly steep hill until we reached their modest apartment building at the crest.

Their front door opened up into a kitchen, with one large window facing out front. Underneath was a counter and sink full of dirty dishes, even though they cooked at his sister's home and sometimes at the neighbor's apartment because they did not have a stove or refrigerator. We walked through to the living area, adorned with two red couches, wooden dressers, a memorial for Julieta's son, and

FIGURE 3. Two syringes and a shared heroin spoon posed on the couple's couch. Many of Julieta and Mateo's photos depicted their drug use. Photo by Julieta.

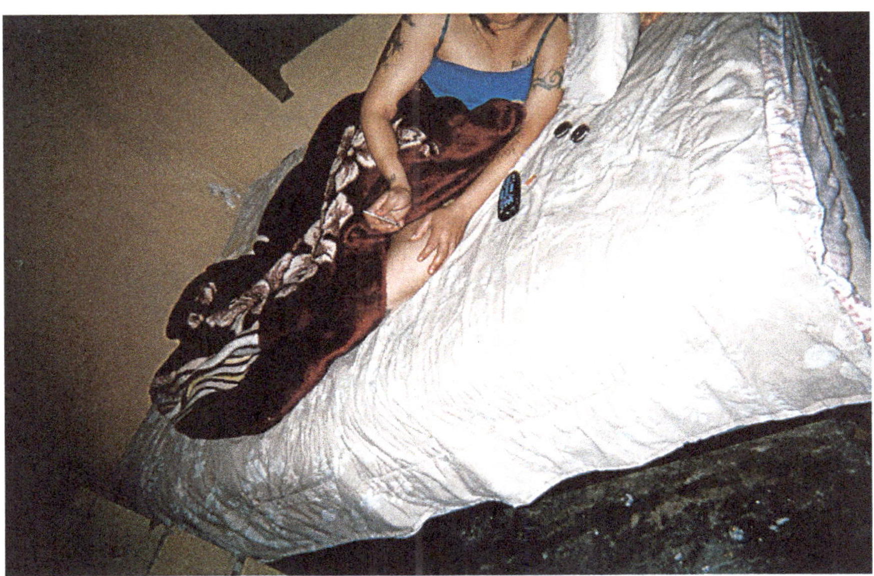

FIGURE 4. Julieta at home in bed with the TV remote, Oreo cookies, and a syringe of heroin. Photo by Mateo.

a bed in the far corner next to the bathroom, in which the door handle was falling off. It was minimalist but comfortable, and they kept the front screen door open most of the time to let the cool breeze come through, except for when they injected.

Mateo was obviously sweaty, anxious, and sick when we arrived, and Julieta asked if we minded if they cured right away. While he prepared the drugs (often a traditionally male activity), she said they were talking about quitting again. Mateo drew up half of the brown liquid in one syringe and half in another, which he gave to her. She excused herself to the bathroom to inject, while he sat on the bed and injected in the top of his right hand. When he finished, he emitted a long, low sigh that indicated his relief. Right after they injected, we looked through their photos. He was quiet and nodding off at first, and she was very talkative, but a little later into the interview, they reversed roles. When they were both alert, they sat close together and Julieta clutched Mateo's arm.

The overwhelming majority of the couples' photos were drug-themed and revealed that they spent most of their days at home together injecting. Several photos into the batch, a series of photos depicting drug preparation came up, and I asked them about the details of the process because I was preoccupied with understanding injection-related HIV risk. Mateo started to explain but then jokingly asked if they could make the "sacrifice" to inject again and show us. Their first injection was "small" anyway. When he was done heating the mixture, he drew it up into two syringes and said, "ladies first" as he handed Julieta a syringe. She asked if we wanted to see her inject but, without waiting for an answer, promptly pulled down her jeans to inject in her usual spot, her left inner knee. Mateo injected in his inner left elbow.

This process repeated multiple times per day. Every day. This is what their life had become in Tijuana. Heroin injection structured their days, which they described as a "hell," in which "every day is the same." Julieta seemed especially distraught about the monotony. Furthermore, as Mateo's health worsened and their addiction deepened, heroin took the place of their sexual intimacy. Julieta worried about Mateo exerting himself too much during sex. Julieta continued to have sex—just not with Mateo. Recall that when I first met Julieta, she was really worried about her HIV/STI test results from the Parejas project. Why was she worried? How do couples like Julieta and Mateo navigate these physical health threats without sacrificing emotional intimacy?

HIV/STI DISCLOSURE

Julieta worked part-time in a nail salon and also maintained several regular clients that she never discussed with Mateo. She used condoms with all but one client; she did not have feelings for him, but he paid her more money for unprotected sex, which went toward Mateo's medical expenses. Like Lucia, Julieta preferred regular clients over riskier one-time clients who were not known to her.

Not only were these client preferences typical across the Parejas sample, but women's strategies in client selection represented a form of harm reduction that kept them physically safer. Furthermore, these benefits extended to their primary relationships. As it turns out, in the Parejas study prevalence (existing cases) and incidence (new cases) of HIV/STIs were relatively low—but not without concern. Among the 424 individual partners tested at baseline, HIV prevalence was 2.6 percent and, overall, 9.9 percent tested positive for HIV/STIs. Just like Lucia, Julieta, and other women had told us, client types mattered for their health and safety: women who reported having regular sex work clients were less likely to test positive for HIV/STIs compared to women without regular clients. Moreover, the protective factor of having regular clients extended to their intimate male partners, who were also less likely to have prevalent HIV/STIs (Robertson et al. 2014c). These epidemiologic trends held longitudinally as well: over the two-year data collection period, acquisition of HIV/STIs over time remained lower among women who had regular clients, and this protection also extended to their intimate male partners (Bazzi et al. 2015). In other words, women's harm reduction strategies in the selection of their sex work clients kept themselves *and* their partners physically safer in terms of avoiding disease.

Clearly, avoiding disease transmission is good news in and of itself. Our findings that women's strategies also protected their primary partners is novel and important. But testing negative also carries social benefits: namely, uninfected partners do not have to disclose a positive test result and raise a potentially hurtful or conflict-provoking topic with an unsuspecting partner. Biological evidence of sexual concurrency (a positive HIV/STI test) represents another level of threat to the primary relationships. Partners preferred silence.

The Parejas project, however, disrupted this strategy. In the study context both partners knew they were being interviewed about health topics and tested for HIV/STIs. For many couples discussing test results became incorporated into their conversations about participating in the project. Indeed, a quantitative analysis revealed that 87 percent of Parejas participants disclosed a test result during the follow-up period of the study (Pines et al. 2015). However, within this high disclosure rate, couples who had been together longer were less likely to disclose positive results. As an uncomfortable topic that threatens trust and emotional intimacy, these findings underscore the high stakes of these long-term relationships.

Julieta tried to evade returning to the office for her test results, but Mateo insisted. Mateo said he trusted her to "take care of herself," a common euphemism we heard for condom use and an example of sexual silence that gestures to but avoids direct communication about HIV/STI risk. He also did not think she had other kinds of sexual partners (or did he not want to talk about it?). Either there was naively no reason for him to worry, or he held his suspicions in silence and pushing to go together for their test results was a way to confront an uncomfortable topic. Julieta's guilt gnawed at her, and she hoped to avoid an uncomfortable conversation.

Like Jaime, discussed earlier in the chapter, Julieta was part of relatively small proportion of partners enrolled in Parejas who pursued outside, nonpaid sexual relationships.[5] Julieta's affair with a married man was brief, and their secret arrangement was purely for "partying" and sex. Like Jaime, she was careful to demarcate the emotional boundaries of this outside partner: "There was no love; there was nothing there . . . nothing more than sex," she confessed. "With the other partner, I had sex with him just for the sex, not because I cared. Because since Mateo got sick, we no longer have sex, nothing. Everything is calmer . . . but sometimes sex is necessary! With the other partner, it was pure partying and chaos [desmadre]."

Julieta's pursuit of pleasure reflects shifting gender roles among sex worker couples in the Mexico-US border region. For women who venture outside of traditional roles of staying home, caring for children, and being the more private partner in heterosexual relationships, new kinds of sexual geographies offer opportunities for sex that have traditionally been available only to men (Hirsch et al. 2007). In traditional Mexican culture (as in many cultural systems, for that matter), men are socialized to pursue multiple partners for pleasure, and women are socialized for love and marriage. Julieta and Mateo's relationship provides another example of shifting gender norms and challenges to hegemonic notions of masculinity. If men can pursue sex for pleasure without compromising their primary relationship, Julieta shows us that women can too. Women like Julieta have opportunities to interact with people outside the home and family system, enabling them to forge new relations. Why wouldn't women similarly explore new sexual opportunities if the circumstances were right? Women, including sex workers, are sexual beings with needs and desires for pleasure just like men. Julieta acknowledged this and indulged, but only in sex that meant "nothing" so that she didn't jeopardize her relationship with Mateo. Even so, she felt guilty and eventually cut off her affair.

Back in the Parejas project office, before the nurse could even tell her the test results, Julieta burst into tears. The thought of learning she could be HIV positive or have an STI was stressful. She tested negative. Luckily, she was able share her negative results with Mateo, who was likewise negative. But she never told Mateo about her affair. In the context of her relationship with Mateo, in which they live relatively isolated as a couple contending with economic precarity, chronic illness, and relapsing heroin addiction, why would she confess her sexual transgressions to a trusting, unsuspecting, and gravely ill partner? Because she tested negative for HIV/STIs, what would be gained and what would be lost from revealing her sexual secrets?

A SOCIAL PHENOMENON OR PUBLIC HEALTH PROBLEM?

The couples featured in this chapter share similarities with each other and other couples enrolled in Parejas: they are emotionally close and love each other but have sex with other people and lie about it. On the surface these secrets and lies seem counterintuitive to arguing for the importance of emotional intimacy in sex workers' noncommercial relationships. It might even justify bringing concerns of HIV/STIs to the forefront of couples' narratives. However, a deeper dive into the couples' stories reveals that infidelity in this context can be read as accomplishing something rather than merely failing at fidelity.

It is first important to situate sexual concurrency within broader historical and sociopolitical contexts. Infidelity is a global phenomenon (Tsapelas, Fisher, and Aron 2010; Fisher 2016).[6] Although cross-cultural anthropological research illustrates that large-scale political, economic, social, and cultural changes have transformed the role of personal relationships to emphasize love and intimacy rather than obligation across diverse contexts, this has not led to corresponding decreases in infidelity (Hirsch et al. 2009, Rebhun 1999; Smith 2008). Nor have shifts toward companionate relationships necessarily led to increased sexual communication between partners (Hirsch et al. 2007). Thus, the stories in this chapter reflect the complexity of all human sexual relationships within a globalizing world. Sex work adds a layer of complication, but these relationships are really no different than any other the world over.

In Tijuana behaviors categorized as sexual concurrency are varied and shaped by broader sociopolitical contexts of economic exclusion, shifting gender roles, the relentlessness of drug addiction, and precarity of survival itself in the highly sexualized geography of the Zona Norte. In one form of sexual concurrency, women engage in freelance sex work, a pervasive and normalized form of economic survival for many vulnerable women in the region. In this context women enact harm reduction strategies in selecting clients to keep themselves and their partners as physically and socially safe as possible. Couples avoid direct discussions of sex work under a "mutual pretense" to avoid hurt feelings or conflict and to preserve emotional fidelity. But sex work also shifts gender dynamics and invades traditional notions of masculinity, which in turn shapes other forms of concurrency with outside sexual partners for pleasure, who are likewise kept secret.

While couples' lived experience of exclusion and vulnerability do not absolve partners of their acts of indiscretion, lies, and secrets, it does help explain how the deep emotional imprints of the world around us shape our behavior. For example, Jaime's infidelity does not reflect discontent within his relationship with Lucia, but it does represent a form of lashing out against the economic exclusion and social marginalization that he—and other men like him—feel regarding their inability to provide and subsequent economic reliance on their partner's sex work. Jaime framed his sexual risk taking as a pursuit of pleasure, but these encounters also counteract some of his feelings of anger, stress, jealousy, and inadequacy. Sex for pleasure allows him to at least temporarily feel "like a man" to restore a sense of masculinity. A similar argument applies to Julieta's stressful situation in the context of relapsing into heroin use and caring for a partner with chronic illness; she also justified her affair, but it never changed her love for Mateo.

While Jaime's and Julieta's encounters were driven by sexual satisfaction, they also reflect what anthropologist Héctor Carrillo (2002) writes about as "rational" forms of sex in his ethnography of sexuality and HIV in Mexico. One of Carrillo's male participants described "rational" sex as that without love and total surrender; it is only about physical pleasure. Only when individuals love their partner can sex be "irrational" in the sense of a full emotional surrender to that person. While having an affair might not seem like a "rational" decision, the calculation of Jaime's and Julieta's pursuits with partners with whom they have no emotional commitment signals an intentionality about their actions and desire not to hurt their partners or break up their relationships.

In other words, we need to reframe our understandings of the ir/rationality of sexual risk and how this changes depending on the social context. Sex has "feeling" in it and a different meaning in sex workers' primary relationships. There is no space for condom use in this context, and virtually no couples in Parejas, including the couples in this chapter, reported consistent condom use. Despite knowing the physical risks for HIV/STIs, condom use in intimate relationships cannot be rationalized because these relationships are about love, emotional intimacy, support, and commitment. On the other hand, concurrent sexual relationships are rational on other levels: women rationalize their sex work and client choice (and calculate condom use with clients in economic terms), drug addiction might rationalize trading sex with same-sex partners, and outside affairs are rationalized as pleasure but not love. None of these concurrent partnerships (client or nonpaying) are intended to break or replace the primary intimate relationship; they function for various other reasons outside of, but not totally apart from, the primary intimate relationship. Rational outside sexual relationships may be for money, drugs, restoration of masculinity, experimentation, escape, or pleasure but *not* for love.

Thus, sexual concurrency is a social phenomenon, yet we primarily treat it as a public health problem. For couples like Lucia and Jaime and Julieta and Mateo, concurrency is not understood, negotiated, and lived in epidemiological terms of disease risk. Concurrency emerges amid a challenging set of life circumstances and is practiced in ways that ultimately prioritize and reinforce the importance of primary intimate relationships. While concerns about HIV/STIs are of course real, disease is not the primary factor driving partners' sexual behaviors. Sexual concurrency is about more than the physical act of sex and risk of HIV/STIs.

What does this mean? A key contribution of this chapter is to highlight the social and emotional contexts of sexual concurrency and assert that failing at fidelity doesn't mean failing in love. As we learn from the couples in this chapter and the broader Parejas study, sex can *end* with outside partners and clients, but *emotions begin* within intimate relationships in which a shared connection makes life meaningful. We need to push beyond an ethnocentric reading of sex workers' relationships that dismisses the possibilities for love in contexts of multiple sexual partnerships. While the tactics couples employ to have sex with other people and hide it might seem counterintuitive to this pursuit, the lengths partners go through to maintain their bonds actually tells us something important about the meaning of these intimate relationships. They matter. They are qualitatively different. Amid challenging life circumstances, partners do whatever they can to hold on to each other.

To be certain, concurrent sexual relationships can endanger primary intimate relationships in terms of HIV/STI transmission. Public health prioritizes disclosure, and it is not necessarily a bad thing to share a result and encourage a partner to get tested. However, given that couples go to such lengths to prioritize the emotional safe haven of their relationship over physical health threats, we need to shift public health disease-prevention strategies to better account for the social meanings of concurrency. These topics are taken back up in the final chapter of this book, but for now I want to reiterate the importance of sex workers' relationships as socioemotional spaces of refuge that are highly valued and need to be protected—even if it means an occasional secret or lie.

We see this in returning to Jaime's story: while he may indulge in secret sex with others "like this, or this, and this, or that"—his heart belongs to Lucia. The photographs he took of her, but not his outside partner, evoked a deep and very different kind of emotional response. I could see it in his eyes, as he clenched his fist to his heart, as he thought deeply about her, belly laughed, and talked about how he loved her. It could have been a performance to keep up with his careful appearance. But I don't think so. The moments were too unscripted.

This chapter urges us to look beyond glosses of sexual concurrency to appreciate the emotional complexity and endurance of sex workers' relationships. Dangerous safe havens may not conform to stereotypical standards of monogamous love, but they are critically important safe spaces in their own right. The strategies that couples deploy around concurrency are a constant negotiation of competing risks that ultimately aim to uphold and keep intact couples' dangerous safe havens. The stories of Celia's and Mildred's relationships in the next chapter extends the analysis of couples' dangerous safe havens in relation to their social networks beyond sexual risk.

3

Love in a War Zone

During my fieldwork Tijuana was gripped by a particularly violent and tumultu-
ous period of the War on Drugs, which continues to shape life along the Mexico-
US border. In 2011, the year in which most of my fieldwork for this book took
place, an average of forty-seven people were killed per day in Mexico, four of
whom were tortured, two of whom were decapitated, three of whom were women,
and ten of whom were young people, suggesting a pervasiveness of violence (Molzahn, Rios, Shirk 2012). That same year Tijuana's overall homicide rate--twenty-
five deaths per one hundred thousand--represented one of the highest in all of
Mexico (Heinle, Ferreira, and Shirk 2014). For sex workers and their partners who
use drugs in Tijuana, the cross-border drug wars enact multiple forms of violence
in their everyday lives, from the psychological terror of widespread death to the
physical threats of violent policing to the institutions that surveil and punish those
struggling with addiction. Amid the myriad violence, it may seem like love is an
impossibility and secondary to basic survival—but is this the case?

This chapter explores how the broader social contexts, institutions, and policies upholding the drug wars along the border shaped couples' everyday lived
experiences and how couples countered their vulnerabilities with their own forms
of resistance. When state institutions fail, and options for care enact further violence among already marginalized individuals, the couples in this chapter turned
inward to their own resources, including networks of family and friends. Although
all intimate relationships are situated within sets of social relations, the familial
contexts of sex workers who use drugs are largely excluded from scholarly considerations of their lives.

Through the stories of Celia and Lazarus and Mildred and Ronaldo, I show how
couples' dangerous safe havens can expand and absorb family, friends, and other
social relationships to create communities of care. These living arrangements
were sometimes chaotic but also represented a key strategy for marshaling household resources and offering social protection. Even as these household dynamics

complicated couples' lives, their intimate relationships remained fundamental to each partners' well-being and in important ways differed from their other relationships. The strength of these bonds were further tested when each couple experienced a period of social separation exacerbated by the violence of the drug wars: for Celia, this was a separation from her partner, Lazarus, and for Mildred and Ronaldo, this was a separation from their daughter. Through their stories we are urged to reconsider what it means to love, care, and rely on one another in the midst of a war zone.

CELIA AND LAZARUS

Celia was only two years old when her family moved from Ciudad Juárez to Southern California, where she spent most of her life. She grew up as one of twelve siblings, three of whom died from complications related to drug use. When she was little, Celia used to play parole officer by sitting behind a desk pretending to do paperwork. Celia liked school, but her brothers did not think it was "cool," so she started to hang around different crowds. Among them she met boyfriends who profoundly shaped her life and addiction trajectory.

Celia first got pregnant at age fourteen. Her boyfriend at the time wanted her to terminate the pregnancy and gave her the money for an abortion, but she spent it at the mall. She remembered giving birth around Easter time because there were "bunny rabbits and shit" hanging on the hospital walls as decorations. She became pregnant again at sixteen, this time with her new boyfriend. He had introduced her to crack. Celia claimed he smoked it even while visiting her in the hospital after she gave birth. Celia eventually started exchanging sex for money to support their drug habit "because I thought he loved me." Before he went to prison for gang-related activities, they promised each other that they would not fall in love or start a family with anyone else. She held up her end of the bargain and even had two abortions to do so. He did not and instead became romantically involved with someone else upon his release.

Celia herself has a significant prison record related to her drug use and armed robbery, and she has been deported three times. Twice she returned to the States on the same day because border security was less militarized in the 1990s. As Celia put it, "You'll do anything when you just want to go home." However, her most recent deportation left her stuck in Tijuana. She arrived with nothing more than the clothes she was wearing and a small amount of cash. On her first night she got a hotel room and got drunk. She was distraught and did not know what else to do. Eventually she got a job working in a bar and started exchanging sex to get by. She was gradually introduced to social contacts who used drugs. She already had a long history of drug use, and the easy availability of heroin and meth in Tijuana deepened her addiction. She wasn't interested in a relationship when she met Lazarus in a Tijuana shooting gallery about a year after she arrived in the city.

Lazarus was also not from Tijuana, but another nearby border city, where his entire family remained. He struggled with the death of his mother when he was young, and he was not raised with care or affection. He grew up with his father and five brothers, but he was often left to his own devices and struggled with poverty and limited education, job training, and direction. He longed for love and affection growing up but instead started using drugs at an early age. Lazarus originally came to Tijuana with the intention to cross into the United States, but he found it "difficult" to do so, primarily because of his drug use. He ended up staying. As both he and Celia shared similarly disadvantaged backgrounds, histories of addiction, and limited support in Tijuana, they gravitated toward each other. They first got together because he was really good at hustling for money, and he helped her inject. She used to know how to inject but had long ago scarred her veins to the point that she needed assistance injecting into her neck. The couple started to spend a lot of time together, hustling for drugs, paying for hotel rooms to get off the streets, and injecting heroin. As he described it, their circumstances made sense for them to be together, and he "insisted" she become his girlfriend because he wanted to fill an emotional void. He knew that she had sex work clients and claimed that he would not get jealous.

As Celia described it, he began to pressure her to have sex, but she wasn't physically attracted to him. She eventually "felt sorry" for him and relented to have sex because he claimed that nothing would change between them. However, as Celia told it,

> It wasn't true because, after we had sex, oh my God. I couldn't get him away from me. He just started being real possessive, jealous, and I don't know. "You said you were not going to be like this. I'm not even your girlfriend. You know, we just had sex." Then he just, you know, kept on and on and on and on, and I would push him away, whatever, and then I used to feel like bad because he's a real good person you know. And real sentimental and stuff, you know, and I don't want to be mean. But then I got real sick and then, you know how when someone takes care of you, like when you're real sick and you think the people who are your friends would help you and they don't, then somebody else does it who you least expected, and that's what he did. He just won me over because he went out of his way for me, and that meant a lot to me, just the little things that he would do. And that's how we started. I guess that's how we became a couple, because he proved to me that he cared about me.

Seven years later Celia reflected on the development of their relationship and admitted, "I ended up falling in love with him because of the way he was, even though he wasn't my type at all." She called him a "border brother," implying he was traditionally Mexican, whereas she had always preferred "gang bangers." She also described him as a "caveman" when she first met him, but she helped refine him, teaching him manners. Celia treated him in a caring and motherly way, given that Lazarus had grown up without love and affection.

Celia was particularly grateful to him for his care after complications from her hysterectomy, as referenced earlier. He looked after her, got her food, bathed her, and helped her get dressed and go to the bathroom. When she got arrested, he would go to the jail to wait for her and try to bail her out if he could afford it, or else he brought her heroin upon her release. Her partnership with Lazarus thus helped her feel "safe" in the context of her daily stressors: "I love him, you know. I'm used to him. I just want to be with him, and I need him. I feel safe around here. I know when he's with me I'm going to eat, right? I'm not going to be sick. He's going to make sure we have our dope, whatever it is that I need, you know. So when he's with me I just feel a little secure on that. And if something were to happen to me, like if I got shot, run over, or whatever, I know he would take care of me."

Celia situated the importance of her relationship in terms of her material and emotional needs, and the security Lazarus would bring if another catastrophic health event occurred. Their shared heroin and meth use formed a core feature of their relationship from the very beginning, and they continued to act as a team, hustling for drugs and using drugs together. To Celia the provision of love and care was inseparable from the materiality of their daily basic needs, including their addictions. However, the couple faced challenges over their sexual relationship and her sex work. Celia was largely uninterested in sex, whereas Lazarus had a strong desire for it, particularly after using meth. Despite his initial claim that he wouldn't be jealous of her sex work, he later admitted jealousy over her suspected clients. Why would she prefer to have sex with those much older men over him?

Their relationship was further complicated by their living arrangement with Celia's two brothers, who constantly teased and tormented Lazarus and took advantage of his ability to hustle for money. Celia's brothers could be intimidating. Chano is more than six feet tall, muscular, and covered in tattoos, and he injects heroin and meth. Oscar is a bit shorter but similarly broad and tattooed. Celia claims the latter went to "juvey" at age thirteen for killing someone and is schizophrenic, though I am not sure if he has been professionally diagnosed. I met and interacted with her brothers throughout the project and gained a sense of what her home life was like, as well as how Celia and Lazarus's relationship functioned within this social context. I screened the couple and enrolled them into the larger Parejas study. I also conducted Celia's quantitative surveys. Her surveys always took several hours, as our conversations went into insightful tangents about her life that were otherwise uncaptured in our structured data collection tools. In one of these interactions, Celia called heroin use a "full time job." When I asked her a series of questions about who decides about her drug use practices ("You, your partner, or both of you?"), she answered, "The drug decides." According to Celia, "This fucking drug doesn't let you rest for nothing, you know. You're constantly going, going, going."

I invited Celia and Lazarus to participate in my project right before they were due for their six-month follow-up surveys and testing. However, right before we were to begin, Lazarus disappeared. He was regularly arrested and taken to the *veinte* (local jail), as people who "look like drug users" are often targeted in Tijuana for police harassment and arrest. But Celia always found out about it, and this time he wasn't in jail. Other times he took off for a few days at a time to get some space from the household chaos, but he always came back. This was the longest Lazarus had ever been away, and Celia did not know where he was.[1] In the meantime I continued to spend time with Celia, which lent insight into how Lazarus had a significant impact on her life and emotional well-being, even in his absence. Yet her heroin addiction meant she had to keep "going, going, going." How did she manage?

RETHINKING "PICADEROS"

Celia lived in a tiny apartment with her two brothers, who were also deported. It was paid for by their mother in Los Angeles, who wired them the US$200 monthly rent. When he was around, Lazarus lived there as well. The apartment was located in what could be considered ground zero in Tijuana's drug war. Off the main strip of the Red Light District, their nondescript three-story building was within easy walking distance from our project office. They also lived in proximity to several *connectas*, or places to procure drugs. All of them had spent a considerable amount of time out on the streets and had profound insight into the area. Defying typical gender roles in the drug economy, Celia was often the one who went into the canal to procure drugs.

Shaping their quick access to drugs was their apartment's proximity to the canal, a significant site of drug use in Tijuana. The canal is a massive concrete structure large enough to allow vehicles to pass through on either side of a recessed waterway. Located just blocks from downtown, the canal's underbelly is out of sight from most of the bustle of the city. It thus provides refuge and acts as a meeting ground for the growing population of migrants, deportees, the unstably housed, and other people who live and spend time there, including Celia and Lazarus. Parts of the canal are often strewn with garbage, and the stench of refuse and stagnant water can be nauseating. Encampments are rhythmically erected and dismantled as the police "sweep" the area and force individuals to resettle elsewhere. Police also regularly target their patrol activities in the canal because it is a well-known area of drug exchange and use. Public drug injection is common. While the scene is mostly male dominated, Celia was one of a handful of women who frequently visited the canal, and she seemed to know everyone. Many of the photos in her project depicted the canal and other street scenes in her daily hustle.

For Celia even walking the several blocks to our project office was a risk because the "asshole" police often harassed people whom they suspected of drug use. Police surveillance, arrest, and incarceration are some of the most ever-present and harmful effects of the drug war, which become embodied in individual subjectivity and sense of self. Tim Rhodes and colleagues suggest that punitive policing practices have inlaid a pervasive sense of powerlessness among vulnerable populations, who embody its consequences in a "fatalistic acceptance of harm and suffering" (2011, 212).

Indeed, Celia internalized her situation; she said that people who get arrested "for looking dirty and looking like dope fiends" were to blame, as it was "their own fault for attracting that attention to themselves and putting them at risk." She also told me that my other white colleague and I were lucky that we don't have to worry about that, referencing the racialized politics of a drug war created to disproportionately scapegoat, blame, punish, incarcerate, and, in Celia's case, deport Black and Brown populations. As a woman, Celia said she could better evade arrest compared to her brothers or Lazarus. She also had a strategy to wear baggy clothes and feign pregnancy should she get stopped by the police, as they typically do not take pregnant women to jail. Such survival strategies became particularly important in Lazarus's absence.

* * *

Given their central location and ties to local social networks of people who use drugs, Celia's apartment functioned as a safe space for people she knew from the street who used drugs. Such places are often called "shooting galleries" or, in this context, *picaderos*. Shooting galleries are often described in the literature as largely impersonal spaces open for public injection in exchange for a fee or drugs. From a public health standpoint, this largely impersonal version of a picadero could bring strangers together into a space where unsanitary conditions and sharing can heighten transmission of HIV/HCV. From an anthropological viewpoint shooting galleries are also social spaces where forms of mutual care circulate in a "moral economy" (Bourgois 1998) wherein people pool money to buy drugs, assist one another with difficult injections, and ensure that people are present to help if overdoses occur. Thus, picaderos impart context-dependent social and public health risks and benefits.

While most scholarship focuses on public spaces of mutual assistance as it relates to drug use, less acknowledged are picaderos based on known social relations of family and friends. I conceptualize Celia's home as an extension of her dangerous safe haven with Lazarus, thus addressing an understudied dimension of this moral economy. While mutual assistance as it relates to drug use is well documented in picaderos, other communal forms of care may circulate and extend beyond sharing drugs and injection assistance. Given the often fetid conditions of the canal and risk of arrest out in the open, Celia's apartment became a social refuge. Drug injection assistance was a core feature of the exchanges in Celia's apartment, but she and her brothers also provided a space where individuals often spent the night, showered, and got a fresh change of clothes. The select groups of individuals who stayed at and frequently visited Celia's apartment helped one another collectively navigate the everyday violence of the ongoing drug wars.

FIGURE 5. A street-vending scene in Tijuana. Celia and Lazarus often sold goods in the streets as part the local informal economy. Photo by Celia.

FIGURE 6. An overcast day at the Tijuana River Canal. Two people sit atop the canal, as others mill about down below. The canal is a common meeting grounds for drug purchasing and drug use. Celia often scored heroin there and seemed to know everyone. Photo by Celia.

FIGURE 7. A scene from inside Celia and Lazarus's extended dangerous safe haven, which served as a picadero for family and friends to inject. Their apartment offered a space of social refuge compared to the conditions of the canal. Photo by Lazarus.

Celia's apartment sat at the top of a narrow concrete stairway, and its front door couldn't fully open because of a dark-blue couch in its way. On the opposite side of the room was a small bed, a rack of clothes hanging over it. Celia's brother Chano slept in the bed, and her other brother, Oscar, had the couch. They had a television with a VCR on top of it, decorated with a depiction of Jesus with two kids at his feet, and the Virgin Mary was on the wall space above it. Celia's bedroom was in the kitchen; her bed was blocked off by a string along the ceiling with pieces of fabric patched together to enclose the space. It was eclectically decorated: red glittery Valentine's Day cards, plastic flowers on the couch cushions stuffed under blankets that served as her bed, and family photos—one of a nephew in prison for murder and another of her mother and older brother, the latter also in prison. Attached to the sparsely stocked kitchen was the bathroom with a shower. There were always piles of newly washed clothes scattered about, as Celia and everyone else in the household participated in an informal economy of selling secondhand clothes in the streets.

The apartment did not fit the archetype of a shooting gallery, nor did we ever feel unsafe with the company there (especially after Celia yelled at Oscar to not "scare us away"). During one visit my colleague and I saw, sleeping in Chano's bed, a gaunt thirteen-year-old boy who used "every" kind of drug. The adults in the apartment said he did not have a mother, and they used to "baby him a lot" and "show him love and friendship" because they felt bad for him. During another week a female friend stayed with Celia and her brothers. The friend bought a lot of heroin and kept them constantly "strung out." Apart from these longer-staying guests, other friends and acquaintances cycled through the space daily.

Without Lazarus to help her inject, Celia had to find others to help her inject in the neck. Lazarus would say, "Girls always go first," and carefully inject Celia before injecting himself. The neck is an exceedingly dangerous area of the body to inject but is common in Tijuana, due to the impurity of the drug market and long careers of injecting that damage veins (Rafful et al. 2015). Celia was already developing a callous there, but she had to trust others to help her. Indeed, my colleague and I witnessed a terrifying event in which her brother attempted multiple times to inject her. But we also witnessed other more expedient forms of injection assistance from "hit doctors" from the canal, who received a hot shower, fresh clothes, shelter, jokes, and friendship in return for their skills.

Contrary to images of people who use drugs as selfish, uncaring, and dangerous "others" best managed through punitive measures, Celia's home became an extension of her dangerous safe haven wherein she and her brothers took people in and provided care. These networks of family and friends helped Celia navigate risk, including her injection drug use. The often animated social relations and multiple forms of care circulating through the apartment contrasted with the violence outside their door. Nevertheless, Celia missed Lazarus. During the period that he was gone, I asked Celia how she had been feeling without him. She answered, "Alone, just alone, fucking just hard on me, you know? Because, like I said, he was there; we were always together, always, always together. . . . The simple fact is that I need him financially and emotionally too, you know? The things that he does, he makes me laugh. I don't feel alone; he's here with me, and I can talk to him about anything."

She had a feeling this was not the end. How could it suddenly be over after nearly eight years together? Despite their issues and the core of the relationship developing over drug use, she felt their relationship ran "too deep" to end so abruptly. "He's got a conscience," she continued, "because he's not like the rest of these guys. I know him that good, just as much as he knows me I know him, so I'm pretty sure he'll come around."

THE REUNION

Celia was right. Lazarus unexpectedly returned home one day. As it turned out, he had grown "tired" of injecting and went to a rehabilitation center outside of Rosarito, south of Tijuana. One day he and Celia had gotten into an argument; he had already been contemplating seeking help to stop using drugs, and he impulsively left without telling anyone.

Although he genuinely wanted help and spent three months at the rehabilitation center, Lazarus received little medical care and few tools to address his drug use. Anthropologist Angela Garcia has aptly described residential rehabilitation centers in Mexico City as a "hybrid institution composed of parts 12-step program, mental asylum, prison, and church" (2015). In Baja California, the state where Tijuana is located, many of the treatment programs I heard about in the course of my research, including Lazarus's experience, resonate with this description. These programs are concentrated in impoverished, drug war–torn areas, where they are run by recovering addicts who use not love but violence, humiliation, Bible study, and menial communal labor to keep individuals busy (and the program functioning). Lazarus took a few sedatives in the beginning to manage the pain of withdrawal, but for the most part his treatment consisted of four twelve-step style meetings interspersed during his fifteen-hour work days. Even after three months, the typical time for these treatment programs, those in charge said he was not permitted to leave. Increasingly desperate, Lazarus and a couple of other guys smashed a window and escaped. He had to walk through the desert for hours so he could hitch a ride back to Tijuana. The moment he showed up at the apartment, he wanted to get high.

Lazarus had been home for about two weeks before I connected with him. He already looked terrible. On that occasion he had not slept in three days because of the meth, and he twitched, fidgeted, and coughed throughout our conversation. Lazarus had returned home to the same drug war outside on the streets and social environment inside his apartment. Without a helpful experience in treatment to navigate these circumstances, it is understandable that he started injecting again. Lazarus cared for Celia, missed her, and longed to hug her when he was apart from her at the center. But part of the care they showed each other was through their drug use. Their extended dangerous safe haven also functioned as a space to care for others while ensuring the collective survival of their family unit. Within this context Lazarus was unsure if he could ever quit using drugs. He pointed out the near impossibility of quitting if a partner continues to use:

> Well, two dope fiends can't be together if one stops and the other one keeps using—the other one is going to start using again because they're going to keep seeing it, seeing it, seeing it. And it's a temptation. Once you got that in your blood system and you're around it, you're always going to be a dope fiend, so if she loves me and I love her, and she really stops and I stop together, you know, we'll help each other out. You know 'cause if she stops and I keep using, I'm going to get her to use because I'm going to want to go out and hustle to get my fix.

Amid Lazarus's ambivalence about quitting, the two were happy to be back together, getting along well, and back to their usual patterns. Many of Lazarus's photos for his project depicted him as back to work, hustling on the streets to provide for Celia and their drug use. Other photos showed the continual flow of friends and acquaintances injecting and hanging out in the refuge of their apartment. For the time being, at least, their dangerous safe haven remained as it ever was.

MILDRED AND RONALDO

Mildred and Ronaldo's relationship in many ways paralleled that of Celia and Lazarus. Mildred and Ronaldo had a caring but often conflictive relationship, but they remained bounded by love. In this case the love for their child served as the centerpiece of the story and their point of resistance to a world of disadvantage around them. Mildred and Ronaldo had been together since she learned she was pregnant. They both had always lived in the northern border region of Mexico. Neither started using drugs until later in life. For Ronaldo this was prompted by the grief from the death of his mother. Mildred had experimented with meth and cocaine but did not even know what black tar heroin was when she was introduced to it through a boyfriend.

After Mildred and Ronaldo met at a mutual acquaintance's home, they quickly formed a relationship that cemented itself with her pregnancy. After he found out Ronaldo traveled to a remote area to kick heroin cold turkey; she was unable to stop using until the last trimester of her pregnancy. She had already been in rehab at least six times in her life and, like Lazarus, described deplorable conditions: "It was horrible. I mean, that doesn't make you stop using drugs; on the contrary you come out with more resentment, with more desire to use." The lack of evidence-based services and social support meant they managed their addictions on their own. She went back to heroin immediately after Zoe was born; Ronaldo did not go back to heroin but started smoking meth.

The dangerous safe haven they constructed was friendly and caring, mostly sustained by their shared sense of responsibility of raising their daughter, Zoe. Mildred said she would "suffer a lot" without Ronaldo. People looked down on her for being a "junkie" and treated her poorly, but he made her feel protected because he was good at fighting and people feared him. "I feel that he supports me in that regard. I feel that if I am alone, I will do worse. People are really mean to me, and he gives me that support despite the fact that sometimes he makes me get upset," she said. Many of these arguments erupted over their mismatched sex drives, due to Ronaldo's meth use (just like Celia and Lazarus).

Ronaldo was one of the few male partners I met who had steady employment. Even so, it did not pay enough to support his family. Mildred engaged in sex work with several clients she could count on for regular financial support. Early on in their relationship, sex work created conflict between Mildred and Ronaldo. To avoid the topic Mildred lied, telling Ronaldo that she sold secondhand clothes and cut hair for cash, as she used to work in a salon. But Ronaldo was not naive: "At midnight, selling clothing? Cutting hair? That's kind of difficult!"

Reflecting on those early days, Ronaldo recounted how sometimes their fights escalated into pushing and kicking, and he was sometimes mean to her, humiliating her and acting macho in front of his friends to put up a front. Now, like most other couples, they avoid the topic. Like other men in the Parejas study, Ronaldo concluded that he had to accept her sex work as a way to contribute to their household needs, and he blamed himself for being unable to provide enough: "Well, what else can I do? The one to blame is me. That is how I feel, and I also feel guilty because we go back to the same story of drugs."

Ronaldo felt guilty that the some of the money they earned supported their drug use rather than everything going toward Zoe. He also worried that something horrible would happen to Mildred when she went out at night, but she said she was more afraid of the police than people who use drugs and solicit sex. As one measure of safety, the couple always used drugs at home rather than in public places. Similar to Celia and Lazarus, their home had also become a type of picadero, where she, Ronaldo, and their daughter lived with Ronaldo's brother, Marco, and his new girlfriend.

In contrast to the centralized tourist chaos of the Zona Norte, where Celia lived and our project office was based, Mildred and Ronaldo lived just on the outskirts of downtown. Nonetheless, this *colonia* (neighborhood) had a bustling informal street economy and active drug scene. During visits to the *colonia*, I saw informal marketplaces spring up on the sides of the road, and neighbors vending *hamburguesas* from carts in front of their homes as dusk approached. The project staff told me that younger males riding bikes were likely running drugs out of certain *tiendas* (shops), but I never asked any of those kids to confirm.

Lodged between a burned-down house on a garbage-strewn lot and a newly constructed two-story home right out of suburban San Diego, the modest single-story home where Mildred, Ronaldo, and their family lived had a tenuous roof and a broken window facing the street. Their front door opened into a dimly lit hallway partially blocked by a discarded toilet lodged in the corner. I always visited them with a colleague, and we sat around a wooden table in the kitchen, which was sparse, with only simple appliances and a half–torn-up *ET* movie poster decorating the sink area. A cluttered living room in the back had several couches, a large television, and other random knickknacks, besieged by several kittens and small dogs. Behind the living area in the very back of the house were two doors: one was Mildred and Ronaldo's bedroom and the other belonged to Marco and his girlfriend. Although Ronaldo was usually working, Marco was always in the background when we visited. He was quiet and polite, and his right arm was nearly completely skin grafted because of a serious abscess from injecting drugs.

Whenever we visited, my colleague and I observed a consistent flow of drug users, mostly men, who were greeted by Marco and escorted into a back bedroom, where we were not privy to their activities. As in Celia's apartment, Mildred and Ronaldo's home functioned as an extension of their dangerous safe haven, a picadero that provided safety and care for known associates. Mildred said the same group of users, all relatives and friends, regularly came in the early morning and late afternoon or evening to cure; many of them held regular jobs during the day and scheduled their heroin use before and after work. She and Marco provided the safe space and sometimes injection assistance in exchange for drugs or a small amount of money. At least one person worked in San Diego but lived in Tijuana to use heroin.

One afternoon a couple showed up; it turned out that she was Marco's ex-partner, who had brought her *sancho* (new boyfriend) and nine-year-old son along. The couple disappeared with Marco into the back bedroom, while the boy entertained himself in the living room by playing with the pets. After they left Mildred explained their relationships to us and commented, "We are very modern," referring to their acceptance of shifting sexual partnerships within their familial group and how this did not disrupt the dynamics of their communal forms of care. For Mildred their home was part of a moral economy that helped the household marshal resources and try to avoid the police. Rather than in public spaces, private homes could keep all actors safe, including any children present. The adults were careful not to directly expose the children to drug use, but how safe are children in these dangerous safe havens?

LOVE FOR ZOE

Globally, many female sex workers have children, yet this is largely neglected in research. When the topic is considered, mothers who engage in sex work—and drug use—are often demonized as neglectful and undeserving parents. However, anthropologists have shown that mothers' stories are far more complex than dominative narratives. Sex workers often face difficult choices of living separately from children but providing financial support versus having children live with them to provide direct material and emotional care, which may also expose children to drug use or other illicit activities (Luna 2020). Most participants in the larger Parejas project had children (84 percent), about a third of whom had children under the age of eighteen living with them. Children profoundly shaped couples' relationships, as they were often the reason partners remained together and sometimes motivated partners to try to engage in health behaviors, like reducing drug use. However, trying to cover basic child-rearing costs often meant women remained in sex work in the context of limited other options (Rolon et al. 2013).

For Mildred and Ronaldo, having Zoe profoundly changed their lives. Amid the couples' personal challenges, Zoe kept them together. Raising Zoe also shaped Mildred's feelings toward Ronaldo: "There is love, from my part there is, and I think that our daughter has made us come together, or maybe she doesn't let us separate, because I wouldn't leave him alone with the girl. I love her a lot. I wouldn't leave and take her away because I feel that she would suffer; either way, he is her dad, with all the defects that he has and his addiction. He loves her a lot and protects her."

Ronaldo loves their daughter very much, and he constantly talked about Zoe. Even as he sometimes expressed frustration and confusion in terms of his feelings about Mildred, he agreed that "our daughter helps us a lot. She helps us stay together." Mildred said he has an "incredible" love for Zoe. He cried when she was born, and "he gets really sad to see the girl hungry and that we have nothing for her. . . . He almost cries. It's incredible; he loves her so much."

Indeed, Ronaldo wanted to raise Zoe in a loving and supportive household. After Zoe was born, Ronaldo tried to change for her benefit and ensure that he offered critical forms of financial, material, and emotional support. Zoe reaffirmed his need to "calm down" and be a provider for the household, as the couple explained one day:

> Ronaldo: I mean, I changed. Before I would wander in the streets a lot. I would be crazier and would wander the streets.
>
> Mildred: He would get into a lot of trouble. . . .
>
> Ronaldo: I would always be at the canal like that *[referring to drug use]* . . . but now with our daughter, I control myself more.
>
> Mildred: You work every day. . . .
>
> Ronaldo: I have to work every day.

The first and only time that I met Zoe, I had accompanied the Parejas field team to follow up with the couple in between visits and update their "locator form," or the documents we used to keep track of couples over the course of the study. We met up in the middle of a street in their neighborhood, as they were out running an errand. Zoe was absolutely adorable, dressed in a tan suede coat lined with sheepskin; she had a pretty smile and enthusiastic personality. She told me she was six at the time. I wondered why she wasn't at school that day.

Later I realized that both parents worried about how their drug use might affect Zoe and raise concerns in school. They contemplated slowing down or stopping their use, but they struggled in the context of limited options for humane drug treatment that would accommodate their family and not separate them during treatment. Ronaldo worried but thought, for now at least, they did a sufficient job of hiding their drug use from Zoe: "She doesn't know about our drug use, you know? The less she knows, the better for her. It has been very difficult, but we have to get over this [stop using drugs], because the day that something happens, we are going to let her down. I would feel bad. I would feel like I was losing something, like everything is lost."

FIGURE 8. Reflecting the often contentious relationship between Mildred and Ronaldo, especially in light of their daughter being taken into state custody, Mildred did not take any photos of her partner. This photo of her dogs was one of her favorites. Photo by Mildred.

Mildred, however, worried that Zoe already knew more than they wanted to her to. She worried that Zoe would be taken away if the school found out, as that had happened to other families:

> Because of heroin, I don't do anything well, I can't gain weight, and I have to change my appearance, and those are some of the reasons why I haven't taken the girl to school. I am afraid that they will take her from me, and I don't know if I should send her with [Ronaldo], and then what are they going to say, "Where's your mom?" The girl talks about everything, and I am afraid that she will tell her teachers that "oh, my mom injects," and they will want to take her from me, because it happened a bit ago at the school that is near the house. The teachers from there sent someone from children's protective services to their house, and that woman is not even an addict. It was just because she would say bad words, and they sent child services, and they took her four kids. I am afraid. People are really mean; it's like they don't think about how much they are going to hurt others.

Unfortunately, these interviews foreshadowed events yet to come.

While their home may have served as a safe space and picadero for friends and family, the constant foot traffic began to draw heightened police surveillance. It all started when the police came into their home without a warrant, looking for information on the whereabouts of a fugitive. When they noticed syringes, they threatened to send Zoe to social services if Ronaldo did not provide them with information on the suspect's whereabouts. He honestly could not help them. The following week the police showed up again and took Mildred and Zoe into custody, along with several syringes—that they had planted this time—for evidence.

The police lied to social services and said that they found Zoe two blocks away from the house because law enforcement cannot legally remove a child from their home without the presence of personnel from social services. Once Zoe was in custody, social services requested her birth certificate, which the couple could not produce. After Zoe was born, they owed Mex$6,000 (about US$450) to the general hospital that they could not afford to pay, so the hospital withheld her documents.[2] The couple said they received poor treatment from hospital staff who suspected that Mildred used drugs and tested Zoe three times to try to find evidence of substances in her system so they could keep her from her parents. Because her parents were unable to pay and procure proper documentation from the hospital, Zoe's life was disadvantaged from the start.

These circumstances demonstrate Mildred and Ronaldo's structural vulnerability, including the stigma and institutional discrimination faced by people who use drugs. Amid the violence of an ongoing drug war, in which drugs are more readily available than evidence-based drug treatment, Ronaldo said it was his daughter who was criminalized and punished. As he put it, the police "did everything brazenly. In other words, without a search warrant, without an order to pick her up, without an order to take her away, and they can't put a minor in a patrol car, you know? Do you think a six-year-old girl is a delinquent? The police treated the girl like a criminal." Ronaldo was angry and upset at their treatment by DIF, or the Sistema Nacional para el Desarrollo Integral de la Familia (National System for the Integral Development of Family), Mexico's child protective services. He felt like he got the runaround with his case, his paperwork was delayed, and his lawyer was available for him only in the mornings—when he was at work. He felt stigmatized for his drug use and unsupported in his case.

Zoe was kept in custody and would be assigned a home placement while the parents demonstrated their fitness to win her back. To regain custody Mildred and Ronaldo underwent state-mandated drug testing, an enactment of biopower that, as French philosopher Michel Foucault notes, regulates and controls health behavior as a means to construct proper citizens ([1978] 1990). Because penalties for women are more severe, due to the stigmatizing of women who use drugs as "selfish" mothers, the couple acquired a drug-free urine specimen to fake Mildred's test results. Ronaldo submitted his own urine, which tested positive for meth. They reasoned that if one of them tested positive for drug use, it might reduce the authorities' suspicion that both used drugs. The positive meth result mandated Ronaldo to twelve sessions of parenting classes for two hours every Friday. He completed the coursework but tested positive again and was mandated to sixteen sessions of "personal reconstruction" classes targeting emotional and psychological issues. Parenting skills, mental health, and coping strategies for emotional trauma are clearly important, but such individualistic approaches also obscure the broader social structures that classified Ronaldo as an unfit parent requiring moral transformation. In many ways the couples' interactions with the state only inflicted further violence and injury in an already fraught situation.

The late Black feminist writer and activist June Jordan asked herself, "Where is the love?" whenever she evaluated life's possibilities. In particular, she urges us to ask how the powerful treat socially vulnerable communities: "How do the strong, the powerful, treat children? . . . the so-called minority members of the body politic? How do the powerful regard women? How do they treat us?" (2003, 269–70). Jordan's questions are part of a long history of Black feminist critiques of state-sanctioned violence and the potential for love to create political change in our communities. Here I find her questions useful to think through the effects of the drug war, including how state apparatuses inflict and enable violence, forcing individuals who use drugs to find alternative sources of redress.[3] People who use drugs in Tijuana are highly stigmatized and frequently subject to harassment and poor treatment. If they have children, is the state more concerned about the welfare of the child or punishing the parents? Jordan suggests that examining the actions of the powerful tells us that our institutions are designed to entrench and perpetuate inequities. Current structures of policing, child welfare, and other institutions do not deserve patience and understanding from those who continue to be harmed; they require a total transformation.

"But what can we do? We can't do anything," Ronaldo lamented. "In other words, everything is by force. If we don't do what they say, what is the DIF going to do?" Any noncompliance on their part threatened their custody case, and, as people who use drugs, they did not perceive themselves as having any power to change that. The couple internalized their poor treatment by hospital staff at her birth, the police, and social services, which left them feeling caught in the crosshairs of a war on drugs they were unable to escape. Zoe's removal brought the couple "closer and created distance," as Ronaldo put it. They struggled with their drug use, the guilt of Zoe's removal, the powerlessness they felt against the system, and the stress on their own relationship. But the couple's response to comply just enough to put them on the pathway to regain custody of Zoe was their way of uniting in solidarity to resist a system that they felt worked against poor people who use drugs.

Zoe was placed with one of Mildred's relatives in another border city, which was a best-case scenario in this situation. They were allowed limited visitation rights. Ronaldo spent more time on public transportation getting there and back home than he did visiting with her, but he dutifully went every Sunday. Sometimes Mildred did too. Throughout their case, Ronaldo dutifully did his part to regain custody. He said he learned a lot in his classes and showed my colleague and me his notebook of emotions he was working through. He was not over his anger and anguish for his family's treatment by state authorities. He clearly missed Zoe. He often became emotionally distraught while trying to hold back tears in his interviews. No matter what questions my colleague and I asked, all of our conversations with Ronaldo circled back to Zoe. Ronaldo could not think of any specific reasons for taking the photographs in his project, including one of a broken bicycle. Afterward I thought about how he told us in an earlier interview that he sold his bike because Zoe was hungry; he needed his bike but he loved his daughter and would sacrifice anything for her.

FIGURE 9. A broken bicycle, one of the few photos that turned out from Ronaldo's roll of film. Photo by Ronaldo.

Ronaldo's photo project was not as fruitful as other couples' work in terms of the photographs produced. However, it was just as insightful in other ways. He drove the conversations to what was really important to him—not HIV and "risk behaviors"—but the love of his daughter. Equally insightful was a comment Mildred made as she walked through the living room at one point while we discussed his photographs. When I asked him why he decided to take photos of what he did—friends working in the backyard, his bedroom, the bicycle—he seemed to interpret my standard questioning as if he had taken photos of the "wrong" things. He asked if he should redo the project. Inadvertently, my project seemed to enact another form of violence, as if the impositions of the health-care system, police, and DIF were not already enough to upset him. Mildred tenderly intervened: "They asked me the same thing, love. I say that the project is good because you feel that they are a little interested in you, and you no longer feel so rejected by society, right? Someone is actually looking at us!"

Indeed, looking into their story provides insights into the familial dynamics and love for children that can characterize extended dangerous safe havens. It reveals a counternarrative to dominant portrayals of parents who use drugs as selfish and uncaring. It also shows that the ways we treat people who use drugs— making them feel "so rejected," as Mildred puts it—only exacerbates the harm and violence in their lives. In reality, child protective cases are extraordinarily difficult situations for everyone involved. Ronaldo bore the brunt of the requirements the couple needed to win her back. He was torn apart by being separated from Zoe and counted down the days until they would learn if they could get her back.

My colleague with whom I conducted this fieldwork clearly struggled with their story, as did I. The candid reflections in her fieldnotes capture the complexity of the situation:

> I was moved by his experience. He made me question the system but also his situation. At the end of the interview I found one of his acquaintances [who came over to inject] disturbing—he wasn't composed—he kept staring at Jennifer with creepy desire and mumbled some things. His partner's acquaintances, also injectors, use their house as a shooting gallery. . . . Is this the right environment for a 7-year-old to grow up? Probably not. But should she be taken away from a father who clearly loves her to death, misses her, and is fighting his addiction and our society to become a provider for his daughter? Definitely not! I was torn after this interview. Made me question life in general, but also made me incredibly grateful for my relatively simple life.[4]

It is easy to make judgments from afar about what a "normal" family "should" look like and what is "best" for children. However, family relations and child caretaking in the context of addiction are really complicated. These situations raise difficult questions about how love and care are expressed when poverty, disadvantage, and violence are part of a family's daily experience. Were Mildred and Ronaldo unfit parents whose drug use rendered them as undeserving of living as a family? Should state authorities be empowered to decide if parents are suitable caretakers? Zoe was in a position of disadvantage from the very day she was born; what about the complicity of the state in producing a precarious life? In circumstances of state-supported violence and precarity, it makes sense for families to turn inward and extend their dangerous safe havens to relatives and friends who help each other survive.

"WHERE IS THE LOVE?"

Turning back to June Jordan's question of "Where is the love?" challenges us to rethink the ways that couples must navigate the state-sanctioned violence of the drug war. When the state deprives its most vulnerable of love in any capacity, individuals must find love elsewhere. Couples crafted dangerous safe havens as one such solution, and, as we see in this chapter, some of these safe havens expand and absorb family, friends, and other social relationships in efforts to create their own communities of care. These extended dangerous safe havens are imperfect responses to the violence and institutional failures of the drug war. These strategies do not change any of the harmful political or social structures of the drug war, as that takes the kind of collective political love and action further discussed in the conclusion. However, the forms of support and mutual aid outlined in this chapter are a starting point of couples' collective survival and offer a social commentary on what happens when we wage war on instead of care for people who use drugs.

In Tijuana the drug-related violence and addiction that couples navigate was not met with evidence-based drug treatment options or supportive social and health services; it was police terror and bureaucratic indifference as usual. Lazarus genuinely wanted help for his drug use, but his experience—typical of many in Parejas—amounted to yet more violence. Mildred and Ronaldo's treatment by various state agencies in their daughter's birth and custody case subjected them to further forms of everyday violence and removal of their child. Celia's and Mildred's intimate relationships were not always easy, but their experiences of separation brought to the forefront the emotional solidarity that underpinned their long-term unions. Even amid the social chaos of their homes and drug-related violence of their lives, their relationships offered forms of love, emotional support, and caretaking that helped them navigate an otherwise oppressive world.

Whereas this chapter examines the structural and social contexts in which dangerous safe havens are forged and strategized, the next chapter turns to the interior emotional experiences of drug use and sex work within these intimate relationships. Circling back to the story of Cindy and Beto gives a fuller picture of how sex workers' relationships can embody social meaning beyond violence and individual risk.

Rewriting Risk

In the light of the window, Cindy was kneeling in a chair and seeking relief from her physical suffering from heroin withdrawal. Visible in the light were the bruises and sores imprinted on her skin from a long history of black tar heroin injection, which permanently scars veins due to its viscosity and unregulated impurities in an illicit drug market. Often Cindy resorted to injecting subcutaneously, which provides slow relief but heightens the risk of skin infections. On this day she injected into the delicate tissue of her breast, which was extremely risky because the tiny veins are liable to rupture. But she was suffering and had few options left. Surrounding Cindy was the material evidence of her life's conditions, including her desk storing chunky high heels for sex work and an assortment of syringes that she and Beto shared. On the top of the desk was a little sparkly pink Christmas tree, a year-round ode to Cindy's love of pink. The decoration provided a bit of reprieve to the heaviness of the scene, as did her artwork and Beto's love messages in magic marker that adorned the walls of their home.

The image I describe was captured by Beto as part of his photovoice project. At the time Cindy was unaware that he snapped her photo because of her intense concentration during this risky task. The photo is devastating. It has always stayed with me. It captures the sense of urgency in the couples' daily heroin injection rituals amid their material constraints, while also suggesting the deep level of intimacy of their dangerous safe haven in which this scenario unfolded.[1]

I open with this scene to make visible the concept of *embodiment*, a critical component of dangerous safe havens. Embodiment evokes the "mindful body" and the interrelationships between sociopolitical forces, the interior emotional experiences of individuals, and the ways that individual bodies navigate their world to forge social relations. Love is an emotional link and foundational to my conceptualization of embodiment. In the context of Cindy and Beto's relationship, love transcended epidemiological risk as emotions guided their embodied practices of sharing syringes and helping each other to get well. Individuals like Cindy, who physically and very visibly embody the war on drugs in their track marks and skin lesions, often face the daily insults of societal judgment, discrimination, and stigma that in turn can become internalized as self-blame. Finding a partner who has embodied a similar lifetime of hardship forms the basis of dangerous safe havens in which couples unconditionally accept and care for each other amid the devastation of addiction and a world that has otherwise shown them no love.

This chapter explores Cindy and Beto's relationship through a lens of love as both an emotional experience and an embodied practice. Their dangerous safe haven represents the embodiment of shared histories of trauma that brought them together and illustrates how health "risk behaviors" that could enact physical harm also express solidarity and emotional commitment. While I examine how injection drug use and sex work shape the dynamics of their relationship—because this is part of their daily reality—I also want to widen the analytical lens beyond indices of risk to consider the everyday circumstances of their lives together. Without romanticizing drug use or minimizing the physiological distress of heroin withdrawal, I also want to draw attention to how their relationship is critically important even beyond their shared addictions. Embodied forms of intimacy and care reflect Cindy and Beto's pursuit of meaningful lives in contexts of disadvantage. But how did they find themselves in such circumstances in the first place?

AN EMOTIONAL DISEASE

Cindy was born in Mexico and smuggled across the border when she was very young, where she was raised by her grandmother in San Diego. She remembered the trauma of crossing the border with a *coyote* at night; he instructed her not to tell her real name to anyone and gave her a fake name to use. She cried because that wasn't her name. She didn't understand why she had to use another name. Growing up on the US side was supposed to bring Cindy a better life. She had gorgeous, impossibly long and thick dark hair and a voluptuous figure that she often showed off in tight jeans. She wanted to be a model while growing up, but her grandmother didn't see the point of Cindy pursuing her own career ambitions because, as she was told, she was only going to get married and have kids anyway.

Cindy grew up in a chaotic household, where her step-grandfather sexually abused her for many years, which her grandmother probably knew about. When Cindy finally gathered the courage to tell a counselor at school, she was told that she and her brothers could be taken from the home and separated into foster care. She thought that would be all her fault, so she retracted her statement. Her mother was mostly absent from her life, due to struggling with substance use, and Cindy sobbed when recounting her feelings of abandonment. She held a lot of resentment toward her mother and recalled a particularly painful time when her mother chose to go to a bar instead of spending time with her, which prompted

Cindy to begin her own experimentation with drugs as a teenager. The first time she used drugs, she went on a three-day meth binge until her friend's father had to intervene and help her. Although she loved school, Cindy dropped out and ran away from home multiple times because she could no longer tolerate the sexual abuse and emotional trauma.

Cindy married when she was young and generally described her relationship in good terms, for the first couple of years anyway. They wanted to have kids. She took care of her nephew for a while and loved taking on a motherly role. However, she couldn't seem to get pregnant. Every month when she menstruated, she grew upset, but she never went to the doctor about it because that would have acknowledged the problem. Things took a turn for the worse when her husband let his brother move into their tiny apartment. His brother stole from them to fund his heroin habit and eventually introduced Cindy to smoking the drug. Her addiction progressed until her husband left her, which sent her further spiraling: "I got really depressed, so I got even more hooked. I started just not showering, not caring, not cleaning the house, not cooking, not eating, nothing; I didn't care. I just started going out, and stealing, and shoplifting and stuff, and selling whatever I got, and giving it to the connect [person selling drugs]. And I ended up starting to sell for the connect." Cindy was moving large quantities of heroin before she was arrested and deported for robbing an ice cream shop at gunpoint. She was never in direct contact with her husband again. They never officially divorced.

Estranged from her family, Cindy got by when she first arrived in Tijuana with the help of another deportee. She cleaned a man's house in exchange for staying with him until she figured out what to do. She lived with several different men and for a while worked in a bar and had a partner who became wildly possessive and wanted her to stay confined at home. When this partner became enraged one day, he slammed Cindy's kitten across the room and killed it. That was a breaking point. Terrified, she packed her bags and snuck out of the house while he was sleeping. Someone later told her that drug dealers from a meth deal gone bad came to the house, nailed all the doors shut, and set it on fire, killing the ex-boyfriend; his ex-wife, with whom he had rekindled a relationship; their newborn baby; his brother; and the brother's girlfriend. Cindy said she "skipped death" by leaving him. Out on her own again, and like many other women with limited options who find themselves in Tijuana by choice or unintended circumstance, sex work became a viable option for her survival. She was already engaged in sex work and deep into her heroin addiction when she met Beto.

Born and raised in Tijuana, Beto had a slight build, shaved head often hidden under a baseball hat, and gentle brown eyes. He grew up in a broken home and suffered verbal and emotional abuse from his mother. He was taken out of the home by child protective services but escaped three times before being taken in by his aunt. His aunt was married to an Iraq War veteran who was quiet and isolated, and the couple gave Beto considerable freedom. Beto started using alcohol and drugs

during his teenage years, ran away again to live on the street, and spent the majority of his adult life in and out of prison. At one point he got married but never
felt emotionally connected to his non–drug using wife, with whom he had two
children. During his marriage he navigated a period of sobriety and held a regular
job, but he never felt content. The couple split up, and he started using drugs again.

Beto called drug addiction an "emotional disease" that stems from one's childhood. In contrast to his trauma and dissatisfaction in life, drugs provided emotional
relief: "You find in drugs what you did not find elsewhere. It is like a refuge, an
escape. . . . You are looking for something, to fill the void, evade thoughts, evade
situations, evade many things. . . . You are looking to find peace for a moment,"
he described when reflecting on his long addiction trajectory.

Cindy and Beto met one day while connecting for heroin. They realized that
they had a lot in common, and their relationship quickly developed. "One of the
reasons she and I understood each other from the beginning," Beto explained, "is
because we had similar lives, the same addiction, the same environment, the same
family state; we have suffered the same things." As adults, Cindy and Beto finally
found comfort with each other. As partners who had already survived so much,
they didn't judge each other for their addictions because they understood its deep
roots. They found support in a shared "emotional disease" from past lifetimes of
embodied vulnerabilities that also shaped their future possibilities.

LOVE AS EMBODIED PRACTICE

Cindy and Beto lived on a compound of land left to Beto's family by his great-
grandmother, the matriarch of a family who had lived in Tijuana for generations.
There was one central house facing the main street, and the descendants had all
been allowed to build small structures on the long, rectangular property. Cindy
drew me a diagram of the compound, depicting a total of fifteen adults and five
children living in an area that must be about a quarter of an acre. Often family
members set up an informal flea market out front, where they sold everything
from glitter Jesus figurines to electric candles, small furniture, and shoes, but
mostly tools and car parts. Beto's uncle ran it; he and Beto used to do drugs and
get in trouble together, but this uncle had been clean from heroin for twenty years.
He and his wife ran a drug rehabilitation center, but they never judged or pres-
sured Cindy and Beto to enroll. They figured that if the couple wanted help, they
would ask for it. Many of the other family members drank alcohol, including Beto's
other uncle, who lived in the main house and was usually sitting out front when
I came by.

Inside the fenced property people were always coming and going, and a San
Diego rock station constantly played in the background (the music was often
picked up in my recordings, wherein the Beatles' "Here Comes the Sun" might be
juxtaposed against a discussion of the couple's heroin use). Cindy said the cops

probably thought that they were a *narcotraficante* family because of all the activity. Yet amid so many people, the couple largely kept to themselves. I never observed much interaction, nor did anyone ever stop to ask why a *gringa* (or two, when a colleague accompanied me) kept coming around to hang out. Cindy and Beto often felt judged as the "heroin users," and they didn't like being around drunk people anyway. They personally never used alcohol as a harm reduction strategy to prevent overdose.

Even surrounded by family and so much social activity, Beto always felt alone until Cindy moved in: "With Cindy, everything is very different, very different. . . . She inspires me; I know that I have someone, because where I live, even though my family is big, even with all those people, I was still alone. And since she came to live there, I don't care. She is everyone as long as I'm with her." Beto had constructed their single-room dwelling on the property, where they carved out the physical, social, and emotional refuge of their dangerous safe haven. Evidence of the safety of their safe haven was inscribed in magic marker all over the walls, where Beto wrote love messages to Cindy: "Yeah, he wrote, 'Mi Sirenita.' He calls me his little mermaid *[laughs]*, and then 'te amo y te amaré por siempre mi flakis', mi flaca, mi flakis, y 'solo tú y yo para siempre', 'tu lugar está aquí en mi corazón', this is your place right here, and then [he drew] a heart. He wrote all those messages for me on the wall," Cindy beamed.

The danger in their safe haven was anchored in the couple's daily heroin use, which structured their time and was a collaborative endeavor that involved weighing multiple, competing physical and social risks. But a closer look at their relationship also reveals the deeper symbolism of their shared drug use and what is at stake in their relationship. While heroin use was a key feature of their lives together, their relationship at once revolved around but transcended the centrality of addiction.

Cindy and Beto shared the labor of drug procurement and use. They took turns purchasing drugs out in front of their compound. Logistically, Beto typically took charge of preparing the drugs, which meant heating and liquefying the black tar heroin in the bottom of a soda can, and equally dividing up the liquid into their syringes. Cindy frequently worked late, so Beto procured and prepared the drugs while she remained in bed. She was often woken up with "Baby, your stuff is ready," and if he were able to buy a sugary donut or other breakfast treat to complement the full syringe, all the better. They shared all utensils throughout the preparation process (e.g., water, cooker, syringes) and kept their syringes in a common area, in which there was little indication of whose syringe was whose. With limited access they used whichever syringe seemed to work best for them at the time. Cindy said they don't use condoms, so sharing syringes "doesn't matter anyway." While they typically injected themselves on their own, they helped each other to inject when one was struggling or in pain.

All of these drug injection practices are epidemiological "risk behaviors" that heighten both partners' susceptibility to infectious diseases and other harms, including viral hepatitis and HIV. Heightened rates of infection gesture to a public health rendering of the concept of embodiment, which social epidemiologist Nancy Krieger conceives of as "how people literally embody, biologically, the multilevel dynamic and co-constituted societal and ecologic context within which we live, work, love, play, fight, ail, and die, thereby creating population patterns of health, disease, and well-being within and across historical generations" (2016, 832). Through this lens of embodiment, our lifetime experiences become physically inscribed onto our bodies in ways that help explain statistical patterns of health disparities at the population level.

The bruises and scarring all over the couple's bodies signaled their lifetimes of embodied insults that manifested in and from drug use. The ongoing drug war and impurities of criminalized drug markets physically imprint viral and bacterial infections, skin infections, abscesses, track marks, and other health harms on the bodies of people who inject drugs. Not only did the couple contend with more distal threats of infectious disease like HIV, but they embodied these other physical risks that also socially "marked" their bodies as drug users. Cindy's difficulty finding veins had even led her to start injecting into a delicate vein in her forehead. She worried that the beginning of a tiny track mark will quickly worsen.

Cindy and Beto recognized these physical health risks of their drug use. However, like many other people who inject drugs, they did not perceive their drug use entirely in terms of "risk," nor did they necessarily prioritize disease avoidance in guiding their actions. Their concerns were just as much social and emotional as physical. Rather than acts of thoughtless destruction, helping each other in their drug use represented embodied practices of caretaking, reinforcing their relationship as a dangerous safe haven amid multiple and competing risks. Akin to anthropologist Angela Garcia's work on intergenerational heroin use among close kin, practices related to drug use were not viewed as harm but are "oriented toward relieving the pain of the other and, as such, they were moral acts, embedded in the everyday context of shared vulnerability and difficult life circumstances" (2014a, 56).

For each partner the seedlings of addiction started early, accumulated in multiple forms of trauma over the life course, and became physically embodied as track marks, scars, and infections. This physical manifestation, in turn, exposes individuals to social discrimination and rejection. It further confines individuals under new forms of surveillance, including being targeted by police for their appearance as suspected drug users. Epidemiological studies in Tijuana have found that being arrested for track marks is associated with HIV infection, which is likely a proxy measure of the stigma, discrimination, and mistreatment that shapes the ill health of people who inject drugs (Strathdee et al. 2008a).

Embodiment thus has physical as well as social dimensions, or what French philosopher Pierre Bourdieu (1977) refers to as the "socially informed body," which moves through the world internalizing the broader environment while navigating the emotional lived experience of inequality and cultivating a subjective sense of what really matters.[2] Couples' embodied practices of caretaking prioritize their emotional unity and hold a key to reinterpreting the meaning of "risk behaviors." Drug use was but one part of Cindy and Beto's love and risk to be navigated amid other interrelated challenges, including economic precarity, sex work, incarceration, illness, and their collective will for survival.

* * *

Following the embodied ways in which Cindy and Beto moved through the challenges of their world together rewrites notions of risk as the couple themselves experienced it. Beto affectionately nicknamed Cindy *la chamuca*, or local slang for "the devil," which also connotes a sense of mischievousness. Rather than anything inherently evil, *la chamuca* references how they considered themselves to be partners in crime in navigating their material circumstances:

> Cindy: I'm not going to be a nag and be like, "No, don't do that and this and that." If I see it's doable and there's no risk, and I know I can back him up or look out for him, I'll be like, "Okay, let's go for it," because I've always been down for things, so I'm like, "Okay, let's go for it." That's why he calls me *la chamuca*, but he thinks it's cool. We talked, and I said, "If I would be nagging you instead of being like, 'Yeah, go for it,' would you not do it?" and he's like, "No, I would just have to hide it from you, and I'd have a hard time doing stuff." It's not like I'm making him do anything. That's how I look at it.
>
> Beto: We're accomplices. . . .
>
> Cindy: Yeah, I always told him, "We're accomplices; we're buddies; we're friends; we're partners; we're everything," you know?

As indicated in this passage, they meant "everything" to each other, and together they negotiated risk taking. They shared a sense of what was possible in terms of their life constraints. Cindy did not "nag" Beto or try to make him into something he is not, but rather they supported each other as they are. As an example, Cindy encouraged him to steal a bike from someone outside in the street whom they had been watching through their window. They described their victim as succumbing to the effects of a "speedball" (a mixture of heroin and meth) in that he was alternately nodding off (from the heroin) and tweaking on the rocks on the street (obsessively focusing on an object, an effect of meth). Their victim was too distracted to notice before Beto snatched the bike and pedaled away. He later sold it for Mex$100 (about US$10) and three tamales. As she often did, Cindy seemed so proud of her man as she told the story.

In terms of day-to-day support, Cindy largely preferred to earn money from sex work to help maintain their drug use rather than Beto "risking himself" to commit crimes. Beto sometimes worked as a mechanic, but it was not enough to reliably support their daily needs. With limited education and a prison record, Beto could not easily find stable employment. Petty theft was a last resort option that left him vulnerable to arrest. Further, Beto embodied his drug use in his own track marks and scars, and he picked at his skin whenever he smoked meth, which also "marked" him as drug user and left him open to harassment by authorities even when he wasn't committing a crime. Cindy felt it was much easier for her to discreetly engage in the quasi-legal activity of sex work with her regular clients and avoid arrest compared to Beto undertaking regular criminal activity and potentially going back to prison.

Like the other women in this book, Cindy managed her sex work in ways that reduced her exposure to harm and maintained the love and emotional intimacy that she and Beto shared. Cindy described sex work as a process of dissociating herself emotionally while she let clients temporarily "borrow" her physical body. Cindy clearly distinguished the boundaries of her work from her relationship with Beto: "I mean, it's a job that I'm doing; I'm not doing it for pleasure; I'm not doing it because I like it, or nothing like that. What I like, I do it with my husband, and only him, and I enjoy it only with him. When I do this, I don't enjoy it. I'm like putting my mind out of my body, and like you're borrowing a body, and my mind is just leaving, you know, to complete the job, get some money, and that's the way I take it."

Cindy was beautiful and crafty and often used her erotic assets to finagle money and other material items from her clients without even engaging in sex. While she cultivated friendly relationships with these regular clients for her financial benefit and physical safety, as did other women in this book, she was careful not to breach the emotional contract she had with Beto by developing feelings for them. She never allowed clients to kiss her; she called that practice "sacred" and reserved only for "someone you love." She also used condoms with clients to demarcate physical and emotional separation. In contrast, using a condom with Beto would not be the same experience, either physically or emotionally. Condomless sex helped her feel "closer" to Beto and reinforced their trust: "You feel more like you're trusting each other; you really, truly, trust him by not using a condom with him."

Cindy loved and trusted Beto with her life. She perceived the benefits of her sex work as outweighing the couples' competing risks, including his heightened risk of arrest and incarceration. Since childhood Cindy had suffered from feelings of abandonment, for which she had often blamed herself. Cindy's mother was largely absent, and prior partners spent time incarcerated and left her in precarious situations. This continued to give her anxiety. One night after she and Beto had gotten high, he walked to the store to buy cigarettes. When he didn't return for a long time, she panicked that he had been arrested. She was ready to walk all the way to the jail in the cold and dark of night to try to bail him out before she found him nodded off on the toilet in the shared bathroom facility of their compound. When she found him, she sobbed and hugged him in relief. Beto was somewhat bewildered by her intense emotional reaction, but he offered comfort and reassurance that he wasn't going anywhere.

The stakes of imprisonment took on an almost mythical quality in a conversation we had one day about prison life. I naively hadn't realized that some of the best quality drugs in Tijuana were distributed from well-connected networks of prisoners, and gang affiliations on the inside can signal a struggle for survival where the stakes are life and death. Inmates are divided into different categories, including Sureños, a term for Latino gang affiliates from Southern California, and Paisas, Mexican nationals who have no gang affiliation. "He didn't use to like Sureños at all," Cindy explained, "and check him out, check him out! He got married to a Sureña *[laughter]*. Same with me though, I didn't use to like Paisas at all, and look at me." On the outside of prison they could laugh about it, but they both grew serious when they explained the context:

> Cindy: Yeah, it's a war to the death, and he being the enemy, it's like, "What's up with you, dude?" Same with me. If I fall into prison, and they know about this, oh, I would be in trouble. But I told him that if that ever happens, God forbid, but if that ever happens, when I went to visit, I would cover my tattoos and all that. I would not speak English. I wouldn't say I was a southerner, so I wouldn't cause problems. . . . We are not supposed to be together. I love my baby.
>
> Beto: If that were to happen, I'd play dumb. But I'm going to stay here.
>
> Cindy: That's right. You're not going back to prison.
>
> Beto: I'm not going to fall into prison anymore. I already have three years out, and before that I was three months on the outside at any given time at the most, and then inside again. Two years, three years, one month, I went out two months, and in again for two years, three years, five years. For eleven years, I had almost three years total on the outside, and the rest of the time, I was inside. And when I was out here, I was also in a rehabilitation center for a while, another kind of confinement.

Sex work, then, is a form of situated rationality and a moral act of care within Cindy's life constraints primarily aimed at supporting the couple and keeping Beto out of prison again. Her carefully cultivated client base enabled her to reduce her own physical risks, while caring for Beto in ways that helped assure their collective social safety. She also supported him in her role as *la chamuca*, encouraging him to engage in "low-risk" activities to contribute financially. All of these embodied practices prioritized the socioemotional sense of security that their dangerous safe haven provided. Beyond finances Cindy's sex work was her way of assuring the longevity of her dangerous safe haven and showing unconditional care for a partner who helped make her feel like a complete person:

> We love each other a lot. We found our other half; we found the one we were looking for. It's cool stuff. I always tell him he's never gonna be alone again; since he has me,

he'll never be alone again. He'll always, always have someone that worries for him, that looks after him, and I told him I might just be a lady . . . but I can take care of him too. There's things that I can do to take care of him, to look after him to make sure he's okay, he's safe. Not just because he's a man he's gonna be the one to take care of me. I can take care of him too, and I'll always take care of him in any way that I can. Always, always, always.

*   *   *

At one point during the Parejas project Cindy asked, "I wonder how other couples are. Are they like us? Are they on the same page, and do they answer the questions like we do?"

From my perspective the answer to Cindy's question is no—not all couples were like them. Though forms of love and care were apparent across couples, as seen in earlier chapters, Cindy and Beto proclaimed to be "in love" with each other. Their relationship had a depth of emotion, and the couple embodied their love and care for each other through daily practices beyond drug use and sex work.

Cindy constantly complimented Beto. She often bragged how smart he was even for having little formal education. Sometimes as she spoke, he looked down sheepishly, and she would rub his head or kiss him on the cheek. Cindy was also impressed by Beto's street smarts. When Beto shared a series of photos of street scenes taken for my project, he told the story of leaving home and living with a community camped out on a hill behind some roadside billboards. They managed to evade the police by running away, which involved jumping down onto a rooftop and sliding down the billboard pole. Cindy had heard some of these stories, but not all of the details, and she was impressed by his ingenuity. She remarked to me, "Survival, huh?" And then to him, "That's pretty cool stuff, smarty pants. Baby you're so cute." Survival indeed: Beto was eventually arrested and incarcerated, only to be released several years later and find out that his street friends had either passed away from drug-related causes or were infected with HIV.

The same will for survival translated to their own relationship, in which HIV and other forms of illness posed a constant threat, particularly given their precarious living conditions and limited access to health care. Cindy was frequently sick, including several bouts of undetermined flu-like illness throughout the project. Solidarity in sickness offers an important example of closeness and care in sex workers' relationships, as we also see in Julieta and Mateo's story in chapter 2 and Celia and Lazarus's story in chapter 3.

During one particularly severe bout of illness, Cindy suffered from a high fever, exhaustion, vomiting, and a stomachache to the point that she was immobilized and thought she "was going to die." In her frustration she told Beto that she was becoming a "hindrance" and she should leave. "She told me . . . that my life was very *heavy* as it was," Beto recalled, and that leaving would free him from her suffering. He told me a different view:

"I told her, 'That's a joke, right? That's what your partner is for: to rely on in the good and the bad. If there is really love and the relationship is serious, then I think that one must be together until the last consequences, whether they are good or bad."

Then Cindy turned to Beto: "You know the truth, not because I don't love you. I love you [*no porque no te quiera, te amo*], and that's why I wanted to leave."

Then she turned to me: "But he told me that it wasn't right, that I should let him decide if he didn't want to be in that situation. He always tells me not to decide for him, not to think for him, to let him think for himself, and that was his thought, his decision, that he didn't want me to change anything. He wanted to keep taking care of me. He was happy like that and it was the support I needed because I was feeling bad, thank God."

Angela Garcia has described a similar "closeness and heaviness" in the relations of heroin-using families who share an embodied understanding of the world (2014b, 209). The moments of "closeness and heaviness" for Cindy and Beto speak to the intensity of their relationship that included, but transcended, their shared heroin addiction. While much of their daily support for each other was geared toward "getting well" in terms of heroin withdrawal, Beto also had a greater sense of responsibility in caring for his sick partner, no matter how "heavy" his life already was. Beto did not leave. In fact, in his quest to care for Cindy, he "borrowed" money from one of her regular clients so he could buy her medication.

Harkening back to the beginning of their relationship shows that not all moments were so heavy in cultivating their closeness. When Beto first invited Cindy to stay with him, she asked if she could bring along her dog, Paloma. Beto hated dogs. To his horror, on their first night together, Paloma slept in bed with them. But Paloma came to play a critical and symbolic role in their relationship. Beto saw how important the dog was to Cindy. Paloma was always around, often waiting with them in the driveway for the drug dealers to drive by to score (or chasing their cars down the street). Most of the time, when they sat in the shade of the driveway waiting to connect, they smoked cigarettes, talked, or read to each other, with Paloma by their side. In fact, a selfie of the couple that Beto snapped depicts them in this scenario. The photo is classic: Beto has a cigarette hanging out of his mouth, and both are wearing dark sunglasses and leaning closely into each other. Cindy pointed out that Paloma was in between them, but only the tip of her ear was caught in the bottom of the frame. Cindy said it was one of her favorite photos from the project because it shows how close they are as a couple.[3]

Feminist scholar Donna Haraway has written extensively about the importance of interspecies bonding between humans and their dogs. As Haraway has noted, the "acts of love" shown in caring for pets "breed acts of love like caring about and for other concatenated, emergent worlds" (2003, 61). Beto's learned love for Paloma was an expression of his love for Cindy, as he recognized the importance of the dog to Cindy. Over time he grew fond of not only Paloma but her subsequent litters of puppies. Paloma had the same father for all three litters of puppies

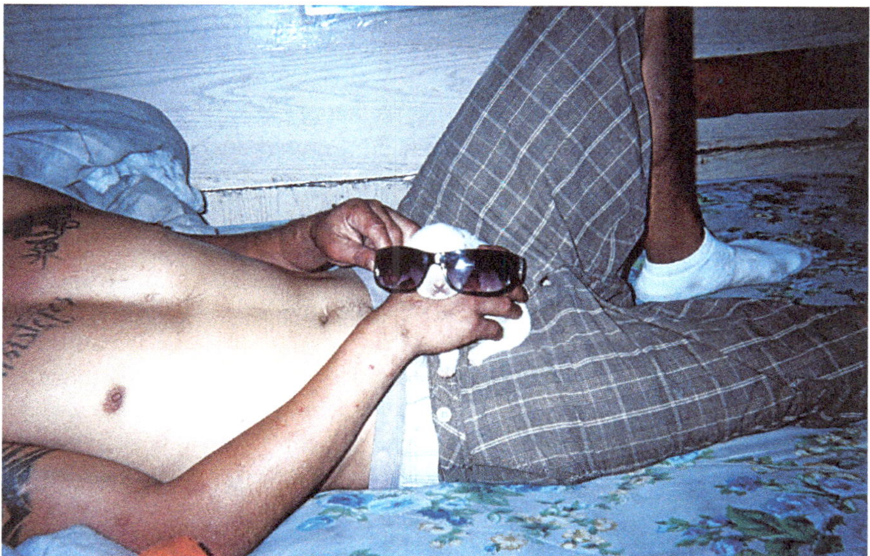

FIGURE 10. Although Beto was not fond of dogs when he met Cindy, his attitude changed because of the love that Cindy had for her dog, Paloma. Beto even grew particularly fond of one of Paloma's puppies, whom they named Sabastian. This was one of Cindy's favorite photos. Photo by Cindy.

over the past few years, and this dog always came back to check on her after she gave birth. Cindy said that, just like she and Beto, the dogs are "in love."

* * *

Many of the embodied acts of love and care that Cindy and Beto showed each other are "obvious" or "typical" among any intimate couple, including sharing, holding hands, speaking to each other affectionately, and accepting pets into the family. These moments also include the simple pleasures of telling jokes and stories, finishing each other's thoughts, and even sharing a good meal or the sugary snacks they loved. Even seemingly insignificant practices like smoking cigarettes were embodied acts of care and imbued with meaning. When they first started dating, Beto always lit Cindy's cigarette first. When one day he lit his first, she worried that he did not love her anymore and started to feel upset. Sensitive to her feelings, he asked her what was wrong, and she confessed her fear. Now, as they both laughed, they assured me that Beto always lights her cigarette first.

To be certain, drug use was interwoven into these more mundane daily practices and rituals. However, it was one piece of a bigger picture that I began to better understand through the course of fieldwork. On one occasion my colleague and I spent the entire day at Cindy and Beto's home. We witnessed several injection episodes, observed them smoke meth (which they said was rare), and conducted an extended interview for the Parejas project, as well as chatted with them and hung out on a much less formal basis. Their morning injections were of typical intensity and duration, and then, as if nothing out of the ordinary had happened, we played darts and talked about Paloma and the latest litter of puppies until it was lunchtime.

We had brought them some leftover carne asada from a party over the weekend, and Cindy suggested it would be "fun" to teach us how to make tortillas. This also provided us with an opportunity to visit the main house in the compound, where Beto's uncle lives. They suggested we buy him a forty-ounce beer in return for using his kitchen facilities to make lunch, which was well received. We took turns hand rolling the tortillas, and Beto took charge of cooking, including making French fries from scratch. He told us that if the tortillas bubbled up as they cooked, it meant one was ready for marriage. Apparently, he was ready.

After lunch the cadence of their daily ritual demanded that they score heroin again. Our original plan was to head back to the project office to conduct "official" data collection, as the couple was to participate in a joint follow-up interview about their experiences in the larger Parejas public health study. Instead, we all went outside and waited to connect. In their driveway, where they often passed the time together, we turned on our recorders and started the interview, including asking them if anything had changed in their relationship over the past year of their participation in the project:

> Cindy: Actually, nothing is new, right? Paloma had more puppies *[laughs]*. But everything else remains the same, and always good. He and I don't let anyone affect us. While he and I are happy with each other, we're fine; then we're good, and nothing else matters, so people can try what they want to break us down, but they can't.
>
> Beto: Yes, this is how it always is. I wonder how common the word love *[amor]* is. . . . If it's only words, or it happens in all couples . . . but it has happened to us; we have never stopped talking or doing things. We never get to extreme situations, where one of us does something that the other does not like, or that does not seem right to the other, or that we have to change the relationship. Since the very first day, everything has been awesome.

This question did not directly ask about love, but Beto tied the durability of their relationship to the ingredients of love, not just as a word but as a way of interacting and embodied practice.

We also learned that the project had inspired them to reflect on their relationship. Beto admitted that he felt nervous to participate at the beginning, but he came to see the interviews as conversations where he could open up about his experiences. Cindy also came to value the Parejas project as a way to have a shared experience with Beto that also helped them communicate as a couple and feel closer. Even in the context of a study on HIV risk, the embodied possibilities to locate love, care, and intimacy were present.

After Beto scored we all went inside to continue the interview as they injected. As it was later in the day at this point, they were not quite as *malilla*, or sick from heroin withdrawal, as they were first thing in the morning, and so they were not as quiet and focused in their injection processes They told us to keep asking them questions, and they were lucid and forthcoming about their experiences in the project.[4] As we saturated the topics in our semistructured interview guide for the main study, we branched out into more casual conversation, including asking how the injection process was going this time around. Beto lamented the trouble they both had from long careers of injection. He said that some men have resorted to injecting in their penis, though he called that "sacred," and he has not tried it. But that reminded him of a story: it is the "legend, er, true story" of Mata Hari. Yet another example of the embodied ways that Cindy and Beto worked together as a couple was through their storytelling. They often took turns telling stories, particularly recounting their lives together and helping each other fill in the details. But they also shared silly moments of exchange, like our conversation that emerged about the "true" story of Mata Hari.

Historically, Mata Hari was a famous Dutch exotic dancer accused by the French of espionage in World War I, though many considered her to be persecuted for breaking moral codes governing women's "proper" roles at the time rather than for any evidence of treason. Cindy and Beto's version of the Mata Hari, however, was quite different. They took turns telling the story of a woman from "high society" so upset and enraged by her partner's philandering that she killed him, wrapped him up in a curtain, and kept him in the closet. One day she realized that she would never find another man like him, and she could not live without him, so she must kill herself to be with him again. She decided to cut off what Beto called his "noble part" and held it close to her as she jumped out of a window and to her death. Beto concluded, "The penis is taken from her and put into a museum. It's a piece of art. It is called Mata Hari, which means 'The most beautiful penis in the universe.'" Although we were all heartily laughing at the absurdity, they both colluded in trying to convince us that it was a "TRUE story."

That night, when writing my fieldnotes, I thought about how they worked together as a team to completely upend our plans to go to the project office in a more structured environment for data collection. I appreciated their comfort in inviting us in, allowing for a less scripted version of themselves that made their home—heroin injections and all—feel like a safe haven to us, even as risk was all around. I began to understand how perceptions of danger can shift when we are with other people we trust, and how this is surely amplified in the context of their intimate relationship. However, I also questioned the "scientific value" of transcribing the entire recording, including the Mata Hari story. After all, those are not the kind of data the NIH was probably expecting out of these interviews.

FIGURE 11. Beto perhaps misfired in this shot of Cindy, which was part of a series of photos of the couple smoking meth with a friend. Although Cindy is mostly cut out of the frame, the photo reveals some of the love messages Beto wrote in magic marker on their walls, translated as "I love you and I'll always love you," "your place is here and in my heart," and "only you and me forever." Photo by Beto.

Yet, how could I ignore it? Cindy and Beto were engaging in a fundamental part of the human experience: making sense of the world and conveying their experiences through storytelling. By mythologizing Mata Hari, they were conveying a symbolic message about their own lives, including a juxtaposition of their desires and frustrations. Anthropologist Mary Douglas has called myths a "contemplation of the unsatisfactory compromises" in life. "In the devious statements of the myth, people can recognize indirectly what it would be difficult to admit openly and yet what is patently clear to all and sundry, that the ideal is not attainable" ([1967] 2004, 52).

I later began to think about how the idea of the perfect romantic version of love that has become the Western—and increasingly globalized—ideal is one of the most troubled subjects of myth. Literary scholar Joseph Campbell (2004) traces this idealized version of love in literature to the poetic works of twelfth-century troubadours: the archetypal myth of Tristan and Isolde reflects the emergence of a companionate love between two tormented individuals for whom only their love for each other could bring true healing amid suffering. Perhaps Cindy and Beto's version of the Mata Hari was yet another rendering of Tristan and Isolde, Romeo and Juliet, star-crossed Sureños and Paisas, or any number of other love stories that reflect the core message of all myths: that everybody must find their own "pathway to bliss."[5]

A life of material disadvantage and heroin addiction may not be the typical stuff of mythical love stories, but building a dangerous safe haven with a partner who understands, loves, and protects in such conditions may be the best pathway to take in an otherwise loveless world. Even as this book has critiqued a singular, perfect image of romantic love, Cindy and Beto embodied a love for each other that manifested in multiple ways, big and small, related to drug use but beyond addiction, and into the mundane and even the absurd. Maybe their version of the Mata Hari was just a silly story they told for their own entertainment as well as ours. But maybe Cindy and Beto can teach us to look past mythologized versions of love to understand that different kinds of relationships can be lived on their own terms, with couples carving their own pathways toward a meaningful life.

'TIL DEATH DO US PART

The last time I saw Cindy and Beto was in the project office, when they returned for a follow-up survey and HIV/STI testing. I chatted with Beto in the waiting room, as it took a while for the nurse to find a vein from which to draw blood from Cindy. When she emerged, he pulled two lollipops out of his pocket and gave one to her. After we said goodbye, I peered outside our second-story window and saw them stop at an ice cream vendor across the street for *paletas* before walking off into the crowded street, holding hands and eating their popsicles.

Cindy and Beto's story lends insight into what it means to love and care for a partner in broader contexts of inequality, marginalization, and disadvantage. Like the other couples featured in this book, they understood each other's embodied life trajectories of trauma and hardship and offered each other multiple forms of support that included but transcended supporting each other's addictions. They shared an emotionally close relationship, in which they considered themselves to be "in love," and their relationship was transformative in their lives up until the end. Unfortunately, Beto's proclamation that couples "must be together until the last consequences, whether they are good or bad" came to tragic fruition when Cindy passed away from complications of an illness.[6]

Cindy's premature death takes us back full circle to a public health rendering of embodiment, in that she literally and biologically embodied her disadvantage and inequity in the form of illness and untimely death. Her death reflects patterns of premature morbidity and mortality that characterize populations of sex workers across global contexts. These patterns are not accidental or natural but rather reflect the structural inequalities that limit opportunities for women like Cindy, drive them into sex work and injection drug use, and shape their options for survival. A socially informed rendering of embodiment also reminds us that even if the couples' love for each other couldn't change the social structures that enacted harm all around them, it did make life worth living, even in a life cut short. But even in physical death, spirits can live on to inspire us. Could one of Cindy's final contributions to the world be to challenge stereotypes about sex workers' ability to find love? Can reflecting on her life and intimate relationship reveal new possibilities for love—including opening up a space for love to transform our own embodied practices?

Grappling with Cindy's untimely death has inspired me to rethink my own research practices. In struggling with questions about friendship, positionality, power, and the implications of research, I found a connection to a reflection written by Gregory Reck about his friendship with his "star" informant, named Celestino, whom he met during fieldwork in Mexico. Reck considered himself to be a good anthropologist and a friend to his participants like Celestino, but he struggled with the complexity of research relationships, including what it really means to those involved and why the work matters. When Reck left the field, he didn't realize that he would never see Celestino again, but that the deep imprint of their relationship would carry on long afterward: "I would never see him again, but he wasn't gone from my life. Not really. He was there all the time. I talked about him in chandeliered ballrooms filled with anthropologists. I wrote a book and several articles about him. He came to my classes, and I introduced him to my students. I told stories about him, about us, as friends. But most of all, I thought about him. . . . At the strangest of times, Celestino would simply appear in my head. He still does" ([1995] 2006, 44). For me the same holds true about Cindy and Beto. I still think about them (and the other Parejas participants) and what our relationships meant. Beyond ugly chandeliered ballrooms, I think we have an imperative to do more.

As the following chapters continue to grapple with sex work, drug use, love, and risk, I also begin to interweave a tone of reflexivity in relation to the broader implications of our research. The stories of Maria and Gwen in the next chapter are equally tragic yet revealing of the power and limitations of dangerous safe havens for couples' health and well-being. Their participation in Parejas also offers an opportunity to consider the role of love in shaping our research methodologies, a theme that also compels us to rethink global health intervention and practice.

5

(Not) Lost to Follow-Up

The first qualitative interview I conducted in the beginning of the Parejas project was with Maria, a forty-six-year-old American woman with a long history of heroin use and engagement in sex work in Tijuana. After a standard introduction outlining the consent form and its largely clinical concern with confidentiality and data security, I asked if she had any questions. "No." I turned on the tape recorder to begin. "Actually, I do have a question. Why are you studying us? Do you think sex workers are weird or something?" After I answered Maria's questions, she was satisfied enough that I was allowed to proceed. While this exchange was not ultimately transcribed as part of the "official" Parejas data collection, I archived our interaction in my personal fieldnotes. Later I began to think about the "official" record—including what is captured and what is lost in our methodological choices and how this shapes the implications of our work.

This chapter examines the complexities of love in two women's lives as a way to also think through bigger questions about research methodology. I focus on the stories of Maria and Gwen, also an American woman who has lived for many years in Mexico. Both were "lost to follow-up" in the Parejas study—research parlance indicating that neither were able to complete all of their study visits over the two-year period and thus could be excluded from longitudinal analyses. Neither woman completed my own project either. Given the tragic circumstances that prevented them from finishing either study, which made their stories somewhat different from the other couples, I could have excluded them from this book. But where is the love in that?

Research methodologies encompass our overall approach and values that drive research projects. Methodologies are guided by our epistemological, ethical, and political commitments and shape the choice of methods in our projects. Methods are tools and techniques to collect and analyze data (e.g., surveys and semistructured interviews). Methods range from the unstructured interactions of anthropologists in the field to more structured, increasingly sophisticated statistical

97

approaches that are simultaneously hailed as "rigorous" and criticized as imposed forms of white logic enacting oppression. The structured, rigorous, and replicable methods increasingly demanded by granting agencies and academic publishing venues compel us to "clean up" the data, "drop" incomplete cases, "throw away" interviews that pilot test questions, and generally exclude interactions outside of officially approved study protocols as "anecdotal" rather than "real data." In contrast, feminist scholars outline alternative methodologies valuing the knowledge produced through unfinished and otherwise liminal spaces.[1] I envision a methodology guided by love as emerging in feminist traditions prioritizing people over procedure and valuing what happens outside of traditional research frames. By tracing my engagement with Maria and Gwen through the course of research, this chapter reveals the love that would be lost if we don't see beyond conventional measures of "rigor" in research.

As it is, American migrant women like Maria and Gwen are typically unseen in academic and popular accounts of sex work in Mexico. Yet they represent two of the estimated 1.6 million Americans living in Mexico, the majority of whom are concentrated in the northern border region of Baja California, where Tijuana is located.[2] Their intersecting identities as white American bilingual women with histories of drug addiction and sex work in Mexico created unique privileges and vulnerabilities that shaped their intimate relationships with monolingual Spanish-speaking Mexican men in Tijuana. Their stories speak to the historical connections in the Mexico-US border region around leisure economies and the deep social ties that mark cross-border life in this part of the world. Examining Maria's and Gwen's lives through the lens of their participation in Parejas reveals the borderlessness of love and shows how much happens in the lives of research participants beyond the parameters of our studies. They also remind us that their participation—however brief—is meaningful and their stories worthy to be told.

MARIA AND GERALDO

Maria and Geraldo met because of drugs, and much of their relationship was structured around their shared struggles with addiction. He knew that she smoked crack when they met and purposefully started coming around her San Diego neighborhood to buy crack and hang out at her house. One day, when they were watching television, she turned to him to comment on a commercial, and he suddenly kissed her. That started the beginning of a complex, nearly twenty-year relationship marked by periods of trauma, separation, incarceration, drug rehabilitation, and, most recently, serious illness. Yet through it all, Geraldo said they will "always be together."

For the first few years of their relationship, they stayed in San Diego and got high on crack until Geraldo went to jail on a charge he doesn't even remember and got deported to Tijuana. Maria followed him and a year later found out she was pregnant. When the time came to deliver, they went to the border crossing so she could deliver on the US side. He went to the border patrol officers to plead with them to let her through the long wait because she was an American citizen. They got her into an ambulance that whisked her off to the US side. They refused his entry, and he missed the birth of his son. The next day the baby died. They both had kept using drugs during her pregnancy and had not thought that it could lead to premature death. His parents blamed her, which created family conflict. They separated for a few years but still kept in touch. Geraldo didn't like to talk about what happened to their son; he had nine brothers and sisters, and he was the only one without children. He always wanted a boy.

During their separation Geraldo started using drugs more heavily and was constantly in and out of jail. Maria was also arrested in California and given the option of six months in jail or a court-ordered drug rehabilitation program. She chose the latter because she could "wear clothes [not a prison uniform] and smoke, so that was a big privilege." She maintained a period of sobriety for several years: "I was living in San Diego; he was living here in Tijuana. I was working. I had two jobs; I did pretty well. I had two dogs, a car. I used to get my nails done every two weeks, and every two months I had an appointment at Supercuts."

But Maria missed Geraldo. She started traveling down to Tijuana to see him, seeking both the danger and comfort of the dangerous safe haven they had built. She knew there was a risk of relapsing, but even with all the comforts and stability of her situation in San Diego, there was something missing without him. One time when she went to visit Geraldo, she had him inject her with heroin. At first, she didn't feel anything, and so she started her drive back to the border, only to call him ten minutes later to say that she didn't feel well and that she couldn't drive anymore. "You don't know how sorry I am" for introducing her to injection drug use, Geraldo later recounted. Maria, however, said she was "tired of being sober anyway."

Years later, when I met them, heroin injection was a significant feature of their dangerous safe haven. But it was much more than that. They shared an emotional commitment complicated by their addictions and the geopolitics of the border that shaped their possibilities to build a meaningful relationship. Although Maria grew to know Tijuana and could navigate her way through the city, it was still always an adopted place, where she stood out. Yet she couldn't return home, as Geraldo's deportation status restricted their possibilities.

In Tijuana their dangerous safe haven made Maria feel safe. She often woke up in the middle of the night feeling scared and wanting his comfort. She worried about losing him because she is the older of the two. Starting to go through menopause, Maria felt that her hard life was beginning to wear on her appearance: "El esta joven todavía y yo me estoy poniendo más chicharrón con cada día a día [He is still young, and I am becoming more like *chicharrón* every day]," she said, jokingly referring to the fried crackling pork skins that are a favorite snack in Mexico. However, he said her age did not matter, and that they still loved each other. Maria joked that "I must love him if I put up with his shit," referring to his large, meddling Mexican family, her hunch that he's had outside sexual partners, and their shared struggles with addiction. Ultimately, she said that Geraldo is "the love of her life." But, like other couples in this book, the emotional protection of the dangerous safe havens could only go so far amid the everyday violence and social marginalization that marked their lives.

* * *

The next time I saw Maria, after her enrollment in Parejas and our qualitative interview, was between data collection visits when it was time to update locator forms, the detailed sheets of information that staff used to follow up with participants. She was heavily made up in thick lavender eye shadow and lip liner so dark it almost appeared black, but no lipstick. She looked exhausted. She complained about having to do the locator and at first would not even sit down. Eventually, she settled in and we talked about topics well beyond confirming her address.

Maria was nearly raped two weeks prior. Reminiscent of the secret keeping common among couples, she hadn't told Geraldo. She didn't want to upset him and deal with the consequences, as she was pretty sure he would want to find the person and exact revenge. She would rather shut that out and stay inside of her dangerous safe haven. She internalized the blame for this violence. She normally does not get inside cars with strangers, but this man was young and good-looking, so she took the risk. When he didn't follow her directions and make a right turn where she indicated, she knew she was in trouble. As he forced himself on her, she tried reverse psychology on him, as she knew that rape was not about sex as much as power and control. She learned that from watching *CSI: Miami*. Her tactics spooked him, and she escaped the situation without being physically harmed.

But the emotional damage was already taking hold. She wondered why it happened to her when she wasn't even young anymore. Worldwide more than one-third of all women have been physically or sexually assaulted in their lifetimes. A systematic review indicates that sex workers are disproportionately affected, as 45–75 percent have experienced violence (Deering et al. 2014). Like the available epidemiological data, our follow-up surveys asked about experiences of rape, sexual assault, and other forms of violence. However, we didn't ask about situations like Maria's in which it "almost" happens, which can be equally traumatizing but, in terms of data collection, represents a form of erasure. We had resources to offer her, but she wasn't interested.[3]

This wasn't the last of Maria's trauma either. By the time the next Parejas follow-up surveys came due, Maria was also beginning to suffer from serious physical health issues. She showed up to the office with no makeup, and I had never seen her in a baseball hat before. Her leg was in severe pain, and so she had to pull herself up the steep stairwell backward to our office, with a staff member helping and encouraging her to rest and take deep breaths on the way up. She had not seen a doctor, and so she was taking an excessive amount of over-the-counter pain relievers, including eight tablets prior to coming to the interview that day.

Although she periodically cried through the survey, she insisted that she wanted to finish. To get through the interview, I gave Geraldo a dollar to get her cigarettes to take her mind off of her pain. She complained that I kept asking her the same questions over and over again. As with many epidemiologic surveys, the content of many of our questions were similar, but the recall periods of behaviors and details elicited about specific behaviors varied. Maria was not in the mood to answer questions she didn't find important, but she also refused to stop the interview.

I never struggled so much with an interview as I did that day, and her case (among others) highlights the problems of positivist conceptions of survey data collection that assume everyone has a replicable interview experience. I consulted with another project coordinator, and we gave the couple part of their study compensation early so Geraldo could purchase heroin and they could inject and relieve some of her pain. Geraldo took for what seemed like *forever* to get the drugs. Back at the office he pulled a syringe full of dark-brown heroin out of a hidden compartment in his backpack and handed it to her. She grabbed it and with barely a thought, jabbed it into her upper right arm. We probably broke multiple study protocols that day, but I could see why people struggling with addiction would do anything not to see their loved ones suffer. Couples like Maria and Geraldo navigated the thin line between injury and care embedded within their everyday relations and collective efforts of survival (Garcia 2010). For a moment at least, I also became part of that nexus of care and violence, as the research took second place to her well-being. Maria made it through the rest of the interview, and she was well enough that the pair even participated in a couples interview later the same day.

However, she was already hospitalized in the United States when, a short while later, I tried to contact them about the photovoice project. As it turns out, Maria left for San Diego just three days after their last Parejas interviews. She had an embolism in her leg (the lodging of an embolus, or a mass that causes blockage in a distant part of the body) and had been taking far too many over-the-counter painkillers without eating enough. Geraldo got scared about her deteriorating health and called her family in San Diego. The hospitals in Tijuana have a horrific reputation for how they treat people who use drugs, and he worried about her care there. Even so, Maria did not fare well in San Diego, as she had a stroke, was diagnosed with endocarditis (a heart infection), and became infected with methicillin-resistant Staphylococcus aureus (MRSA) while in the hospital. She was under their care for about four months and received methadone to manage the heroin withdrawal.

Remaining behind in Tijuana, Geraldo participated in my photovoice project to show a glimpse of his life separated from Maria.[4] He told me he did not care about my project, but he was doing it only because Maria liked me, and she would want him to do it. His decision-making in her absence reflects the fundamental importance of their relationship. His behavior was still driven by what he thought would make Maria happy.

Geraldo knew Maria was okay because her grandmother called him to keep him up to date, while warning him that she needed time to recover. Because of his deportation status, he could not see her, but he also worried about her wanting to come back to Tijuana and start using heroin again. It pained him, but he resisted talking to her, even the day I offered to let him use the office phone:

> Jennifer: Do you want to talk to her right now? We can use the phone here, and I can call her mother's house. What do you think?
>
> Geraldo: No, so . . . how can I tell you? I don't want to talk to her right now, Jennifer, because if I talk to her, and it's okay, she will want to come here; do you understand me? And I don't want her to come because I don't want her to be using it anymore, and I know that if I talk to her, she is going to tell me things, and they will make me want to see her, and I am going to tell her to come here, and I am going to be very sorry for that. I don't want her to come here, I would prefer to go over there with her, and for me to also stop using than for her to come here, Jennifer. Here, it is the same wherever I go. Where I go is pure drug use, and I don't want her to use again, I want her to recover well. And I assure you that if I talk to her, Jennifer, she will want to come. I really want to talk to her, Jennifer, seriously, I really want to talk to her, but if I talk to her, she will want to come here. She might cry, but I don't want her to come here.

Geraldo was concerned with Maria's recovery, even as he emotionally struggled with wanting to be with her. He felt strongly that being back in the drug scene of Tijuana would jeopardize her health. His emotions often bubbled over in his interviews. He grew visibly upset several times during our interactions, as I tried to be sensitive and not be too invasive in my questions yet still open a space for him to talk. He wanted to stop using drugs and be with her, but without viable options for his own drug treatment, he felt stuck. In his photovoice project he took multiple photos relating to his drug use, which he said had escalated in her absence as a means of coping with his stress.

However, the most revealing photo was not one from his photovoice project but one he carried with him in his tattered leather wallet. It had been taken many years ago, after he had gotten out of prison and Maria had been abstinent on the US side. He lovingly pointed out that she looked *gordita*, or fat, which in this context was used in an endearing way, referring to her as healthy rather than skinny from drug use. The photo was a symbol of the strength of their dangerous safe haven. Not only did this moment speak to the emotional and sensorial power that photographs evoke, but it gestured to a deep and enduring love in their relationship.

Like each of the male partners featured in this book, the underappreciated role of men's love and emotional commitment is a key component of dangerous safe havens. In her insightful book analyzing men, masculinity, and love, bell hooks (2014) notes that men long for love just the same as women. However, men are not typically socialized to share emotions, and we as researchers often uphold these norms by not even asking about it. Thus, men's emotional needs often go unnoticed, which can significantly damage their sense of self and well-being, including how they cope. Seeing his long-term partner suffer from a grave illness and feeling powerless in terms of visiting, Geraldo was deeply emotionally impacted by the situation. He was suffering and wore it in his entire way of being, but he had no outlet other than heroin.

Geraldo gave me Maria's family contacts in San Diego, but when I called, her mother was suspicious that he had put me up to it. When I explained that I was genuinely concerned for Maria, she softened up a bit. She said she would pass along my number so Maria could make the choice to contact me once she got out of the hospital. Clearly, Maria's family knew Geraldo and seemed to have mixed feelings about the happiness and harm they imagined him to bestow on her. Hardly any research has explored the broader family dynamics of sex workers' relationships, but a study of social networks with a subsample of Parejas couples found that extended families shaped partner notions of well-being in critical ways. People *missing* from couples' networks—who tended to be family members—were particularly important to partners. Often these relationships were strained by drug use, as partners didn't want their families (especially children) to see them active in their use (Wagner et al. 2018). Separation was thus conceived of as a way of caring for important relationships and wanting something better for their loved ones. These findings resonate with Geraldo's struggles in his separation from Maria; even when apart, their emotional bond and the effect they had on each other's behaviors remained strong.

Eventually, Maria was discharged from the hospital and communicated with me through texts to let me know how she was doing. These messages were often composed of blocks of emojis rather than actual written text. I visited her at her mother's home in San Diego and talked to her about her recent experiences and plans for the future. She moved more slowly but laughed more often and more heartily than I had previously observed. By that point she had been in contact with Geraldo, who said he planned to quit using heroin. They wanted to get married. She was growing tired of being home and wanted to go back to Tijuana to see him as soon as she felt better. She wondered how their relationship would be together if they were both sober. She also wondered if she would want "just one more shot" if she returned to Tijuana. But she wanted to take that risk because she knew she loved and missed him.

Maria and Geraldo's story illustrates how intimate relationships are always dynamic processes shaped by broader structural forces that permeate interior emotional experiences and personal commitments. Some of this story was captured as official data of Parejas, but many other aspects of the story lived only in the fieldnotes I recorded over two years of our personal interactions. Due to Maria's illness, the couple officially completed only a one-year period of follow-up in Parejas. Their story also reveals how much of these couples' lives remain obscured even in well-designed, mixed-methods longitudinal public health studies. There is much more love and emotional durability in these relationships than remains to be seen through a research lens.

GWEN

I first met Gwen in the lobby of our project office. We needed to take her photo for the credentials we gave out for the Parejas project, so I asked her in Spanish if she could stand against the white wall as a backdrop, and she answered that it would be fine in English. Within the first few minutes of meeting her, I learned that she was originally from the southeastern United States but had lived in Mexico for many years and had been in Tijuana since the last time she got out of prison. Thirty-two years old, Gwen had participated in other research projects conducted by our team and always dropped by the office for her follow-up interviews and to check on her STI test results. She is HIV positive, but her HIV-negative partner did not like to use condoms. Our interaction stayed with me.

Soon after, we needed to pilot test the interview guide for the one-year follow-up qualitative interviews for Parejas. I thought Gwen's candor would be helpful for testing and refining the questions. She was not part of the original qualitative sample, which also rendered her an ideal candidate because the data from pilot interviews are typically "thrown out," as the feedback from piloting is often valued for shaping the data collection instrument rather than the actual data collected. Gwen was incredibly helpful. In fact, we ultimately led off the interviews with her suggested questions: "What was your original motivation to join the Parejas project? Have your reasons for participation changed over time?" In addition to her pilot interview, we shared a long and intense conversation about her life history, and I invited her to participate in the photovoice project. Gwen's partial account gives insight into a migrant life in Tijuana, where she tried to forge a loving relationship. However, her story reveals the contexts in which the danger outweighs the safety of dangerous safe havens.

Gwen had an intense sadness etched on her face from a lifetime of hardship. Her childhood was mostly blurry to her, likely a reaction from severe trauma. She remembered moving to the West Coast when she was young to live in a very rural and isolated area with her mother and siblings. She was sent to live with her father over the summers, even though he had been sexually abusing her since age four or five. When she was eleven, he raped her, and she was forced to drop out of school because of the resulting pregnancy. She was then shunned from both households and lied about her age to land a blue-collar job to support herself. She went to live with a much older man, which she noted as essentially introducing her to sex work. She described herself as angry and violent since her youth as a reaction to her loveless and abusive family situation. "So pretty much I started prostituting since I was . . . I mean, it wasn't as it is now as a job, but I've been depending on men to take care of me since I was eleven, twelve years old," she explained.

After the state took custody of her child, Gwen was hospitalized for nearly a year after an attempted suicide. When released, she went to Nevada to be with her mother. She again lied about her age and worked fast-food jobs and had her first formal experience with sex work around age thirteen. When Gwen turned sixteen, her mom announced that she was getting remarried to a Mexican national. Gwen traveled to southern Mexico for the wedding and decided to stay. A local family took her in, and she got a job in a factory, learned Spanish, and became accustomed to the local culture and life. She fondly recounted the local public plaza on the weekends, where they sold shaved ice. To Gwen "It was nice, probably the only time I can remember in my life being happy." But it lasted for only about two years.

In this cultural context families granted permission for their daughters to court potential partners (in this case Gwen was like a surrogate daughter to her host family). Reminiscent of anthropologist Jennifer Hirsch and colleagues' work in rural Mexico (Hirsch et al. 2002, 2007), Gwen described a social geography structured around traditional gender roles, concerns for family and reputation, and socially sanctioned courting rituals. Gwen's host family told her she was not allowed to see the boy who caught her interest, a family relative named Javier, who they considered to be a "drug addict." Although they told Gwen she could date anyone else in town except for him, Gwen said he "stole" her away. They literally loaded her stuff on the back of his bicycle, and she left her surrogate family for good.

Gwen smuggled Javier into California without proper documentation, where they lived together for several years. She had two children with him and got her GED and a job driving long-distance trucks to support the family. She also helped smuggle other people across the border until she got caught and went to prison. During this time Javier had an affair with their babysitter and fathered a child with her. He was eventually deported and took all the children with him back to Mexico. Gwen served seven years in prison and has not seen any of them since. After she was released, she felt as though she "lost everything." As she described, "I lost my kids. . . . I didn't know what to do. I'd been in jail for so long, and I got used to being in jail." After a brief stint engaging in sex work in Las Vegas, she decided to head back to Mexico. She came to the Zona Norte in Tijuana to buy a *globo* (hit) of meth and never left.

Gwen observed that other women in the Zona earned relatively easy money through sex work, and, with limited options of her own, she tried her luck at it there too. Other sex workers helped her learn where to stand, what to charge, and what to do to stay safe on the job. Gwen had traded sex off and on to survive for several years, but she felt she was "never any good at being a prostitute." She did not want a client so much as to find the right person who would understand her troubled story and help her out of it: "I think I've always wanted to find somebody who was going to save me, and take me away, and fall in love. . . . I was always looking for that somebody to rescue me; I always wanted somebody to come and say, 'You know, you don't have to do this anymore. Come here, I'm going to take you.' I was even stupid, sometimes I wouldn't even charge for sex."

Gwen's lifetime of cumulative trauma shaped her interior emotional experiences and desire to find love. Her bad relationships with men emerged from an absence of love growing up. She internalized blame for this and cast herself as undeserving of love while at the same time longing for it. As bell hooks (2001a) notes, family is the primary place where individuals learn about love, but those, like Gwen, who do not grow up with love are expected to somehow find it in intimate relationships as adults. While some do, it is difficult and elusive for many others. Individuals may spend their entire lives searching for someone to undo the damage caused by the abuse, neglect, and lack of love they have experienced throughout their lifetime. Gwen "always wanted to find somebody" but struggled to forge a relationship that could "rescue" her. Her use of sex work as a strategy to find love and intimacy resonates with other sex workers across global contexts who similarly try to build better lives for themselves (e.g., Brennan 2004; Cheng 2010; Ratliff 1999; Stoebenau et al. 2009). For sex workers like Gwen, love offers hope.

In the meantime, however, Gwen was influenced by all the injection drug use around her. She too started to inject meth and heroin. As her addiction deepened, she found it harder to keep herself together and attract clients. She felt "stuck" in downtown Tijuana: "I didn't go anywhere else. I didn't know anything else to do, and just prostituting. I mean, I had so many marks on my body from the syringes that I couldn't even pick up two dollars to get a hit, and that's when I sometimes slept in the canal. I walked over to where the *alcantarillas* [sewers] are. Sometimes I would fall asleep on the street, behind the cars. . . . I almost ended up dying out there."

Gwen was walking down the street one day when a man yelled down to her from a second-floor balcony. She looked disheveled, and he offered her a hot shower and change of clothes, reminiscent of what Celia and her brothers do for other people who use drugs and spend time on the streets (as depicted in chapter 3). Edward took care of the apartment building and allowed people to come by and use drugs in the privacy of his apartment and off the streets. Gwen was special though, and the two ended up forming a three-year relationship. This relationship represented Gwen's dangerous safe haven immediately prior to Parejas; Edward was a source of material and emotional support who helped her get off the streets, and he may have saved her life. However, the subjective sense of safety and emotional support that he provided could not counteract the very real risk in their relationship that would change her life forever: Edward infected her with HIV.

Gwen found out her HIV status by participating in a long-standing research study for people who inject drugs in Tijuana. After she informed Edward of her status, they went to the doctor together, and testing revealed he had a dangerously compromised immune system. The doctor told them it was likely that Edward had been infected for at least a decade. Gwen thinks he became infected through trading sex with men, and she attributes her own subsequent infection not to their unprotected sex but to sharing a syringe. He did not normally inject, but one day he asked her to inject him because he wanted to know "what it feels like." On this one occasion, nearly three years into their relationship, she trusted him and they shared the syringe. As it turns out, Edward knew he was infected through their entire relationship, but he did not tell her. Gwen harbors a lot of anger and resentment because of this. It was his own form of secret keeping that helped their dangerous safe haven to endure. But after her diagnosis, it no longer felt safe for Gwen, and she left him.

Immediately afterward, Gwen met Ricky, the partner she enrolled with in Parejas. While their relationship started out as mutually supportive, he quickly became possessive and jealous, and her sex work started to create conflict. Increasingly, they got into verbal and physical fights. I met him once in the office, and we had an informal conversation. He was condescending and made me feel really uncomfortable. Gwen was smart and acutely aware of her life constraints, including the limitations of her relationship with Ricky. Her critical analysis of intimate relationships in Tijuana—including her own struggles to find love—insightfully links how the structural and social challenges for women engaged in sex work and drug use along the border shape their pursuit of relationships as refuge, even if it does not always work out as planned:

> Here in downtown Tijuana, almost nobody is from here; it's like you either got deported or something has happened, but you get here, and you're by yourself. I noticed the hardest part about being a prostitute and a drug addict was you get sick one day, one day you don't get money to pay for a hotel room, you don't have the money to get well, you don't have the money to eat, and the next day you didn't sleep, you didn't shower. It's even harder to prostitute the next day because you didn't have a place to stay the night before. . . . I mean, you're not going to get a client like that. . . . So you always need that somebody, and . . . it's easier to make friends with a man, and it's usually more of an . . . "I help you; you help me." If somebody robs me, there's a man at least to stand there, or come help me . . . so I don't feel like I'm alone.
>
> And then, because it's harder for men to get a job . . . you kind of get in that game. "Oh poor thing, he can't find a job," but he helped me out, and I'll help him out. . . . But you end up getting used to that person, and it's easier to stay with the person you're with than go with somebody new. . . .
>
> Like me, it's easier to stay with Ricky than it is to actually think that somebody else is going to accept me with HIV, is going to accept me with an alcohol and drug problem, is going to accept me being a prostitute. I mean, it's like you don't really have that option anymore that somebody is going to say, "Well, I want you to be the

mother of my children. I want to make a home, and we're going to have a wedding with a white dress, and everything is going to be . . ." [her voice trails off]. I mean, it's just not going to happen.

By the time I met her, Gwen was trying to change her life. She had recently gone to a drug rehabilitation program, only to get kicked out when they found out she was HIV positive. Now she was regularly attending Narcotics Anonymous meetings as part of an effort toward recovery. She got a job at a beauty salon and was cutting back on her sex work.

In addition, for the first time in several years, she was seeking medical care and restarting a regimen of antiretroviral therapy to treat her HIV. Previously, she had used a fake name to acquire free HIV medication through the Mexican health system, but she had been off her medication for some time. During her interviews she was coughing a lot and seemed physically run down. She recently reenrolled in a clinic in San Diego and connected with a case manager to help her to navigate the bureaucracy and paperwork. The meds made her feel sick to her stomach, but they told her it would subside, and then she could start interferon treatment for her coinfection with hepatitis C.

As part of this larger effort at change, she and Ricky separated. As she made changes in her life, her dangerous safe haven started to feel more dangerous, and she described her feelings for him as "cautious." Even though Ricky told her that he too was cutting down on his drinking and meth use, she did not see any evidence. As soon as they separated, he moved back in with his ex-wife, a stripper at a local nightclub and the mother of his child. He swore to Gwen that they were not sexually active, but they were together for the living arrangements. She did not believe him. Given his refusal to use condoms with Gwen despite her HIV status, she also felt that it was unlikely he was practicing safe sex with his ex-wife. Gwen reflected on this point and called him "selfish" because he could potentially be infected and in turn infect this other partner with the similar kind of negligence that led to Gwen's infection (Ricky's baseline HIV test was negative).

When I invited Gwen to participate in the photovoice project, her face lit up and she eagerly accepted. I gave her a camera, and she quickly snapped an unexpected photo of me. I acknowledged that I knew her situation might be a little bit different because she and her partner were no longer living together, but nonetheless I was interested in learning about his role in her life. She laughed and commented that through the photos "his role would become apparent." Unfortunately, however, I was never able to find out. I never saw Gwen again. In Parejas we followed only the women and not the men if partners were lost to follow-up or broke up, so I am not sure what happened to Ricky either.

I looked for Gwen. I visited the beauty salon where she worked and called around to jails. The rumor was that she got caught smuggling marijuana across the border. Maybe she was incarcerated, or maybe worse. At one point before her stint in a California prison, she had worked with human smugglers, who she said were dangerous people. But this is rumor and speculation. No one on the study team was ever able to confirm what happened to her.

FINDING A REASON

In their edited volume that aims to "put people first" in global health studies, anthropologists João Biehl and Adriana Petryna (2013) ask, "What would it mean for our research methodologies and writing if we embraced the unfinishedness, seeking ways to analyze the general, the structural, and the processual while maintaining an acute awareness of the inevitability of the incompleteness of our own accounts?" Although Maria's and Gwen's stories are partial, and both were officially lost to follow-up in Parejas, this chapter suggests that there is much to learn from unfinished stories in relation to both experience and methodology.

Telling Maria's and Gwen's stories through their involvement in a research study shows the complexity of women's experiences that are only ever partially captured in any research project. Their stories speak to the ways in which dangerous safe havens constitute an important, if often elusive, strategy to find love, emotional security, and meaning in life. Their experiences also remind us that dangerous safe havens are not always objectively safe spaces from the everyday violence that surround sex work and drug use in the border region.

If we adopt a methodology of love to guide our work, we have an ethical obligation to do justice to the stories that have been entrusted to us. Such methodologies urge us to embrace the knowledge that emerges from liminal spaces to push beyond epistemologies demanding "unbiased" research and "clean" data sets as the preeminent way of knowing. Methodologies that embrace compassion, care, understanding, and the other key "ingredients" of love throughout our research processes and writing open up new possibilities for understanding. This means embracing what appears messy and unfinished. This also means that drawing on the embodied nature of fieldwork and the relationships we build are important ways of knowing. Rather than erase or pathologize experiences of sex work and drug use, methodologies guided by love give attention to what is critically important in the lives of those with whom we work.

For Maria, it was important that we understand the humanity in her struggle of drug use. At the conclusion of our first interview, in which she turned the tables and interviewed me on my role in research, she also asked for my reaction after our conversation:

Maria: Did you learn anything from me?

Jennifer: Of course I did.

Maria: Oh okay. That you never want to be like me? Oh no, don't say that you
          don't ever want to be like me, 'cause then you will. I have learned that
          you can never be judgmental. Everything I have said I would never do, I
          have done.

Maria's pointed questioning and call for nonjudgmental treatment is a cry to be treated with love and understanding. She did not want to be viewed as "weird" and judged because of her drug use, sex work, and all that has happened to her. She wanted to be understood as a person who has lived a complicated life and cultivated an equally complicated but caring intimate relationship. Her nearly twenty-year relationship has endured far longer than the "normative" marriage these days. She found love with Geraldo, and struggling in their addiction together did not diminish that.

Gwen also wanted to find a bigger meaning in the research. Like others in Parejas, she had originally joined for the monetary incentive that paid per interview. Over time she came to value the project and how it helped her, especially in her recent efforts to try to stop using drugs and engage in HIV care. At several different points Gwen reflected on everything that had happened to her in her lifetime. She wondered if her suffering could help others: "It is something that I have to talk about. I mean, it's part of my story. I think I always wanted there to be a reason. . . . At least if it is something that's happened to me, I ended up being HIV positive, with hepatitis C, all the consequences that I had to go through because of my drug use, if I could help somebody else, then there will finally be a reason. . . . You know, something good can come out of all the bad that I had to live through."

Without our chance encounter in the office—and without valuing her pilot interview for its content, inviting her into my project, and putting the partial pieces together for this book—her story might have been lost. A methodology grounded in love opens up space for insights that may not have been originally intended in our studies. Even if the methods we use in the process are flawed and incomplete (e.g., invasive surveys, pilot interviews that get tossed, lost photos), the time, effort, and personal stories people choose to share is a gift to be valued.

Even as this chapter provides insight into the intimate relationships of Maria and Gwen, their status as "lost to follow-up" in the study also provides an opportunity to reflect on the production of research. Without a methodological commitment to love, research continues to be an allegiance to the status quo, which often privileges the researchers over the reasons that individuals like Maria and Gwen participate in our endeavors in the first place. To this end their stories offer a launching point for reflections on best practices in research and lessons for building more compassionate health programs and policies.

Conclusion

Love as a Pathway to Health Equity

In the years since I completed this project, I have driven through Tijuana on multiple occasions, only to feel unsettled. On these trips I've noticed how the numbers of people milling around in the Tijuana River Canal and sex workers lining the streets seem to be a permanent fixture of the cityscape. Despite Parejas and several other multimillion dollar NIH projects, implementation of national legislation to decriminalize drug use, and grassroots efforts to provide health care and harm reduction services, how much has substantively changed in the lives of socially vulnerable communities of sex workers and people who use drugs in Tijuana? In what can feel like an overwhelming impossibility for creating change, difficult questions arise in terms of why we do research, what impact we hope to make, and where we go from here.

Critical theories offer a powerful lens to help make sense of the injustices of the world. Integrating critical political and personal perspectives can unmask how structures of violence and oppression shape and constrain life possibilities and become embodied as health inequities. However, theory is also generated *"in order to act"* (Rhodes 2009, 194; emphasis in original). To this end I hope that my book has lent insight into an underappreciated topic of scholarship and inspires debate, dialogue, and fruitful interdisciplinary collaboration. I also want to push this further to suggest that love is not just a trendy scholarly topic, anodyne sentiment, or idealist but unreachable utopian version of society. Rather, I suggest that if we build on the work of revolutionaries before us and reframe our commitments in solidarity with the most vulnerable among us, *love can carve a pathway to health equity.*

One of the goals of my work is to offer suggestions for programming, policy, and research practice to improve the lives of female sex workers who use drugs, as well as their intimate male partners, families, and communities. The recommendations in this chapter are grounded in a political love and adopt a lens of harm reduction—as a political philosophy and a set of practical strategies—to reenvision the work before us. I close out the book by offering a reflexive articulation of best practices and lessons learned through this research, including what we might do differently if our work were guided by love.

HARM REDUCTION AS BELOVED COMMUNITY

We already know much of what we need to do to create and implement better policies, programs, and research to improve the health and well-being of sex workers who use drugs, along with their loved ones. Yet we are still lagging in terms of achieving health equity for socially marginalized couples. In reviewing several recent comprehensive sources making recommendations to address sex worker health, I found that these publications either erased women's intimate partners completely or referenced their partners only in terms of the potential for intimate partner violence or the need to decriminalize partners' behaviors, such as drug use.[1] *Love and intimate relationships remain largely absent from global health interventions for sex workers.*

My thinking around interventions is guided by a multidimensional construct of love. Not only is interpersonal love a topic worthy of our attention in understanding and improving the human condition, but love can also guide our politics and help us reimagine our work. Revolutionary scholars understand love as a powerful political force that can transform unequal social relations and unjust material conditions. Embracing a *political love* means that our political commitments are guided by the ingredients of love—care, commitment, trust, respect, and the like— and that we take this up in concrete, collective actions to remake the world. In this sense, if a political love were to inform public policy, programming, and research, it would mean mapping out decisions and community-driven efforts that would affect the good for *everyone*, especially those who have been historically marginalized and left behind.

One way to channel the power of love and recenter our efforts toward transformative health and social justice is through the notion of the "beloved community," or what the late Reverend Dr. Martin Luther King Jr. envisioned as an inclusive, interconnected consciousness based in love and compassion ([1967] 2010). At its core the "beloved community" fits into a broader analytic of love as a mode of critical analysis and call to political action. The beloved community means recognizing how all lives are interconnected. Countering neoliberal logics and capitalist processes that exacerbate inequalities by valuing certain lives over others, the beloved community calls for efforts to shift "from a 'thing' oriented society to a 'person' oriented society" (186). Similarly, in outlining her call to build a political love as "concrete, revolutionary practice," Black feminist theologian Keri Day (2016, 105) advocates that love should inform how we organize and behave as communities. Without a political love we foreclose the possibilities of creating a caring and just society, where we live together with respect, compassion, empathy, and the other "ingredients" of love in practice.

Engaging in such political commitments to love and changing harmful discourses and practices may seem abstract and difficult. However, there are multiple ways to enact change. Anthropologists are already integrating the social justice commitments of the beloved community into reenvisioning health care and training the next generation of physicians to practice humanistic medicine.[2] I take another perspective to suggest that *harm reduction* can anchor our political commitments and inform new research practices. My approach to harm reduction articulates with a political love that can compassionately address sex work and drug use in our world. As both a philosophy for thinking and a set of tools for doing, harm reduction links the political with the practical and always centers a love for people first. For many in the movement, harm reduction *is* the beloved community in action.

As a philosophy and movement for social justice, harm reduction is grounded in the belief that everyone has a right to health and should be treated with respect and compassion. As a practice, harm reduction is a set of practical strategies and ideas aimed at reducing the negative health and social consequences of drug use, which applies to meeting the needs of sex workers as well. Harm reduction thus holds transformative potential as a pathway to health equity because it is both a social theory of how we should operate in the world and a set of practices to counter the current harms the world offers us.[3]

Harm reduction (here forward encompassing both philosophy and practice) is premised on the notion that many (if not most) of the harms related to drug use and sex work do not emanate from those behaviors per se but rather are created by the systems that stigmatize, dehumanize, and punish individuals who engage in these behaviors. Harm reduction attempts to change dehumanizing discourses reducing people to "things" to be cast aside and ignored. Instead, harm reduction is a loving practice guided by the foundational principles of respect, acceptance, and dignity. It does not minimize or ignore the real harms associated with drug use and sex work but rather acknowledges that these behaviors are part of our world, and there are better ways to reduce these harms and keep people healthy and safe besides punishment.

Harm reduction services are noncoercive and nonjudgmental and "meet people where they're at" to empower their decision making. As a set of sensible and practical strategies, typical services include education about safer sex and drug behaviors (e.g., information need not be only abstinence-based); safer-sex supplies (e.g., condoms); safer drug use supplies (e.g., syringes, injection equipment, smoking supplies); naloxone (opioid overdose-reversal medication); HIV/HCV testing and linkages to care; referrals to drug treatment; and options for many other health, social, and legal resources. Importantly, harm reduction looks beyond sex and drugs to see people as whole beings who often have many unaddressed needs, including access to preventative health care, mental health services, housing, food, and other basic needs.

Perhaps the most powerful offering of harm reduction lies in its potential to build a beloved community in which people respect and care for one another. In response to the violent systems of oppression that punish people who use drugs and engage in sex work, harm reduction offers a space of nonjudgmental care and compassion. Harm reduction organizations are often linked with other community-based empowering organizations, abolitionist and mutual aid groups, and other grassroots political-mobilizing efforts. Often harm reductionists actively organize at local levels to change legislation and policies. Some advocate outright breaking the law if those laws are not in the best interest of community health and well-being. Others adopt a spiritual orientation, which is particularly conducive to thinking about love as a concrete guide to action. Harm reductionist Reverend Erica Poellot describes the movement as a "revolution of love that resists the forces of death and destruction and is building a new world of life and creation" (2020, 12). In this sense, harm reduction offers a productive starting point for thinking through how love can change the way we address drug use and sex work and move toward health equity.

INTEGRATED HEALTH PROGRAMS FOR SEX WORKERS

Historically, interventions for sex workers have focused largely on sexual risk for HIV and other sexually transmitted infections (STIs) through a lens of biomedical individualism. While HIV/STI prevention remains a key area of concern for sex workers, we need to rethink approaches to programming that are more reflective of sex workers' lived realities and complex needs. As I have argued in this book, ideals of finding love and companionship are no different for women who engage in sex work and use drugs, and attention to women's intimate relationships should be integrated into programming. We should further recognize the experiences of *both* partners in relationships, including men's perspectives that remain largely ignored in health programming. Couples navigate competing health and social risks though the construction of dangerous safe havens that prioritize emotional security, intimacy, and support. Interventions need to acknowledge that "risk" has multiple meanings for couples and is always socially situated.

Findings from my work urge us to move away from biomedical concepts of sexual risk and toward a more loving discussion about sex in the context of subjectivity, emotional intimacy, and pleasure. A growing body of literature has consistently demonstrated that sex workers are less likely to use condoms with intimate partners with whom they share an emotional connection versus clients.[4] My book builds on these findings, providing ethnographic evidence of the emotional and material importance of sex workers' intimate relationships to *both* partners.

Increasingly, couples are considered as a social unit of intervention.[5] Such programs may leverage relationship characteristics, recognizing how love, emotional intimacy, trust, conflict, and care profoundly shape relationship dynamics, and that any efforts to change health behaviors should consider the couples' dynamics in tailoring services. For example, partner communication is important and interconnected with multiple issues within relationships. As we have seen throughout this book, couples maintain forms of sexual silence that do not directly confront certain health issues, including sex work and HIV/STI risk. These silences serve as protection against hurting a partner's feelings and potentially generating conflict, but there may be better ways to promote healthy communication and coping strategies that do not threaten partners' emotional well-being. Motivational interviewing is a guided style of communication that empowers people to make changes based on how they make meaning and understand their particular situation. Assisted disclosure of HIV/STI test results could also be useful, in that providers could thoughtfully help couples discuss their results and negotiate safer-sex strategies.

Individuals in relationships create and adopt their own forms of harm reduction beyond formal services to keep themselves and their partners safe and healthy. Programs should build on the positive aspects of relationships, using strengths-based approaches rather than relying on standard risk-based discourses. Overall, integrating love and emotional intimacy with biomedical and epidemiological considerations of health could shift programming for sex workers in several key ways sketched out here.

Rethinking Program Content

Underlying all programmatic efforts is the imperative to rethink sexual "risk." This means taking sex workers' emotional connections and sexual pleasure seriously while adopting a more realistic harm reduction approach. Condom use to prevent disease transmission should be situated within relational contexts and consider the subjective importance of different types of sexual relationships. It makes sense to work within women's worldviews and encourage condom use with clients as a way to separate income-generating sexual partnerships from their emotionally meaningful partnerships.

Almost no couples in the entire Parejas study used condoms in their often years-long relationships, and trying to promote that now without raising suspicion and breaking trust makes little sense. Safer sex within intimate relationships could focus on negotiated safety approaches, such as agreeing to use condoms with outside partners but not within the primary relationship, engaging in regular HIV/STI testing, and accessing biomedical interventions like preexposure prophylaxis (PrEP) to prevent infection among HIV-negative individuals.

As part of these broader efforts to accommodate realistic patterns of condom use and counter the threat of HIV/STIs, PrEP is an important intervention topic in which the technologies have quickly advanced and recommendations have changed since the time of this research.[6] Yet, as the medicalization of the HIV epidemic continues favoring technological and clinical interventions (e.g., medications), it often comes at the cost of social considerations. Clearly, PrEP is a breakthrough, and everyone who wants to use it should have access, especially the sex workers in lower- and middle-income countries who are inexplicably disadvantaged in terms of accessing PrEP. However, we must still consider the importance of the social context in delivering biomedical interventions. Research has shown that PrEP can raise suspicion and trust issues and even instigate violence within relationship contexts, which may render individuals such as those who participated in Parejas as less likely to be adherent, reducing its effectiveness.[7]

Any such HIV/STI prevention and safer-sex programming should be offered as part of comprehensive sexual and reproductive health services that take sex workers' intimate relationships and childbearing preferences into account. However, programs rarely consider sex workers as parents or pay attention to the health and social outcomes of the children of sex workers, particularly sex workers who also use drugs. This remains a critical gap. As told through the story of Mildred and Ronaldo in chapter 3, the family had multiple challenges with health-care and child-welfare systems to navigate from the very moment their daughter, Zoe, was born. However, punitive approaches can exacerbate already difficult situations. Some scholars have called for the abolishment of "child welfare" systems altogether, arguing that current structures punish poor and racialized groups and expand police power rather than ensure familial welfare (Roberts 2022). More holistic approaches, including working with case managers and advocates trained in harm reduction, and granting families access to the economic, material, and social support they need, could lessen the likelihood of children being taken from homes while promoting family well-being. In many cases providing a supportive, encouraging, and loving environment for families rather than punitive threats of child removal could change familial dynamics and even motivate some families to reduce chaotic drug use or enter drug treatment. Programs for sex workers could play a key role in recognizing the importance of women's families, providing linkages to services, and advocating for broader policy changes that support rather than punish families.[8]

Overall, there is often a curious lack of attention to the overlap between sex work and drug use in health programming. Even though there is strong global evidence of drug use among sex workers, which is a particularly salient issue in cities with robust drug markets like Tijuana, little formal guidance exists on how to best deliver these services. Most of the time such services are offered separately and may be guided by aims of reducing drug use and promoting abstinence-based drug treatment (Iversen et al. 2021). As advocates from the Global Network of Sex Work Projects and the International Network of People Who Use Drugs rightly point out, sex workers who use drugs require regular access to all the services relevant to both sex workers and people who use drugs rather than our largely siloed approaches.[9]

Programs should be grounded in a harm reduction approach to drug use rather than focusing measures of program "success" in terms of abstinence. Some couples in Parejas showed interest in drug treatment and vacillated back and forth about pursuing it, except that humane, evidence-based programs designed for couples are largely absent in Tijuana. Other couples were not ready to quit or cut down. Following harm reduction principles compels us to accept these different realities and take a different approach. Drug use should be considered socially and relationally, moving from pejorative "codependency" models that emerge in programs based on individual self-recovery toward acknowledging an "interdependency" based on the social nature of drug use. As shown throughout this book, drug use is foundational to dangerous safe havens and embodied as practices of caretaking. In addition to working toward accessible and evidence-based treatment options, helping couples stay safer in their drug use means supporting the strategies they already use to protect themselves (e.g., not sharing syringes outside of the relationship, using at home rather than in public). Messaging around keeping partners (and others) safer in their drug use as practices of love, care, and trust would be effectively bolstered with regular access to the tools needed to reduce drug-related harms (e.g., sterile syringes, overdose-reversal medication).[10]

Building Relationships as a Key Intervention

While offering comprehensive health services to couples is critical, it is not just the *content* of programs that is important but also their *delivery* by trusted providers. At their foundation programs should be rooted in love: harm reduction principles of acceptance, nonjudgmental care, and compassion can create safer spaces to foster relationships and build the beloved community. The global literature shows that stigma, judgment, discrimination, lack of empathy, and provider insensitivity are widely reported among disadvantaged groups, including sex workers and people who use drugs.[11] These social barriers mean that individuals do not feel safe accessing care and may delay care until conditions become life-threatening. Individuals may also forgo vital social services and benefits to which they may be entitled if interactions are discriminatory or otherwise unhelpful. Personnel and approaches to service delivery matter.

The importance of building relationships is illustrated in a particularly frank conversation with Cindy and Beto about the Parejas study and what they desired in future programs. They both emphasized how important it was to have people with whom they could build a relationship and work up to discussing the difficult issues they faced in their lives. Cindy appreciated developing trust with project staff over time. Otherwise, she felt like she had to reopen wounds to strangers at subsequent visits. Here, she discussed her experiences in the Parejas research project, but her sentiments translate to other types of health programming. I think it is valuable to quote Cindy at length:

I wasn't rude to [the other interviewer], but if I had been given the choice, if somebody had told me, "Are you comfortable with your interviewer? Or do you want somebody else?" I would have liked to at least have had another option. Like Beto was saying earlier, you know, during the first interview you may want to say something, but you kind of just touch the subject on the surface, and then you back off and you don't say it, and then when you go home you feel like, "Well, the interviewer was kind of nice, and I remember she didn't look like she was judging me." You know, you start thinking about all that, and then at home you're like, "Next time I'm going to tell her this, or I'm going to tell her that," and then the next time you share more. And another thing I like, when I talk about something, I'm like, "Remember Jen, when I told you this?" and then she remembers.

That feels good. That helps our self-esteem as well, and it helps us feel more confident with you guys. It's really hard to talk about all this stuff, especially your past; it's hard to talk about all that stuff. You know, it's weird to just be saying it to some stranger that you've really never met before, and just as you start feeling comfortable with them, then the next time you come, you're expecting to see them, and you see somebody new that you've never met before either, and you're like ahh. . . . You know, you go back into your shell, all over again, and it's a process, all over again. I mean, it's hard within ourselves; it was a battle for me within myself to bring myself to the point where I could share enough just during the one session that I had with someone, and so the next time it's like, I've gotten that out of the way already, and I don't need to go through that again. It was hard for me emotionally to go through all of that. And then when you get a new person, having to go through that all over again takes a lot out of the person.

Jen told us, "If anything is wrong, or if you don't like anything, or this and that, or if you have any suggestions, you would help me a lot." She made it feel more like she's not just using us to complete her paper or her work, or whatever, but she's also receiving help from us. You know, we're not just receiving help for her, but she's getting help from us, and that gives you more value as a person as well.

There's a lot of people who are not in the situation that Beto and I are in, and I feel that we're pretty confident with ourselves, but there's so many people who are not over their issues or maybe even need help. Maybe they're in a situation that's harmful for them, and they need someone they can trust and speak to, but they don't dare to do it. . . .

You never know what's in every person's life. And like I said, you don't just trust someone; you've got to earn their trust. So that's a job for you guys [as researchers or providers]; you are trying to earn our trust. . . . If you have the same person, and you're building trust with them, you can expect to think, "I think they're pretty comfortable with me. Next time I can probably go a little deeper."

Considering the lifetime of disadvantage that Cindy had embodied, it could be emotionally challenging to open up and discuss painful events. Tackling sensitive issues is best developed with trust over time and points to the need for trauma-informed care. Cindy also challenged us as providers and researchers to create opportunities for genuine participation in shaping programming.

Creating spaces to give people "value," as Cindy put it, also begins to cultivate a love of self that has been stripped away through lifetimes of trauma. The importance of self-love has a long history in Black feminisms, which emphasize the importance of loving oneself as an act of resistance in a world that doesn't want them to exist.[12] A healthy and positive self-love then enables individuals to find communion with others. In a loving state of being, individuals develop new subjectivities about the self and other and recognize that they are not individually morally deficient as they have been labeled and made to feel all their lives. Instead, self-love gets past individual blame to the recognition of repressive structures that call for transformation (e.g., stigma in health care, institutional barriers to services, the wars on drugs). Efforts to cultivate self-love through supportive, trusting relationships with program staff and others can begin to address the roots of addiction and raise consciousness toward social change and collective healing.

POLITICAL LOVE AS POLICY

Tailored, comprehensive, and compassionate programs for sex workers, like those outlined here, are vitally important. However, their effectiveness is also contingent on the political climate and broader social contexts that shape conditions of oppression and ill-health in the first place. Criminalization, stigma, and discrimination against sex workers who use drugs, as well as their intimate partners, reduces couples to their perceived disease risk and can keep them from accessing vital services. Discourses of deservingness question the value of investing in programs addressing sex work and drug use and feed into policies that surveil and punish rather than care for stigmatized groups who are already disadvantaged due to factors such as gender, race, class, migration status, and sexuality, among other lived experiences. As a counternarrative, drawing on political love as a guide reimagines the possibilities for policy.

No country in the world has completely decriminalized both sex work and drug use (Iversen et al. 2021), speaking to the globally pervasive lack of political love and imagination in addressing community health concerns. An increasing number of global organizations are calling for full decriminalization of sex work in parallel with an end to the global wars on drugs and a full shift toward harm reduction.[13] Mexico provides an interesting case study in terms of how decriminalization efforts form a backdrop for better understanding and addressing couples' unmet health needs. While Mexico's policies appear well intended to produce more progressive and public health–based outcomes, a critical reading reveals that such efforts remain grounded in largely punitive models of punishment, control, and political theater.

Policies regulating sex work through local ordinances in Tijuana seemed to have little direct impact on the women with whom I worked. Although sex workers are to register and get regular health checkups, the women in this book evaded the system and did not benefit from it. The kind of sexual exchange that they practiced was less formal, public, and surveilled compared to the venue-based sex workers in Tijuana's world-famous clubs. But nondiscriminatory access to comprehensive and confidential health services for all sex workers—not simply surveillance systems based on perceived disease threats—is needed to address health inequities.

To be certain, sex worker rights and laws ensuring safe labor conditions are important. Empowerment approaches, wherein sex workers organize themselves into collectives, are also promising in many contexts to strengthen their political clout and rights.[14] However, the women in Parejas were largely not in the formal labor market, nor was sex work a marker of social identity, as they mostly avoided discussing sex work to preserve their intimate relationships. Research on sex worker empowerment in Tijuana has also found low levels of participation among sex workers who use drugs (Urada et al. 2021). Thus, it seems unlikely that organizing around sex work would be most beneficial to these particular women.

In terms of drug policy, Mexico's *narcomenudeo* reforms federally decriminalize possession of small amounts of drugs for personal use and mandate drug treatment instead of incarceration on the third apprehension on possession charges. These reforms were introduced in 2009 and were in the process of being implemented during the Parejas study. On the ground it was too early to see any effect of the policy shift on the couples' lives. However, their stories provide evidence of the need for large-scale changes in drug policy and law enforcement. What has happened since? And how might reading drug policy through a lens of political love shed light on what is happening now and what should happen next?

Drug policy reform is necessary but insufficient by itself to address a complex, multifaceted social and health issue like drug use. Political perceptions of and investment in public health infrastructure and harm reduction are corollary to policy reform efforts. Moreover, there have been unintended consequences related to public health and medicalized models of addiction. Among some politicians this approach justifies calls for involuntary drug treatment, which facilitates the containment of undesirable populations under a guise of medical care. However, involuntary drug treatment is largely ineffective, and, worse yet, what often counts for "treatment" across Mexico is based on punitive approaches using violence and humiliation.[15] Every couple in this book struggled with addiction, but access to evidence-based and humane drug treatment was virtually absent, as illustrated by Lazarus's experience in a rehabilitation center, described in chapter 3. Residential treatment programs also rarely account for how intimate relationship dynamics and families impact drug treatment outcomes, as programs are typically segregated by gender and often do not have support for couples with children. As such, these programs represent yet another form of structural violence enacted on people who use drugs, in which they are individually blamed for their "failure" to "succeed" rather than acknowledging a system unable to effectively support people who genuinely want help. In short, although drug treatment sounds like a better alternative to incarceration, in practice the conditions in treatment centers in much of Mexico remain deplorable and counter to real change.

On-the-street police enforcement of drug policies is also a concern. Globally, there is a significant literature on the detrimental health and social effects of violent and arbitrary policing on people who use drugs and on sex workers.[16] In the wake of the 2020 transnational movement in solidarity with Black lives demanding attention to historically entrenched police violence, global calls to scrutinize the linkages between public health and policing have taken on an overdue sense of urgency.

At the time of this research, policing was a constant concern of couples, primarily related to their drug use. The stories throughout the chapters suggest the violence that policing enacted in couples' lives, including harassment for their appearance, obstacles for obtaining or carrying syringes, and threats of arrest, incarceration, and involuntary treatment. Not only do such police practices carry health consequences, but fear of the police also left social, psychological, and emotional imprints on individuals, who constantly worried about the safety of their partners. Male partners were often particularly targeted for harassment and arrest, leaving some of the women to take on more public roles—and risks— from engagement in sex work to support the couples' drug use to procuring drugs in the street-level drug economy. Mildred and Ronaldo were even targeted in their own home, where their daughter was removed into state custody because the police planted evidence and operated outside of their jurisdiction. In all, the negative effects of the policing system were a constant and clear threat to couples' well-being.

Since Parejas, police-education interventions have been developed and implemented in Tijuana, with a primary focus on promoting greater respect toward people who use drugs, an enhanced understanding of drug-law reform, and the health benefits of safe access to harm reduction services (Strathdee et al. 2015). These interventions have increased police knowledge (Arredondo et al. 2017), and researchers have also noted cases in which individual officers have changed their attitudes to become more supportive of people who use drugs. Despite this, researchers also found statistically significant increases in arrests preceding local political elections that likely reflected efforts to secure votes as tough-on-crime candidates (Arredondo et al. 2018). Furthermore, coordinated efforts among state and federal policing agencies, municipal judges, and drug center staff to "clean up" the canal through massive crackdowns have relocated individuals into drug rehabilitation centers against their will and otherwise displaced people under quality-of-life ordinances, such as loitering and other minor violations (Morales et al. 2020). As it stands, corruption, inadequate police knowledge and training, and an inefficient justice system undermine the effectiveness of Mexico's drug policies (Strathdee et al. 2015; Zedillo et al. 2019). Unless police training about public health issues is sustained and politically supported, along with options for evidence-based, noncoerced drug treatment, Mexico's drug policy cannot reach its public health potential as it is currently conceived.

However, if we return to the idea of a political love as informing public policy, then we need a bolder critique of current political structures and the viability of the policing system as it currently operates, including questioning assumptions that armed agents of the state are necessarily effective public health champions and caregivers. One alternative approach is to engage in serious discussions about abolition. This means dismantling carceral systems that punish people who engage in sex work and use drugs (including those operating under the guise of "rehabilitation") in favor of building alternative systems better able to respond to community needs. Abolitionist approaches recognize the purposeful structural racism and systemic oppression encoded into the architecture of our institutions, which renders reform a futile task. This harkens back to June Jordan's question "Where is the love?" discussed in relation to the institutions of the drug war in chapter 3, including the child welfare and policing systems (2003, 269). Thinking about how the poor and most vulnerable in society are treated by those holding institutional power should reveal to us a lack of political love that requires urgent transformation. Ultimately, attempts at police reform do not broadly reduce community harms, and public health collaborations with police can end up amassing more resources for law enforcement than addressing health issues. Instead, at its core, abolition is about transformation and imagination. Alternative approaches favor building community services to provide care and resources in lieu of punitive state intervention. This means creating an infrastructure that situates sex work and drug use in the context of intersecting health and social needs in our communities, including addressing inequities in economic opportunities, education, housing, food security, and other basic needs. These alternative approaches necessitate shifting resources from carceral systems to communities themselves and are grounded in harm reduction principles to support rather than criminalize and punish people. While abolition may seem speculative and even unrealistic to some, police violence and human rights violations against sex workers and people who use drugs represent a global public health crisis that requires revolutionary acts of imagination. Abolition offers an alternative and aligns with the ideals of building the beloved community.[17]

In line with abolitionist imaginations, broader efforts are needed to expand access to harm reduction and build critical linkages across health and social services (that do not include the police). Harm reduction is politically permitted in Mexico and could keep people safer in their drug use and sex work, but the scope and coverage of services remains largely inadequate, as only a few harm reduction organizations are currently operating in all of Mexico. Despite its promise, there are also obstacles in expanding services in terms of political and financial support. Syringe services programs in lower- and middle-income countries are often supported by global health organizations, including the Global Fund, a major organization dedicated to ending the epidemics of HIV/AIDS, tuberculosis, and malaria. From 2011 to 2013, which partially overlaps with the Parejas project, the Global Fund supported syringe services programs in Mexico. Even so, most of the couples in the Parejas project inconsistently accessed these services. Problems with funding have only exacerbated the conditions of scarcity that I witnessed during my work. Since Parejas the Global Fund withdrew its support, which has resulted in a significant decrease in provision of sterile syringes, less geographic coverage of services, less use of services, and increases in syringe sharing among people who inject drugs (Cepeda et al. 2019; Bórquez et al. 2019). Additionally, the federal government has since suspended funding for civil society organizations responsible for delivering HIV treatment and prevention services, representing a devastating blow to sustainable public health efforts across Mexico (Agren 2019a, 2019b).

Amid these challenges, harm reduction programming (e.g., access to sterile syringes, the opioid overdose-reversal medication naloxone) is offered in Tijuana in a drop-in center in the Zona Norte and by mobile services to expand the geographic reach. In addition, the Clínica de Heridas (Wound Clinic) is a volunteer-run mobile clinic, serving people who use drugs and suffer from injection-related wounds (abscesses), particularly migrants experiencing homelessness and US deportees who have been dispersed throughout Tijuana due to police victimization and violence (Mittal et al. 2016). This outreach was started by a local physician who saw a tremendous unmet need in the community and took action.

Another critical harm reduction strategy is overdose prevention programs, sometimes called safe injection facilities or safe consumption sites, where individuals have a safer place to use drugs, with access to sterile supplies and medical attention should they overdose. Such sites make public health sense but remain politically controversial. In the nearby border city of Mexicali, a local organization started the first such site in Latin America while offering other harm reduction services and support for women who use drugs (Agren 2019c). Evidence from chapter 3 shows that some couples extended their dangerous safe havens to friends and family, not only as safer sites to use drugs but also as spaces where other forms of mutual aid (e.g., a shower, clothes, temporary shelter) could be accessed. The concept of safe consumption sites could also work in Tijuana, if run by and for communities who use drugs and granted critical political and financial support.

Taken together, without broader political commitment, programs and policies are stymied in addressing health and social inequities among sex workers and people who use drugs. Thus, when the state cannot—or will not—take care of its most vulnerable, community organizing for harm reduction can fill in the gaps. Such efforts reflect abolitionist futures and require fundraising, volunteering, building mutual aid networks, and creating other grassroots caregiving efforts so that communities have access to the resources they need to take care of one another and remain safe and healthy. These efforts are grounded in a political commitment to build the beloved community. Is there also a role for research?

TOWARD A MORE LOVING RESEARCH PRACTICE

As researchers who work with socially disadvantaged populations who engage in stigmatized and illegal behaviors, we must step back and reflect on our own roles in perpetuating oppression and how we might approach research from a more loving framework. Traditional academic practices have assumed an authoritative role for researchers who "collect" data from their "subjects" and publish these findings in prestigious venues for audiences of other academics. Although these ideas about research and associated practices exist on a continuum and are slowly shifting toward greater community engagement, the truth is that "research as usual" is more likely to advance careers than transform lives.[18]

In their contribution to the edited volume on activist research *Engaging Contradictions*, critical theorists Joy James and Edmund Gordon (2008) suggest that love offers a "counter-narrative" to the narcissism of typical academic procedures too often driven by self-absorption, competition, and career ambition. James and Gordon call for dismantling traditionally "apolitical" research values and maintain that a potent combination of "love and outrage" ought to sustain our efforts—that is, love for our communities and outrage over the social and health injustices they endure. Research is always guided by our politics and situated within broader power structures; we need not only acknowledge this but revolutionize our approaches by asking ourselves, Who are we as researchers? What are our political commitments? Even if we do not come from a similarly oppressed background as those with whom we work, are we willing to take on the cause? Are we just observers, liberal allies, or coconspirators for social and health justice?

Variously called activist, anti-oppressive, and community-engaged, among other labels, what I refer to under an umbrella term of "transformative research" (which goes beyond any singular discipline) calls for methodologies grounded in a political love. Transformative research is carried out in collaboration in all phases with communities not as the "subjects" of study but as cocurators of knowledge for action. Integrating love as a basis for transformative research practice compels us to rethink data itself in terms of how we how produce it, to what ends that data is used, and how research processes are always situated within unequal power relations that we can work to unmask and alter. This means bringing our work outside of the university system to produce solutions in collaboration with communities. In other words, shifting our research methodologies means that love can carve a pathway to health equity. We simply cannot achieve health equity through research as usual.

A critical part of reorienting our research practice means looking to communities themselves for guidance. Many activist groups have already thought deeply about undoing extractive research conventions and recentering priorities. Excellent models are available for guiding principles of transformative research.[19] I am particularly drawn to the "Ethical Research Manifesto" of the North Carolina Survivors Union (NCSU), a community-based drug user union in the United States. They begin by acknowledging that researchers "need us more than we need them" and call for greater community participation "from planning to dissemination." They recognize that research, if aligned with community-driven values, can be beneficial for all those involved. The manifesto lays out a set of guiding principles that align with a political love; in fact, love itself is second on their list of research values:

> Love
> We know it is not a traditional research value, but love is at the core of all of NCSU's work. We love our community fiercely and compassionately. The research we do with you will be rooted in this love, and we invite you to open yourself up to it as well. It is not enough to engage in principles of nonmaleficence or beneficence; our research must care for our community and hold its interests at the forefront. Join us here—we have fun! (NCSU, n.d., 1)

While *love* and *fun* are not typical descriptors of academic research, is there any reason for them to be excluded? What might change if these principles were included?

Concretely, what does transformative research about sex work and drug use look like? To close out the chapter, I reflect on the entire research process that underlies this book to think through what was done well and where to improve. This section is by no means intended to criticize any other researchers or offer a proscriptive approach. The shortcomings detailed here are mine alone. My recommendations emerge from my own reflections, experiences, and particular interdisciplinary career trajectory. The reflections are applicable to multiple academic contexts, but research always needs to be appropriately adapted to the local context.

Research Design and Questions

Being in dialogue with communities to jointly arrive at a research topic and specific questions is foundational to transformative scholarship. The Parejas study successfully achieved this objective, as the investigators listened and responded to sex workers' concerns that their intimate partners were being left out of research and health services. My specific study focusing on love was at least partially grounded in this principle; the questions about the role of love in shaping HIV risk emerged from my early observations and conversations in the field, including interactions with Cindy. My focus on love came from a well-intended space of wanting to question prevailing discourses of disease and violence in sex work research, yet my study remained tethered to HIV to explore these concepts. Was this hopeful or still resigned to a paradigm of suffering?

Admittedly, genuine collaboration in designing research from the beginning of the process can be challenging for multiple reasons, none the least of which is that community members are busy with their lives and may not have the time, access, desire, or skills to prioritize research or conceptualize their needs within scientific paradigms. Furthermore, the power structures of the research enterprise often dictate which research priorities are "fundable" and who is able to ask particular kinds of questions. To access many forms of health-related funding, we must construct narratives of urgency and privilege notions of risk, but this can unintentionally marginalize communities in the process.

One key recommendation is to volunteer and work in other nonextractive capacities prior to initiating any new research project (and throughout the research process) so that researchers get to know the community, the salient issues, and their potential role (if any) to contribute in that context. Forming a Community Advisory Board (CAB) or similar entity composed of research participants and community members can also guide researchers in decision making throughout the entire research process. In my case I felt fortunate in that I joined an already established research group who had developed trust among sex workers and people using drugs in the Red Light District of Tijuana and were already learning about pressing health needs in the community, which led to the Parejas study. I felt more secure in my work knowing that the clinic gave back to the community in providing free health services and a space for engagement. I also worked hard to personally build relationships beyond the research protocols. But I could have taken a more transformative approach to foster dialogue and inclusion through a CAB and other forms of involvement in the community, including hiring and training participants to help conduct the research, as my current research orientation has shifted toward.

The Production of Data

Health-related research entails a process of documenting deeply private and sometimes life-threatening concerns, whether by manipulation of huge databases or intimate ethnography. Whether we anonymize data from private medical records or collect detailed life histories from key confidants, transformative research approaches respect that the word "data" derives from the Latin word for "gift." Data are gifts; they represent individual lives, and they deserve love and care. Conceptualizing data as gifts gestures to a reciprocal methodology, emphasizing how we treat people, develop trust, and collaboratively work toward change (Strega and Brown 2015).

One of anthropology's most redeeming qualities is its commitment to building relationships. But typical methods of participant observation—with an emphasis on observation and documentation—could be pushed even further to become *observant participation*, which places greater emphasis on active participation during the research process (Vargas 2008). While there is value in description, flipping the emphasis toward participation opens up new ways of interacting in communities. It urges us to think beyond "data collection" to new modes of practice while being reflexive about our roles. While I tried to be open and develop caring relationships with couples in a traditional participant observation framework, I still wonder what pushing this further would have resulted in.

My use of photovoice and interviews with photographs as prompts was intended to invite greater input from couples and enable them to drive the conversations to topics I might not have known to ask about. Given the sensitive nature of the study, I kept my process more individually focused than traditional photovoice projects that engage community members to hold workshops and public exhibits to draw attention to specific issues. My visual approach was mostly successful and I think enjoyable for partners (except for Maria's partner, Geraldo, who told me he enrolled in the project only because she would want him to). Partners like Mildred found the process generative, commenting to her partner, Ronaldo, that it made her feel like someone finally paid attention to her life. If collaborative and directed by the community, photovoice with a public-engagement component could effectively catalyze social change.

I also advocate pushing creative methods even further, going deeper into the arts, health humanities, and experimental methodologies. From my work with the couples featured in this book, I see artistic methods as useful for exploring lived experiences of trauma, sharing stories, and potentially reducing stigma and generating empathy in the community. Many of the partners, especially the women, liked to produce art, draw, and write in journals to express their feelings. I could imagine the collective healing potential of art in lives that have long been silenced and oppressed. As Gloria Anzaldúa (2013) notes, such "creative acts" tap into something broader than the self—they form an embodied experience in which individuals connect with others who have similarly struggled. Through this experience they are able to foster a deeper kind of consciousness. Integrating creative expression into research could generate possibilities for consciousness raising as a means to articulate a political love working for transformation.[20]

Interpretation and Analysis of Data

Data analysis and interpretation are critical parts of the research process from which participants and community members are often excluded. Researchers may be concerned about introducing "bias" into the analysis process, but participants' insights can sharpen our analytical edge and lead to unexpected insights. Methodologies guided by love appreciate community members not as raw sources of data to be extracted but as experts in their own lives who can help us make sense of complex issues (Freire [1970] 2018; Hale 2008; Strega and Brown 2015).

There are a range of ways to facilitate collaborative analytical processes, and the Parejas project lends insight into one such approach. The design and analysis of our initial qualitative interviews from both field sites were based on a collaborative model incorporating input from our transdisciplinary, binational team, whose members worked in multiple study capacities, from data collection to more conceptual roles. This model integrated multiple perspectives from the ground up, informing the questions we asked as well as processes of coding, analysis, and writing. In addition, in the one-year follow-up qualitative interviews, we implemented a process sometimes called "member checking," in which we went back to couples to assess our preliminary understanding of the data. Much of the backbone of this book is built on these foundational understandings of how couples valued their relationships, coped with outside sexual partners, and adopted communication styles and risk-reduction measures that prioritized the emotional intimacy of their relationship over physical health threats.

Member checking can provide valuable insights, but there are multiple ways for researchers to engage participants and even the broader community into analytical processes. Methods can range from participants reading and commenting on a researcher's writing to holding community events to generate actionable next steps. Whatever process is appropriate to the study, valuing different kinds of expertise and facilitating greater inclusion in analytical discussions shifts participants' roles to coproducers of knowledge. Coconstructed analytical processes could also lead to better solutions to health problems than researchers could devise on their own, thus strengthening the potential of research as a pathway to health equity and encouraging us to rethink the real impact of our work.

Rethinking Dissemination and Research "Impact"

Based on traditional academic measures, my project is a "success" in that you are reading this book, and there are more than thirty other publications in peer-reviewed journals about the Parejas study that contribute to the scholarly literature. To be clear, publications are important academic currencies and build systems of knowledge. However, if our research is multipurpose in that it is to be theoretically generative and crafted in order to act, shouldn't there be multiple ways of assessing our contributions? How does a methodology guided by love urge us to reprioritize sharing knowledge and evaluating the impacts of research?

Practically speaking, we can increase our impact if we disseminate our work in a mix of venues to reach multiple audiences. Experimental formats broaden the conversation, including a growing trend toward open-access publications, online formats, and public writing. In addition to publications, community-dissemination events, art exhibits, podcasts, digital storytelling, and other creative ways of producing and engaging with research materials can engage broader publics. An open-access book to share the stories of sex workers and their intimate partners and offer reflections and tools for others to improve on the research process is my modest contribution to these broader efforts. In all, creative and collaborative efforts that go beyond conversations in small disciplinary circles are the next horizon for academia.

Beyond measures of scholarly productivity, anthropologist Charles Hale (2008) asserts that capacity building and problem solving in communities should be key aspirations of research and evaluated accordingly. Working with structurally vulnerable communities requires us to go outside of academia and make connections in spaces where academic credentials mean little if action does not follow. In other words, we should also assess our impact by asking, *Did our research produce knowledge to address a problem or guide social transformation?* Key challenges remain in transforming incentive structures and valuing community engagement in the academy, but transformative research requires a sustained commitment to move beyond traditional measures of academic success to tangible action. As Gloria Anzaldúa reminds us, "Change requires more than words on a page—it takes perseverance, creative ingenuity, and acts of love" (2013, 574).

*   *   *

I end my book by mapping out a more loving approach to programming, policies, and research to support sex workers who use drugs, along with their intimate partners, in the hope we can achieve real change. Of course, all of these issues could be explored with greater depth, and there are many other issues beyond the scope of this conclusion that impact sex workers' and their partners' health and quality of life. At their core these recommendations emphasize the need for meaningful participation by sex workers and people who use drugs, who are experts in their own lives and know best what they need. In addition, these recommendations call for the holistic provision of care, respectful programming and research that can engender trusting relationships, and meaningful collaboration between academia and communities, including research that goes beyond traditional boundaries of knowledge production. The success of any of these suggestions, however, requires us to move forward with a more revolutionary political commitment to love—a genuine desire to build the beloved community that engenders understanding and ensures the welfare of all.

In closing, I will always carry the memories of fieldwork in Tijuana with me, for better or worse. There is always room for improvement and more work to be done to address the historically entrenched health inequities along the border and elsewhere. Imperfect as this work may be and partial as the narratives are, I care deeply for the people in this book, who are not always granted that right. Sex workers and their intimate partners are capable and deserving of love, and their experiences should not be excluded from our efforts to pursue global health equity. I hope that these couples have contributed to such efforts through their stories of love and humanity. I also hope that other research participants, scholars, service providers, community members, coconspirators, and others take this work even further to harness the power of love's revolutionary potential.

Afterword

In the years since this project was completed, much has changed, but many of our greatest health challenges remain fundamentally the same. Globally, we continue to contend with a relentless HIV pandemic, myriad health and social consequences from unimaginative and punitive global drug policies, and enduring forms of stigma and criminalization against sex workers and people who use drugs that prevents them from accessing vital services and leading lives of dignity. Most recently, we have collectively experienced the interlinked and devastating effects of the global coronavirus pandemic, historically entrenched racialized police violence, and the ongoing opioid crisis ravaging North America. All of these issues lay bare the deep global health inequities that shape our life chances. This moment speaks to the urgency of the work that still lies before us, while also highlighting how much we need one another if we are to make any substantive progress toward health equity. The stories in this book remain vital as ever in reminding us that our relationships matter. The world often seems bleak, but I remain optimistic about the transformative power of love.

Riverside, California—2022

INTRODUCTION: DANGEROUS SAFE HAVENS

1. Many global public health studies use acronyms like FSW for female sex worker. I have been a coauthor on multiple papers in which this is used. However, my personal preference is not to use acronyms in place of people. In this book I use the language of partners, couples, men, women, members of families, individuals, and people to reference the "participants" in my study (also a deliberate choice of words that grants agency to those involved in research). Furthermore, although some of the Parejas used the term "prostitution" to describe the women's work, I adopt the more neutral (but not entirely unproblematic) term "sex work" to acknowledge that exchanging sex is a form of labor. I further modify this term by referring to the women in this book as "freelance sex workers" to signal the agency in their work in that they are not based in formal venues and do not have a boss.

2. Sincere gratitude goes to anthropologist Alisse Waterston for introducing the term "dangerous safe havens" during our panel "Steps Towards an Anthropology of Affect" during the 2012 American Anthropological Association meeting (Syvertsen 2012).

3. Critical medical anthropology was proposed by Singer and Baer; see, for example, Singer and Baer (2018).

4. First articulated by Galtung (1969), the concept of structural violence was popularized in anthropology by Farmer; see, for example, Farmer (1999).

5. See, for example, Csordas (1993), Desjarlais (1997), and Garcia (2010).

6. There is a rich scholarship and long history of incorporating love into critical analyses by Black and Latina/Chicana feminist writers. Many of these scholars see self-love in light of a loveless world of hatred as an act of resistance and call for a political love to change the way we see the world and how we act for social justice. I want to thank my colleague San Juanita García for bringing her copy of *Methodology of the Oppressed* (Sandoval 2000) to a writing retreat in Indio, California, and suggesting that Sandoval's writing about love could inform my project. Sandoval draws on a long line of revolutionary thinkers, including Che

Guevara, Frantz Fanon, Gloria Anzaldúa, Roland Barthes, and others to make a beautiful argument for the power of love as a revolutionary force to propel social change. In my book I draw primarily on the work of Anzaldúa ([1987] 2012), Freire ([1970] 2018), hooks (2001a, 2001b), Day (2016), Dominguez (2000), and Jordan (2003) but want to pay respect to other Black feminist writings about love, including the Combahee River Collective (1983), Lorde (1984), Collins (2004), and Nash (2013).

7. The literature focusing on poor health outcomes among sex workers is significant; see, for example, reviews by Shannon et al. (2015, 2018) and Deering et al. (2014).

8. My thinking about risk is largely inspired by Lupton (1993).

9. Anthropologists have studied love from a wide range of perspectives, including as a political construct (Berlant 2011; Hardt 2011; Zigon 2013), as a cross-cultural experience (Jankowiak and Fischer 1992; Jankowiak 2008), and as a biocultural phenomenon (Fisher 2004).

10. According to the US Department of Homeland Security's *Yearbook of Immigration Statistics* (2012), from 2009 to 2011, the period when I traveled most frequently to Tijuana, the numbers of "aliens returned by nationality and by country" for Mexico was 469,610 in 2009; 354,507 in 2010; and 205,811 in 2011. While not all these individuals were deported to Tijuana, the city is the primary deportee-receiving community in Mexico. Scholars have calculated that more than 815,000 deported Mexican migrants were displaced to Tijuana between 2008 and 2013, which roughly corresponds to my entire period of fieldwork during Parejas (Pinedo et al. 2018).

11. There is a rich tradition in ethnographic scholarship on drug use and addiction. See, for example, Agar (1973), Bourgois (1999), Bourgois and Schonberg (2009), Garcia (2010), Knight (2015), Maher (1997), Page (1990), Romero-Daza, Weeks, and Singer (2003), and Sterk (1999, 2000).

12. Additional notes on my methods feel warranted (especially for global public health audiences). Visual methods hold tremendous power to help people see in different ways, but I also hold no illusion that providing people with cameras erodes power imbalances or liberates individuals from their daily hardships. While I call my process "photovoice"—as it creates a visual space for voice through photos—I ultimately did not choose to pursue a collaborative workshop process with the couples or create a public exhibit of the photos, as traditional photovoice projects often do (see Wang et al. 1998). I had a hard time reconciling how to use the photographic material beyond the interviews and my dissertation (in which I blurred images so as not to reveal identities). Although I had additional written consent to use specific images for specific purposes, including in this book, I ultimately decided to err on the side of caution and not share most of the photos from the project because I worry about their misuse.

Ethnographic drug research methods also have unique strengths, but a long line of anthropologists have grappled with their emotional and ethical challenges. One core question that ethnographers must grapple with is how we can observe destructive behavior like drug use and not intervene. For now I note that if any of the couples had wanted assistance for drug treatment during my fieldwork, which they contemplated at times, they certainly knew that I and everyone else on our Parejas research team would do our best to help them. But it was also not my place to force treatment on people. In retrospect, however, I could have been more proactive in promoting harm reduction and advocating for funding and services, a point I explore further in the conclusion.

13. See, for example, Cole and Thomas (2009), Hirsch and Wardlow (2006), and Padilla et al. (2007).

14. See, for example, Corbett et al. (2009) and Rhodes and Cusick (2000).

15. See, for example, Betancur and Cortés (2011), Gerber and Kohler (2021), Rebhun (1999), Segovia and Ravanal (2021), and Zelizer (2005).

16. See Valdez, Kaplan, and Cepeda (2000) for a discussion of the "paradoxical autonomy" that sex work creates for Mexican American women who use heroin; see, for example, Abel (2011), Lamas (2017), and Sanders (2004) for analyses of how sex workers negotiate and maintain their emotional well-being in the context of their work.

17. See, for example, Brennan (2004), Cabezas (2009), Cheng (2010), Ratliff (1999), and Williams (2013).

18. See, for example, Goldenberg et al. (2011) and Hoang (2015).

19. Of course, women and others around the world are also trafficked against their will and controlled by pimps and managers. I don't mean to discount the brutal inhumanity of these experiences. However, here I am focusing largely on women who are voluntarily in the sex trade and who exercise some level of agency in their work.

20. See, for example, Bailey and Figueroa (2018), Castañeda and Ortiz (1996), Maher et al. (2013), Murray et al. (2007), Sanders (2002), and Stoebenau et al. (2009).

21. See, for example, Bellhouse et al. (2015), Jackson et al. (2009), Onyango et al. (2019), and Warr and Pyett (1999).

22. See, for example, Lam (2008), Lazuardi et al. (2012), MacRae and Aalto (2000), Simmons and Singer (2006), and Rance et al. (2017).

23. See, for example, Rhodes and Quirk (1998), Rhodes and Treloar (2008), Rhodes et al. (2017), and Rance et al. (2018).

24. See, for example, Morris et al. (2015, 2019).

25. See Syvertsen (2019).

26. Robbins (2013) writes about how the focus of anthropological inquiry has shifted over time from the "savage" to the "suffering" and to more recent movement toward the "good," which promotes a disciplinary focus to more hopeful and humanistic strands of inquiry. See also Ortner (2016) for an overview of theoretical trends in anthropology since the 1980s and Zigon (2013), who, in writing about love as a heuristic to analyze ethics and morality, draws a connection between "love" and the "good" in anthropology.

27. Quoted from bell hooks (2001b, 17), whose work explores the history and shifting meanings of love among Black communities in the United States.

1. PAREJAS

1. The US Bureau of Transportation Statistics (2011) keeps data only on northbound border crossings; my estimate includes car and bus passengers and pedestrians and is based on data from 2011, the year the majority of my fieldwork was conducted. See US Department of Transportation (n.d.).

2. Thanks in part to revitalization projects and the growth of tourism in the nearby Guadalupe Wine Valley and coastal beach towns, Tijuana and surrounding areas of Baja California have become trendy travel destinations (though the coronavirus pandemic has complicated travel). This is reflected in an episode of the late Anthony Bourdain's popular

television show *No Reservations*, in which he appeared pleasantly surprised by his experience in Baja California. The episode provides a counternarrative to the often negative media coverage of the region to audiences in the United States (Baja 2012).

3. I learned about the term "whorearchy" in an excellent harm reduction training run by sex workers; see Knox (2014) for an insider explanation.

4. I refer to the "War on Drugs" and "drug war" or "drug wars" interchangeably; texts and media make distinctions between the United States' drug war and Mexico's drug war, but these are interrelated. The entire "war" terminology is problematic and rooted in former president Richard Nixon's declaration of a War on Drugs, which has been revealed as a systematic political assault on Black and Brown people rather any helpful attempts to mitigate addiction and promote healing.

5. Thank you goes to Steffanie Strathdee for sharing this candid story with me and allowing me to include it in this book. Sadly, she also recently told me that Yolanda, one of the sex workers whose passionate arguments helped inspire the Parejas project, passed away from an overdose. Much gratitude to Yolanda for her contributions to the world and may she rest in peace.

6. There are approximately thirty-two academic publications about Parejas and its substudies available for interested readers to learn further details. Most are available through PubMed, a free full-text archive of literature maintained by the National Library of Medicine; see PubMed (n.d.).

7. This section draws primarily from Syvertsen et al. (2013) as well as additional unpublished data from the baseline qualitative interviews that were analyzed but did not make it into that publication.

2. WHERE SEX ENDS AND EMOTIONS BEGIN

1. Composite characters are often used in highly sensitive research to blur individual identities; here I add and change some details by integrating other data collected in my project to construct an additional layer of protection. I do not make up any details from my imagination, except for the physical descriptions of the couples.

2. Jaime's concern with respect and their shared concerns about reputation articulates with anthropologist Jennifer Hirsch's research in the interior of Mexico, where the couple hails from; see, for example, Hirsch et al. (2007).

3. See chapters 3 and 6 for more discussion on drug rehabilitation in Mexico, as well as other literature documenting abusive conditions, including Bazzi et al. (2016), Garcia (2015), Harvey-Vera et al. (2016), Rafful et al. (2020), and Syvertsen et al. (2010).

4. See, for example, Connell and Messerschmidt (2005), Connell (2014), and Gutmann (1996, 2007) for examinations of shifting notions of gender and masculinity.

5. Outside partnerships, or "past year cumulative concurrency," was measured by obtaining the dates of sex with up to five other recurring sexual partners from the past year (i.e., partners with whom participants repeatedly had sex), including women's regular clients. The analyst compared dates of sex with various partners, including enrolled study partners, to identify periods of overlap and determine the past-year cumulative prevalence of recurring concurrency. In the baseline surveys 16 percent of the 421 partners reported having recurring outside sexual partners during the previous year. Concurrency was higher

among women than men, but when excluding women's regular sex work clients, the percentages were roughly the same, as 8 percent of women and 6 percent of men had outside noncommercial partners. See Robertson et al. (2013b).

6. Some of the literature on fidelity is cross-cultural and comparative, and some is grounded in the biological, evolutionary, and psychological bases of what it means to be human. For example, Helen Fisher (2004, 2016) is a popular bioanthropologist who has written extensively about the biochemical foundations of love and fidelity, but her work has also been critiqued by some cultural anthropologists as reductionist and deterministic.

3. LOVE IN A WAR ZONE

1. Celia went through considerable trouble to try to hide that Lazarus was missing because she feared getting kicked out of Parejas (even though we followed the women no matter what happened to their partners). She first tried to tell me Lazarus had just gotten a new job selling drugs at the canal, and his schedule was too busy to participate in interviews anymore; she even brought a colleague and me over to the canal and pointed out "Lazarus" to us from afar. Next she brought another man into the project office to try to pass off as Lazarus. She looked down at the floor, and I could tell she was lying, but she insisted that he looked different because he was "really tan" from working outside at his new job in the canal. Eventually, she admitted that Lazarus had suddenly left, and she had not heard from him.

2. This practice is no longer in place under universal health coverage in Mexico. Unfortunately, Mildred and Ronaldo's daughter was born before Mexico's national health-insurance program, Seguro Popular, was fully implemented. It was introduced in 2003, but universal coverage was not reached until nine years after implementation. It is unknown how many drug-involved or otherwise vulnerable families are continuously marginalized by lack of access to health care; see Knaul et al. (2012).

3. Jordan asked, "Where is the love?" at a 1978 conference about Black feminisms. She raises the question based on her experience as a Black woman resisting a world of anti-Black hatred and gender-based and sexual violence. Asking ourselves to think about where is the love in everyday life seems widely applicable to our oppressive world, especially in relation to the racist, sexist, and classist tactics of an ongoing drug war. Jennifer Nash's work (2013) also helped me think through this question and inspired me to grapple with Jordan's work.

4. Gratitude goes to María Luisa Mittal, who accompanied me on this fieldwork, helped me to understand the complexity of their story, and gave me permission to use her candid fieldnotes in this chapter. Of note, the "disturbing" acquaintance that she describes in this scene was one of the only times in the entirety of my fieldwork in Tijuana that I felt unsafe, but we exited the situation without incident.

4. REWRITING RISK

1. I describe this scene not to offer gratuitous details but to highlight the urgency of addiction and the lengths that individuals will go to when they are suffering from withdrawal. Cindy referred back to that photo in a separate conversation to relay to me how much she struggled with injecting on a daily basis. This was part of her reality. While the photo is haunting in composition and content, and I have used it in presentations, I ultimately

decided against publishing it here. I do not want it to be taken out of context or to detract from my larger point of the chapter, which is that Cindy and Beto's relationship was more complicated and meaningful than drug use alone. This point is also articulated in Syvertsen and Bazzi (2015).

2. Significant literature on embodiment carries considerable potential for cross-disciplinary conversations bridging public health and social science. From public health I find Nancy Krieger's (2016) work particularly helpful. I encourage readers to look up her prodigious volume of work. From anthropology my understanding draws from Thomas Csordas's classic work and engagement with Pierre Bourdieu, in which he writes that "a theory of practice can best be grounded in the socially informed body" (Csordas 1990, 7). To Bourdieu the "socially informed body" has been cultivated by experiences across the life course that shape not only the traditional five senses but "the sense of necessity and the sense of duty, the sense of direction and the sense of reality, the sense of balance and the sense of beauty, common sense and the sense of the sacred, tactical sense and the sense of responsibility, business sense and the sense of propriety, the sense of humor and the sense of absurdity, moral sense and the sense of practicality, and so on" (1977, 124). The sense of humor and absurdity that Bourdieu references informed my decision to keep Cindy and Beto's story of the Mata Hari in the later part of the chapter.

3. This was also my favorite photo, probably of the entire project. However, I was unable to obtain the necessary additional permissions for revealing their identities because I have not been able to reach Beto and Cindy passed away. Otherwise, this is one example where I would have chosen to share a very personal photograph because it shows a loving and positive side to a type of relationship that is often stigmatized and misunderstood.

4. Our plan was to go to the office for data collection to ensure a quiet, private space and create an interviewing atmosphere that was mostly similar for all the participants. While some might argue that interviewing a couple in the field while they are injecting heroin might compromise the validity of the data, I would argue otherwise. Building relationships with the couple and finding ourselves in that position revealed a trust that flowed both ways and might suggest more openness on their part to be forthright in what they shared with us. It is also useless and cruel to try to interview people experiencing heroin withdrawal, which is what Cindy and Beto feared would start to happen if we went to the office and undertook the process there. Long-term heroin injectors are using for maintenance and daily functioning; in time it becomes nearly impossible to function without it. Interviewing in general can be problematic in many different ways, including the scripted performativity of formal interviews and social-desirability bias, which arguably could be stronger in interviews conducted in a clinical setting. The data from people who are "high" on heroin can be just as trustworthy or problematic as data from anyone else, even in "controlled" settings. I would argue that the quality and integrity of data all comes down to the relationships that we build with participants.

5. Technically, a legend is based on facts and becomes exaggerated so that the story takes on heroic qualities, while a myth refers to symbolic storytelling that is not grounded in fact. Thus, the story of Mata Hari can be considered a legend rather than a myth, but Cindy and Beto's version was so outlandish that it might as well be a myth.

6. Although I never found out why Cindy passed away, I know from the study data that she was not HIV positive or suffering from an STI. In combing through her transcripts, I saw that she once told me that early death from cancer was part of her family medical

history. Perhaps her death was not directly related to her sex work or drug use after all, and her dangerous safe haven kept her as safe as possible to the end.

5. (NOT) LOST TO FOLLOW-UP

1. Working in interdisciplinary spaces has exposed me to very different methodological approaches and sets of tools to answer questions. Largely positivist methodologies call for structured, rigorous, and replicable methods, which have become the expectation in many spaces, including large research projects like those funded by the National Institutes of Health. These are the methods I am referring to in terms of "official" data collection and analysis. While these approaches are conventional and often go unchallenged, they have also been criticized as white supremacist and colonial and can reproduce structures of oppression; see, for example, Zuberi and Bonilla-Silva (2008). Statistics can be useful but have their limits, methodological transparency is helpful, and methodological critiques are valid. Building on the work of feminist scholars (see, for example, Fierros and Delgado Bernal 2016; and Sandoval 2000) is one approach to opening up new ways of seeing, experiencing, and knowing. If our methodological approach is informed by love, we can accept the inevitable messiness of research because our comitments to social and health justice and the relationships we build during the work is most important—and we still learn valuable information along the way without having to erase the stories entrusted to us.

2. It is difficult to track down reliable data on the number of Americans living in Mexico, but I use data from US Department of State (2021)

3. In retrospect, I wonder if I could have done more to help her. I asked if Maria needed help or wanted referrals to services, but she said she was okay. She seemed like she just wanted to talk, and so our long conversation that afternoon continued on to cover the drug market and "asshole" cops and eventually to head lice and our mutual fear of cockroaches. I am by no means trained as a counselor, and it is not typically within the purview of anthropology to offer mental health–service provision, but sometimes people just want someone to listen and spend the time.

4. I have written about the content of Geraldo's photovoice project in Syvertsen, Bazzi, and Mittal (2017). In this chapter I have chosen to focus on Maria's story and what was otherwise left out of the Parejas record.

CONCLUSION: LOVE AS A PATHWAY TO HEALTH EQUITY

1. See publications reviewing the state of the evidence, including Shannon et al. (2018), Goldenberg et al. (2021), and NSWP and INPUD (2015). Of note, these are valuable resources with excellent recommendations that guided my thinking in this chapter; my point is simply that sex workers' intimate relationships remain missing from mainstream public health policy recommendations.

2. I am referring to efforts to create structural competency in medicine, which means that physicians and medical students are trained to identify the structural and social factors driving health inequities and can use this information to better engage with their patients; see Metzl and Hansen (2014) and the Structural Competency Working Group (2020).

3. My understanding of harm reduction is heavily informed by the National Harm Reduction Coalition (n.d.), a US-based coalition dedicated to facilitating dialogue and action

to end racialized, punitive drug policies; its work carries global implications. Harm Reduction International (n.d.), a global nongovernmental organization, is also an excellent resource.

4. See the discussion of the literature related to love and health in the introduction.

5. Excellent models for couples-based programs are available, including El-Bassel et al. (2011), McMahon et al. (2015), and Wechsberg et al. (2015).

6. The science of preexposure prophylaxis (PrEP) has rapidly changed over the past several years, as multiple clinical trials have provided evidence for the effectiveness of regularly using antiretroviral medication to prevent HIV infection among negative persons. Shortly after Parejas data collection ended, PrEP gained numerous approvals for its use in HIV prevention. In 2012 the US Food and Drug Administration approved a once-daily pill form of PrEP and in 2019 approved a second formulation for some high-risk populations. In 2014 the World Health Organization recommended PrEP for use among men who have sex with men and by late 2015 expanded their recommendations of PrEP to all individuals "at substantial risk of HIV infection" as a choice within a comprehensive HIV-prevention package. Other forms of PrEP have also been under testing and development, including gels, vaginal rings, and injectables. In Parejas we asked couples about their perspectives on microbicide gels for HIV prevention, of which they were generally accepting, except for concerns about the potential for it to create mistrust and conflict within their relationships; see Robertson et al. (2013a).

7. For qualitative studies that complicate PrEP use among couples, see, for example, van der Straten et al. (2014) and Roberts et al. (2016); for a review of social science approaches to understanding PrEP use among female sex workers, see Syvertsen et al. (2014).

8. The Academy of Perinatal Harm Reduction and Harm Reduction Coaltion have developed an excellent toolkit on "Pregnancy and Substance Use"; see Kurzer-Yashin and Sue (2020). The Parejas research team also published a paper using case studies to examine the challenges of raising children in the context of sex work and drug use; see Rolon et al. (2013).

9. I like the briefing paper published by the Global Network of Sex Work Projects and the International Network of People Who Use Drugs for their perspective and suggestions on needed services (though intimate relationships are not covered; see NSWP and INPUD 2015). Iversen et al.'s chapter (2021) is also helpful in synthesizing the literature and making recommendations. They estimate the global prevalence of lifetime drug use among female sex workers to be 29 percent, which should suggest that more attention is needed in terms of the overlap between sex work and drug use. See also El-Bassel et al. (2011), McMahon et al. (2015), and Wechsberg et al. (2015), which suggest that couples-based public health interventions are moving toward addressing sexual and drug-related risk among vulnerable couples.

10. See the discussion of the literature related to emotions and drug use in the introduction to this volume.

11. There is a growing body of literature on how people who engage in sex work and use drugs face multiple forms of stigma from providers of medical care and social services; see, for example, Lazarus et al. (2012); Paquette, Syvertsen, and Pollini (2018); Syvertsen et al. (2021); Van Boekel et al. (2013); and Wanyenze et al. (2017).

12. Cultivating self-love is an important part of building a multidimensional conception of love linking the political to the personal. Self-love is a rebellious act that allows

individuals to value themselves for who are they are and the potential of what they can do; loving oneself is a first step in raising collective states of consciousness toward transformation of the social world. See, for example, the Combahee River Collective (1983), Lorde (1984), and Collins (2004).

13. Decriminalization of sex work removes criminal prosecution and helps ensure the labor rights of sex workers. A number of international organizations have publicly called for decriminalization, including the Global Network of Sex Work Projects, World Health Organization, Joint United Nations Programme on HIV/AIDS, Amnesty International, United Nations Development Program, and United Nations Population Fund. Similarly, drug decriminalization is the removal of criminal penalties for drug-law violations (usually possession for personal use). Likewise, support for decriminalizing drugs is rapidly expanding and supported by global organizations such as the International Network of People Who Use Drugs, World Health Organization, Drug Policy Alliance, International Red Cross, American Public Health Association, American Civil Liberties Union, Human Rights Watch, and National Association for the Advancement of Colored People. Studies suggest that decriminalization of sex work could significantly reduce global HIV infections (Shannon et al. 2015). Decriminalizing drug use could also lead to reductions in risk behaviors and better engagement in HIV care (DeBeck et al. 2017).

14. For research into sex worker empowerment, including challenges and best practices, see Kerrigan et al. (2015) and Gil et al. (2021). Empowerment approaches can work well, but my point here is that, because practices of sex work vary so much, multiple approaches are needed.

15. Unfortunately, literature documenting inhumane and abusive conditions in drug-treatment centers in Mexico continues to grow. When I first arrived at UCSD for my fellowship in 2009, as I helped get the Parejas study up and running, I also analyzed data from the original qualitative study that informed El Cuete, a decades-long cohort study that has provided critical information about injection drug use and drug markets in the border region. There was not enough space in the journal article to include all the heartbreaking stories that I read in the transcripts (see Syvertsen et al. 2010). Despite treatment being an integral part of Mexico's drug reforms, subsequent work has found that the abuses continue, including Bazzi et al. (2016), Garcia (2015), Harvey-Vera et al. (2016), and Rafful et al. (2020). Recent modeling studies have found that access to opioid-agonist treatment rather than compulsory, abstinence-based drug rehabilitation programs could have a greater public health benefit in terms of curbing the HIV epidemic. In contrast, compulsory treatment can negatively impact patients' well-being and treatment success, which could lead to poor mental health outcomes, increased syringe sharing, overdose, and increases in HIV transmission (see Bórquez et al. 2018).

16. See, for example, Baker et al. (2020); DeBeck et al. (2017); Strathdee, Beletsky, and Kerr (2015); Footer et al. (2016); West et al. (2020); and Werb (2011).

17. A robust discussion of abolition in global public health and drug research is needed, but it is beyond the scope of this chapter. Some excellent resources to learn about what this means and what we can do to promote change include Agid et al. (2021); Abolition for the People (2020); and the *Abolition Journal* (2020). See also Cullors (2018); Davis (2003); Iwai, Khan, and DasGupta (2020); and Kaba (2021).

18. Much of this section is inspired by the edited volume *Engaging Contradictions* (Hale 2008), but there is also an ever-expanding literature on activist, anti-oppressive, and

community-engaged research; see, for example, Schensul et al. (2014), Strega and Brown (2015), Speed (2006), Wallerstein and Duran (2010), and Wallerstein et al. (2017).

19. The North Carolina Survivors Union is a community-based organization and part of a larger drug user union, the National Urban Survivors League. Although this organization is based in the United States, its manifesto has global implications (NCSU, n.d.). Another excellent resource is provided by the Vancouver Area Network of Drug Users (VANDU, n.d.). See also the Drug Policy Alliance's (n.d.) Department of Research and Academic Engagement for other trainings and resources.

20. There is tremendous potential to harness the power of arts in producing and disseminating research; for an excellent guide on integrating public health, arts, culture, and community, see Sonke et al. (2019).

Abel, Gillian M. 2011. "Different Stage, Different Performance: The Protective Strategy of Role Play on Emotional Health in Sex Work." *Social Science and Medicine* 72 (7): 1177–84.

Abolition for the People. 2020. "Abolition for the People: A Movement for a Future without Policing and Prisons." Kaepernick Publishing. Accessed October 6, 2020. https://level .medium.com/abolition-for-the-people-397ef29e3ca5.

Abolition Journal. 2020. "If You're New to Abolition: Study Group Guide." Accessed June 25, 2020. https://abolitionjournal.org/studyguide/.

Agar, Michael. 1973. *Ripping and Running: A Formal Ethnography of Urban Heroin Addicts.* New York: Seminar Press.

Agid, Shana, Melissa Burch, Priya Kandaswamy, Erica Meiners, Dylan Rodriguez, and Setsu Shigematsu. 2021. "Resource Guide for Teaching and Learning Abolition." Critical Resistance. Accessed May 14, 2022. https://criticalresistance.org/wp-content/uploads /2021/08/CR_GuideforTeachingLearningAbolition-1.pdf

Agren, David. 2019a. "AMLO's Mexico Leads to Drastic Cuts to Health System." *Lancet* 393 (10188): 2289–90.

———. 2019b. "Is the HIV/AIDS Response in Jeopardy in Mexico?" *Lancet HIV* 6 (8): e493–94.

———. 2019c. "Verter: Helping Drug Users Near the USA-Mexico Border." *Lancet HIV* 6 (8): e495.

Anzaldúa, Gloria. (1987) 2012. *Borderlands/la Frontera: The New Mestiza.* San Francisco: Aunt Lute Books.

———. 2013. "Now Let Us Shift . . . the Path of Conocimiento . . . Inner Work, Public Acts." In *This Bridge We Call Home: Radical Visions for Transformation*, edited by Gloria Anzaldúa and Ana Louise Keating, 540–78. London: Routledge.

Arredondo, J., T. Gaines, S. Manian, C. Vilalta, A. Bañuelos, S.A. Strathdee, and L. Beletsky. 2018. "The Law on the Streets: Evaluating the Impact of Mexico's Drug Decriminalization

Reform on Drug Possession Arrests in Tijuana, Mexico." *International Journal of Drug Policy* 54:1–8.

Arredondo, J., S.A. Strathdee, J. Cepeda, D. Abramovitz, I. Artamonova, E. Clairgue, E. Bustamante, M.L. Mittal, T. Rocha, A. Bañuelos, H.O. Olivarria, M. Morales, G. Rangel, C. Magis, and L. Beletsky. 2017. "Measuring Improvement in Knowledge of Drug Policy Reforms Following a Police Education Program in Tijuana, Mexico." *Harm Reduction Journal* 14:72.

Bailey, Althea E., and John Peter Figueroa. 2018. "Agency, Lapse in Condom Use and Relationship Intimacy among Female Sex Workers in Jamaica." *Culture, Health and Sexuality* 20 (5): 531–44.

"Baja." 2012. *Anthony Bourdain: No Reservations*. Season 8, episode 8. New York: Travel Channel.

Baker, Pieter, Leo Beletsky, Liliana Avalos, Christopher Venegas, Carlos Rivera, Steffanie A. Strathdee, and Javier Cepeda. 2020. "Policing Practices and Risk of HIV Infection Among People Who Inject Drugs." *Epidemiologic Reviews* 42 (1): 27–40.

Barthes, Roland. 1977. *A Lover's Discourse: Fragments*. Translated from French by Richard Howard. New York: Hill and Wang.

Bazzi, Angela Robertson, Gudelia Rangel, Gustavo Martinez, Monica D. Ulibarri, Jennifer L. Syvertsen, Samuel A. Bazzi, Scott Roesch, Heather A. Pines, and Steffanie A. Strathdee. 2015. "Incidence and Predictors of HIV and Sexually Transmitted Infections among Female Sex Workers and Their Intimate Male Partners in Northern Mexico: A Longitudinal, Multilevel Study." *American Journal of Epidemiology* 181 (9): 723–31.

Bazzi, Angela Robertson, Jennifer L. Syvertsen, María Luisa Rolón, Gustavo Martinez, Gudelia Rangel, Alicia Vera, Hortensia Amaro, Monica D. Ulibarri, Daniel O. Hernandez, and Steffanie A. Strathdee. 2016. "Social and Structural Challenges to Drug Cessation among Couples in Northern Mexico: Implications for Drug Treatment in Underserved Communities." *Journal of Substance Abuse Treatment* 61:26–33.

Beletsky, Leo, Karla D. Wagner, Jaime Arredondo, Lawrence Palinkas, Carlos Magis Rodríguez, Nicolette Kalic, and Steffanie A. Strathdee. 2016. "Implementing Mexico's 'Narcomenudeo' Drug Law Reform: A Mixed Methods Assessment of Early Experiences among People Who Inject Drugs." *Journal of Mixed Methods Research* 10 (4): 384–401.

Bellhouse, Clare, Susan Crebbin, Christopher K. Fairley, and Jade E. Bilardi. 2015. "The Impact of Sex Work on Women's Personal Romantic Relationships and the Mental Separation of Their Work and Personal Lives: A Mixed-Methods Study." *PLOS One* 10 (10): e0141575.

Berlant, Lauren. 2011. "A Properly Political Concept of Love: Three Approaches in Ten Pages." *Cultural Anthropology* 26 (4): 683–91.

Betancur, Catalina, and Andrés Felipe Marín Cortés. 2011. "Cuerpo, comercio sexual, amor e identidad: Significados construidos por mujeres que practicaron la prostitución." *CES Psicología* 4 (1): 32–51.

Bezares Buenrostro, Héctor E. 2019. "Violencia, espacio y vida cotidiana en la guerra mexicana contra las drogas: Un análisis de Tijuana." *Revista Austral de Ciencias Sociales* 37:231–52.

Biehl, João, and Adriana Petryna, eds. 2013. *When People Come First: Critical Studies in Global Health*. Princeton: Princeton University Press.

Bórquez, Annick, Daniela Abramovitz, Javier Cepeda, Gudelia Rangel, Patricia González-Zúñiga, Natasha K. Martin, Carlos Magis-Rodríguez, and Steffanie A. Strathdee. 2019.

"Syringe Sharing among People Who Inject Drugs in Tijuana: Before and After the Global Fund." *Salud Mental* 42 (4): 149–56.

Bórquez, Annick, Leo Beletsky, Bohdan Nosyk, Steffanie A. Strathdee, Alejandro Madrazo, Daniela Abramovitz, Claudia Rafful, Mario Morales, Javier Cepeda, Dimitra Panagiotoglou, Emanuel Krebs, Peter Vickerman, Marie Claude Boily, Nicholas Thomson, and Natasha K. Martin. 2018. "The Effect of Public Health-Oriented Drug Law Reform on HIV Incidence in People Who Inject Drugs in Tijuana, Mexico: An Epidemic Modelling Study." *Lancet Public Health* 3:e429–37.

Boullosa, Carmen, and Mike Wallace. 2015. *A Narco History: How the United States and Mexico Jointly Created the "Mexican Drug War."* New York: OR Books.

Bourdieu, Pierre. 1977. *Outline of a Theory of Practice.* Cambridge: Cambridge University Press.

Bourgois, Philippe. 1998. "The Moral Economies of Homeless Heroin Addicts: Confronting Ethnography, HIV Risk and Everyday Violence in San Francisco Shooting Encampments." *Substance Use and Misuse* 33:2323–51.

———. 1999. "Theory, Method, and Power in Drug and HIV-Prevention Research: A Participant Observer's Critique." *Substance Use and Misuse* 34 (14): 2155–72.

Bourgois, Philippe, and Jeff Schonberg. 2009. *Righteous Dopefiend.* Berkeley: University of California Press.

Brennan, Denise. 2004. *What's Love Got to Do with It? Transnational Desires and Sex Tourism in the Dominican Republic.* Durham, NC: Duke University Press.

Bringas Rábago, Nora Leticia, and Ruth Gaxiola Aldama. 2012. "Los espacios de la prostitución en Tijuana: Turismo sexual entre varones." *Región y Sociedad* 24 (55): 81–130.

Bucardo, Jesus, Shirley J. Semple, Miguel Fraga-Vallejo, Wendy Davila, and Thomas L. Patterson. 2004. "A Qualitative Exploration of Female Sex Work in Tijuana, Mexico." *Archives of Sexual Behavior* 33 (4): 343–51.

Burgueño, Fernando Guereña, Abram S. Benenson, Jesús Bucardo Amaya, Adela Caudillo Carreño, and José de Jesús Curriel Figueroa. 1992. "Comportamiento sexual y abuso de drogas en homosexuales, prostitutas y prisioneros en Tijuana, México." *Revista Latinoamericana de Psicología* 24 (1–2): 85–96.

Cabezas, Amalia L. 2009. *Economies of Desire: Sex and Tourism in Cuba and the Dominican Republic.* Philadelphia: Temple University Press.

Campbell, Howard. 2010. *Drug War Zone: Frontline Dispatches from the Streets of El Paso and Juarez.* Austin: University of Texas Press.

Campbell, Joseph. 2004. *Pathways to Bliss: Mythology and Personal Transformation.* Novato, CA: New World Library.

Carrillo, Héctor. 2002. *The Night Is Young: Sexuality in Mexico in the Time of AIDS.* Chicago: University of Chicago Press.

Castañeda, Xóchitl, and Victor Ortiz. 1996. "Sex Masks: The Double Life of Female Commercial Sex Workers in Mexico City." *Culture, Medicine and Psychiatry* 20 (2): 229–47.

Castillo, Debra A., Maria Gudelia Rangel Gomez, and Bonnie Delgado. 1999. "Border Lives: Prostitute Women in Tijuana." *Signs* 24 (2): 387–422.

Cepeda, Javier A., Jose Luis Burgos, James G. Kahn, Rosario Padilla, Pedro Emilio Meza Martinez, Luis Alberto Segovia, Tommi Gaines, Daniela Abramovitz, Gudelia Rangel, and Carlos Magis-Rodriguez. 2019. "Evaluating the Impact of Global Fund Withdrawal on Needle and Syringe Provision, Cost and Use among People Who Inject Drugs in Tijuana, Mexico: A Costing Analysis." *BMJ Open* 9 (1): e026298.

Cheng, Sealing. 2010. *On the Move for Love: Migrant Entertainers and the US Military in South Korea*. Philadelphia: University of Pennsylvania Press.

Choudhury, Shonali M. 2010. "'As Prostitutes, We Control Our Bodies': Perceptions of Health and Body in the Lives of Establishment-Based Female Sex Workers in Tijuana, Mexico." *Culture, Health and Sexuality* 12 (6): 677–89.

Cole, Jennifer, and Lynn M. Thomas, eds. 2009. *Love in Africa*. Chicago: University of Chicago Press.

Collins, Patricia Hill. 2004. *Black Sexual Politics: African Americans, Gender, and the New Racism*. New York: Routledge.

Combahee River Collective. 1983. "Combahee River Collective Statement." In *Home Girls: A Black Feminist Anthology*, edited by Barbara Smith, 264–74. New York: Kitchen Table.

Connell, Raewyn. 2014. "Rethinking Gender from the South." *Feminist Studies* 40 (3): 518–39.

Connell, R.W., and James W Messerschmidt. 2005. "Hegemonic Masculinity: Rethinking the Concept." *Gender and Society* 19 (6): 829–59.

Corbett, A. Michelle, Julia Dickson-Gómez, Helena Hilario, and Margaret R. Weeks. 2009. "A Little Thing Called Love: Condom Use in High-Risk Primary Heterosexual Relationships." *Perspectives on Sexual and Reproductive Health* 41 (4): 218–24.

Csordas, Thomas J. 1990. "Embodiment as a Paradigm for Anthropology." *Ethos* 18 (1): 5–47.

———. 1993. "Somatic Modes of Attention." *Cultural Anthropology* 8 (2): 135–156.

Cullors, Patrisse. 2018. "Abolition and Reparations: Histories of Resistance, Transformative Justice, and Accountability." *Harvard Law Review* 132:1684.

Davis, Angela Y. 2003. *Are Prisons Obsolete?* New York: Seven Stories.

Day, Keri. 2016. *Religious Resistance to Neoliberalism: Womanist and Black Feminist Perspectives*. New York: Palgrave Macmillian.

DeBeck, Kora, Tessa Cheng, Julio S. Montaner, Chris Beyrer, Richard Elliott, Susan Sherman, Evan Wood, and Stefan Baral. 2017. "HIV and the Criminalisation of Drug Use among People Who Inject Drugs: A Systematic Review." *Lancet HIV* 4 (8): e357–74.

Deering, Kathleen N., Avni Amin, Jean Shoveller, Ariel Nesbitt, Claudia Garcia-Moreno, Putu Duff, Elena Argento, and Kate Shannon. 2014. "A Systematic Review of the Correlates of Violence against Sex Workers." *American Journal of Public Health* 104 (5): e42–54.

Desjarlais, Robert R. 1997. *Shelter Blues: Sanity and Selfhood among the Homeless*. Philadelphia: University of Pennsylvania Press.

Dominguez, Virginia R. 2000. "For a Politics of Love and Rescue." *Cultural Anthropology* 15 (3): 361–93.

Douglas, Mary. (1967) 2004. "The Meaning of Myth." In *The Strutural Study of Myth and Totemism*, edited by Edmund Leach, 49–70. New York: Routledge.

Drug Policy Alliance. n.d. "Department of Research and Academic Engagement." Accessed May 14, 2022. https://drugpolicy.org/about-us/departments-and-state-offices/research -academic-engagement.

El-Bassel, Nabila, Louisa Gilbert, Elwin Wu, Susan S. Witte, Mingway Chang, Jennifer Hill, and Robert H. Remien. 2011. "Couple-Based HIV Prevention for Low-Income Drug Users from New York City: A Randomized Controlled Trial to Reduce Dual Risks." *Journal of Acquired Immune Deficiency Syndrome* 58 (2): 198–206.

Farmer, Paul. 1999. *Infections and Inequalities: The Modern Plagues*. Berkeley: University of California Press.

Fierros, Cindy O., and Dolores Delgado Bernal. 2016. "Vamos a Platicar: The Contours of Pláticas as Chicana/Latina Feminist Methodology." *Chicana/Latina Studies* 15 (2): 98–121.

Fisher, Helen. 2004. *Why We Love: The Nature and Chemistry of Romantic Love.* New York: Holt.

———. 2016. *Anatomy of Love: A Natural History of Mating, Marriage, and Why We Stray.* New York: Norton.

Footer, Katherine H.A., Bradley E. Silberzahn, Kayla N. Tormohlen, and Susan G. Sherman. 2016. "Policing Practices as a Structural Determinant for HIV among Sex Workers: A Systematic Review of Empirical Findings." *Journal of the International AIDS Society* 19:20883.

Foucault, Michel (1978) 1990. *The History of Sexuality: An Introduction.* Vol. 1. New York: Vintage.

Freire, Paulo. (1970) 2018. *Pedagogy of the Oppressed.* New York: Bloomsbury.

Galtung, Johan. 1969. "Violence, Peace, and Peace Research." *Journal of Peace Research* 6 (3): 167–91.

Garcia, Angela. 2010. *The Pastoral Clinic: Addiction and Dispossession along the Rio Grande.* Berkeley: University of California Press.

———. 2014a. "The Promise: On the Morality of the Marginal and the Illicit." *Ethos* 42 (1): 51–64.

———. 2014b. "Regeneration: Love, Drugs and the Remaking of Hispano Inheritance." *Social Anthropology* 22 (2): 200–212.

———. 2015. "Serenity: Violence, Inequality, and Recovery on the Edge of Mexico City." *Medical Anthropology Quarterly* 29 (4): 455–72.

Gerber, Ana Sofía, and Florencia Ravarotto Kohler. 2021. "Alguien, alguna vez, amó a un* trabajador* sexual." *Polémicas Feministas* 5:1–13.

Gil, Cynthia Navarrete, Manjula Ramaiah, Andrea Mantsios, Clare Barrington, and Deanna Kerrigan. 2021. "Best Practices and Challenges to Sex Worker Community Empowerment and Mobilisation Strategies to Promote Health and Human Rights." In Goldenberg et al. 2021, 189–206.

Goldenberg, Shira M., Steffanie A. Strathdee, Manuel Gallardo, Tim Rhodes, Karla D. Wagner, and Thomas L. Patterson. 2011. "'Over Here, It's Just Drugs, Women and All the Madness': The HIV Risk Environment of Clients of Female Sex Workers in Tijuana, Mexico." *Social Science and Medicine* 72 (7): 1185–92.

Goldenberg, Shira M., Ruth Morgan Thomas, Anna Forbes, and Stefan Baral, eds. 2021. *Sex Work, Health, and Human Rights.* Cham, Switzerland: Springer.

González de la Rocha, Mercedes. 2006. "Vanishing Assets: Cumulative Disadvantage among the Urban Poor." *Annals of the American Academy of Political and Social Science* 606 (1): 68–94.

Gutmann, Matthew C. 1996. *The Meanings of Macho: Being a Man in Mexico City.* Berkeley: University of California Press.

———. 2007. *Fixing Men: Sex, Birth Control, and AIDS in Mexico.* Berkeley: University of California Press.

Hale, Charles R, ed. 2008. *Engaging Contradictions: Theory, Politics, and Methods of Activist Scholarship.* Berkeley: University of California Press.

Haraway, Donna Jeanne. 2003. *The Companion Species Manifesto: Dogs, People, and Significant Otherness.* Chicago: Prickly Paradigm.

Hardt, Michael. 2011. "For Love or Money." *Cultural Anthropology* 26 (4): 676–82.

Harm Reduction International. n.d. "Harm Reduction International." Accessed May 14, 2022. www.hri.global/.

Harvey-Vera, Alicia Yolanda, Patricia González-Zúñiga, Adriana Carolina Vargas-Ojeda, Maria Elena Medina-Mora, Carlos Leonardo Magis-Rodríguez, Karla Wagner, Steffanie Anne Strathdee, and Daniel Werb. 2016. "Risk of Violence in Drug Rehabilitation Centers: Perceptions of People Who Inject Drugs in Tijuana, Mexico." *Substance Abuse Treatment, Prevention, and Policy* 11:5.

Heinle, Kimberly, Octavio Rodriguez Ferreira, and David A. Shirk. 2014. *Drug Violence in Mexico: Data and Analysis through 2013.* San Diego: Department of Political Science and International Relations, University of San Diego.

Heinle, Kimberly, Cory Molzahn, and David A. Shirk. 2015. *Drug Violence in Mexico: Data and Analysis through 2014.* Department of Political Science and International Relations, University of San Diego.

Heyman, Josiah. 1994. "The Mexico–United States Border in Anthropology: A Critique and Reformulation." *Journal of Political Ecology* 1:43–66.

Hirsch, Jennifer S., Jennifer Higgins, Margaret E. Bentley, and Constance A. Nathanson. 2002. "The Social Constructions of Sexuality: Marital Infidelity and Sexually Transmitted Disease-HIV Risk in a Mexican Migrant Community." *American Journal of Public Health* 92 (8): 1227–37.

Hirsch, Jennifer S., Sergio Meneses, Brenda Thompson, Mirka Negroni, Blanca Pelcastre, and Carlos Del Rio. 2007. "The Inevitability of Infidelity: Sexual Reputation, Social Geographies, and Marital HIV Risk in Rural Mexico." *American Journal of Public Health* 97 (6): 986–96.

Hirsch, Jennifer S., and Holly Wardlow, eds. 2006. *Modern Loves: The Anthropology of Romantic Courtship and Companionate Marriage.* Ann Arbor: University of Michigan Press.

Hirsch, Jennifer S., Holly Wardlow, Daniel Jordan Smith, Harriet M. Phinney, Shanti Parikh, and Constance A. Nathanson. 2009. *The Secret: Love, Marriage, and HIV.* Nashville: Vanderbilt University Press.

Hoang, Kimberly Kay. 2015. *Dealing in Desire: Asian Ascendancy, Western Decline, and the Hidden Currencies of Global Sex Work.* Berkeley: University of California Press.

hooks, bell. 2001a. *All about Love: New Visions.* New York: HarperCollins.

———. 2001b. *Salvation: Black People and Love.* New York: Perennial.

———. 2004. *The Will to Change: Men, Masculinity, and Love.* New York: Washington Square Press.

INEGI (Instituto Nacional de Estadística, Geografía e Informática). 2010 "Census of Population and Housing Units." https://en.www.inegi.org.mx/programas/ccpv/2010/.

INPRFM (Instituto Nacional de Psiquiatría Ramón de la Fuente Muñiz), INSP (Instituto Nacional de Salud Pública), and Secretaría de Salud. 2011. *Encuesta Nacional de Adicciones 2011: Reporte de Drogas.* Mexico City: INPRFM.

Iversen, Jenny, Pike Long, Alexandra Lutnick, and Lisa Maher. 2021. "Patterns and Epidemiology of Illicit Drug Use among Sex Workers Globally: A Systematic Review." In Goldenberg et al. 2021, 95–120.

Iwai, Yoshiko, Zahra H. Khan, and Sayantani DasGupta. 2020. "Abolition Medicine." *Lancet* 396 (10245): 158–59.

Jackson, Lois A., Tod Augusta-Scott, Marilee Burwash-Brennan, Jeff Karabanow, Karyn Robertson, and Barbara Sowinski. 2009. "Intimate Relationships and Women Involved in the Sex Trade: Perceptions and Experiences of Inclusion and Exclusion." *Health* 13 (1): 25–46.

James, Joy, and Edmund T. Gordon. 2008. "Afterword: Activist Scholars or Radical Subjects?" In Hale 2008, 367–74.

Jankowiak, William R. 2008. *Intimacies: Love and Sex across Cultures.* New York: Columbia University Press.

Jankowiak, William R., and Edward F. Fischer. 1992. "A Cross-Cultural Perspective on Romantic Love." *Ethnology* 31 (2): 149–55.

Jordan, June. 2003. *Some of Us Did Not Die: New and Selected Essays.* New York: Civitas Books.

Kaba, Mariame. 2021. *We Do This 'Til We Free Us: Abolitionist Organizing and Transforming Justice.* Chicago: Haymarket Books.

Katsulis, Yasmina. 2009. *Sex Work and the City: The Social Geography of Health and Safety in Tijuana, Mexico.* Austin: University of Texas Press.

Katsulis, Yasmina, Vera Lopez, Alesha Durfee, and Alyssa Robillard. 2010. "Female Sex Workers and the Social Context of Workplace Violence in Tijuana, Mexico." *Medical Anthropology Quarterly* 24 (3): 344–62.

Kelly, Patty. 2008. *Lydia's Open Door: Inside Mexico's Most Modern Brothel.* Berkeley: University of California Press.

Kerrigan, Deanna, Caitlin E., Kennedy, Ruth Morgan-Thomas, Sushena Reza-Paul, Peninah Mwangi, Kay Thi Win, Allison McFall, Virginia A. Fonner, and Jennifer Butler. 2015. "A Community Empowerment Approach to the HIV Response among Sex Workers: Effectiveness, Challenges, and Considerations for Implementation and Scale-Up." *Lancet* 385 (9963): 172–85.

King, Martin Luther, Jr. (1967) 2010. *Where Do We Go from Here: Chaos or Community?* Boston: Beacon.

Knaul, Felicia Marie, Eduardo González-Pier, Octavio Gómez-Dantés, David García-Junco, Héctor Arreola-Ornelas, Mariana Barraza-Lloréns, Rosa Sandoval, Francisco Caballero, Mauricio Hernández-Avila, and Mercedes Juan. 2012. "The Quest for Universal Health Coverage: Achieving Social Protection for All in Mexico." *Lancet* 380 (9849): 1259–79.

Knight, Kelly Ray. 2015. *Addicted, Pregnant, Poor.* Durham, NC: Duke University Press.

Knox, Belle. 2014. "Tearing Down the Whorearchy from the Inside." Jezebel. Accessed May 14, 2022. https://jezebel.com/tearing-down-the-whorearchy-from-the-inside-1596459558.

Koff, Harlan. 2015. "Informal Economies in European and American Cross-Border Regions." *Journal of Borderlands Studies* 30 (4): 469–87.

Krieger, Nancy. 2016. "Living and Dying at the Crossroads: Racism, Embodiment, and Why Theory Is Essential for a Public Health of Consequence." *American Journal of Public Health* 106 (5): 832–33.

Kurzer-Yashin, Dana, and Kimberly Sue, eds. 2020. *Pregnancy and Substance Use: A Harm Reduction Toolkit.* New York: Academy of Perinatal Harm Reduction/Harm Reduction Coalition.

Labonté, Ronald, Eric Crosbie, Deborah Gleeson, and Courtney McNamara. 2019. "USMCA (NAFTA 2.0): Tightening the Constraints on the Right to Regulate for Public Health." *Globalization and Health* 15:35.

Labonté, Ronald, Deborah Gleeson, and Courtney L. McNamara. 2020. "USMCA 2.0: A Few Improvements but Far from a 'Healthy' Trade Treaty." *Globalization and Health* 16:43.

Lam, Nguyen Tran. 2008. "Drugs, Sex and AIDS: Sexual Relationships among Injecting Drug Users and Their Sexual Partners in Vietnam." Supplement, *Culture, Health and Sexuality* 10 (S1): S123–37.

Lamas, Marta. 2017. "Trabajo sexual e intimidad." *Cuicuilco: Revista de Ciencias Antropológicas* 24 (68): 11–34.

Latapi, Agustín Escobar, and Mercedes González de la Rocha. 1995. "Crisis, Restructuring and Urban Poverty in Mexico." *Environment and Urbanization* 7 (1): 57–76.

Lazarus, Lisa, Kathleen N. Deering, Rose Nabess, Kate Gibson, Mark W. Tyndall, and Kate Shannon. 2012. "Occupational Stigma as a Primary Barrier to Health Care for Street-Based Sex Workers in Canada." *Culture, Health and Sexuality* 14 (2): 139–50.

Lazuardi, Elan, Heather Worth, Antonia Morita Iswari Saktiawati, Catherine Spooner, Retna Padmawati, and Yanri Subronto. 2012. "Boyfriends and Injecting: The Role of Intimate Male Partners in the Life of Women Who Inject Drugs in Central Java." *Culture, Health and Sexuality* 14 (5): 491–503.

Lorde, Audre. 1984. *Sister Outsider: Essays and Speeches*. Berkeley: Crossing.

Loucky, James, and Donald K. Alper. 2008. "Pacific Borders, Discordant Borders: Where North American Edges Together." In *Transboundary Policy Challenges in the Pacific Border Regions of North America*, edited by Donald K. Alper, John Chadwick Day, and James Loucky, 11–38. Calgary: University of Calgary Press.

Luna, Sarah. 2020. *Love in the Drug War*. Austin: University of Texas Press.

Lupton, Deborah. 1993. "Risk as Moral Danger: The Social and Political Functions of Risk Discourse in Public Health." *International Journal of Health Services* 23 (3): 425–35.

Lusk, Mark, Kathleen Staudt, and Eva Moya. 2012a. "Social Justice in the US-Mexico Border Region." In Lusk, Staudt, and Moya 2012b, 3–38.

———, eds. 2012b. *Social Justice in the US-Mexico Border Region*. New York: Springer.

MacRae, R., and E. Aalto. 2000. "Gendered Power Dynamics and HIV Risk in Drug-Using Sexual Relationships." *AIDS Care* 12 (4): 505–16.

Maher, Lisa. 1997. *Sexed Work: Gender, Race, and Resistance in a Brooklyn Drug Market*. Oxford: Oxford University Press.

Maher, Lisa, Julie Mooney-Somers, Pisith Phlong, Marie-Claude Couture, Serey Phal Kien, Ellen Stein, Anna Juong Bates, Neth Sansothy, Kimberly Page, on Behalf of the Young Women's Health Study Collaborative. 2013. "Condom Negotiation across Different Relationship Types by Young Women Engaged in Sex Work in Phnom Penh, Cambodia." *Global Public Health* 8 (3): 270–83.

McMahon, James M., Enrique R. Pouget, Stephanie Tortu, Ellen M. Volpe, Leilani Torres, and William Rodriguez. 2015. "Couple-Based HIV Counseling and Testing: A Risk Reduction Intervention for US Drug-Involved Women and Their Primary Male Partners." *Prevention Science* 16 (2): 341–51.

Metzl, Jonathan M., and Helena Hansen. 2014. "Structural Competency: Theorizing a New Medical Engagement with Stigma and Inequality." *Social Science and Medicine* 103:126–33.

Middlebrook, Kevin J., and Eduardo Zepeda. 2003. "On the Political Economy of Mexican Development Policy." In *Confronting Development: Assessing Mexico's Economic and*

Social Policy Challenges, edited by Kevin J. Middlebrook and Eduardo Zepeda, 3–54. Stanford: Stanford University Press.

Mittal, María Luisa, Angela Robertson Bazzi, María Gudelia Rangel, Hugo Staines, Kelly Yotebieng, Steffanie A. Strathdee, and Jennifer L. Syvertsen. 2018. "'He's Not My Pimp': Toward an Understanding of Intimate Male Partner Involvement in Female Sex Work at the Mexico-US Border." *Culture, Health and Sexuality* 20 (9): 961–75.

Mittal, María Luisa, Patricia González-Zúñiga, Claudia Rafful, Austin James Parish, Kenya Lazos-Torres, Teresita Rocha-Jiménez, Jaime Arredondo, Peter J. Davidson, and Steffanie A. Strathdee. 2016. "Building Binational and Interdisciplinary Capacity for a Sustainable Mobile Wound Clinic for Persons Who Inject Drugs (PWID) in Tijuana, Mexico." *UCSD Public Health Research Day*. La Jolla, CA: Institute for Public Health.

Molzahn, Cory, Viridiana Rios, and David A. Shirk. 2012. *Drug Violence in Mexico: Data and Analysis through 2011*. Trans-Border Institute. San Diego: Trans-border Institute, University of San Diego.

Morales, Mario, Claudia Rafful, Pieter Baker, Jaime Arredondo, Sunyou Kang, Maria L. Mittal, Teresita Rocha-Jiménez, Steffanie A. Strathdee, and Leo Beletsky. 2020. "'Pick Up Anything That Moves': A Qualitative Analysis of a Police Crackdown against People Who Use Drugs in Tijuana, Mexico." *Health and Justice* 8:9.

Morris, Meghan D., Erin Andrew, Judy Y. Tan, Lisa Maher, Colleen Hoff, Lynae Darbes, and Kimberly Page. 2019. "Injecting-Related Trust, Cooperation, Intimacy, and Power as Key Factors Influencing Risk Perception among Drug Injecting Partnerships." *PLOS One* 14 (5): e0217811.

Morris, Meghan D., Anna Bates, Erin Andrew, Judith Hahn, Kimberly Page, and Lisa Maher. 2015. "More Than Just Someone to Inject Drugs With: Injecting within Primary Injection Partnerships." *Drug and Alcohol Dependence* 156:275–81.

Morris, Martina, and Mirjam Kretzschmar. 1997. "Concurrent Partnerships and the Spread of HIV." *AIDS* 11 (5): 641–48.

Morrison, Toni. (1970) 2007. *The Bluest Eye*. New York: Vintage International.

Murray, Laura, Luis Moreno, Santo Rosario, Jonathan Ellen, Michael Sweat, and Deanna Kerrigan. 2007. "The Role of Relationship Intimacy in Consistent Condom Use among Female Sex Workers and Their Regular Paying Partners in the Dominican Republic." *AIDS and Behavior* 11 (3): 463–70.

National Harm Reduction Coalition. n.d. "National Harm Reduction Coalition." Accessed May 14, 2022. https://harmreduction.org/.

Nash, Jennifer C. 2013. "Practicing Love: Black Feminism, Love-Politics, and Post-intersectionality." *Meridians* 11 (2): 1–24.

NCSU (North Carolina Survivors Union). n.d. "Ethical Research Manifesto." Accessed May 14, 2022. https://docs.google.com/document/d/1hda_MbF62ycxvM72qngHJLg2zNBg1qv TrvM3TeE51Ik/edit?ts+=+5f57e67a.

NSWP (Global Network of Sex Work Projects) and INPUD (International Network of People Who Use Drugs). 2015. *Sex Workers Who Use Drugs: Experiences, Perspectives, Needs and Rights; Ensuring a Joint Approach*. Edinburgh: NSWP/INPUD.

Ojeda, V.D., S.A. Strathdee, R. Lozada, M.L.A. Rusch, M. Fraga, P. Orozovich, C. Magis-Rodriguez, A. De La Torre, H. Amaro, W. Cornelius, and T.L. Patterson. 2009. "Associations between Migrant Status and Sexually Transmitted Infections among Female Sex Workers in Tijuana, Mexico." *Sexually Transmitted Infections* 85 (6): 420–26.

Onyango, Monica Adhiambo, Yaw Adu-Sarkodie, Rose Odotei Adjei, Thomas Agyarko-Poku, Carol Hunsberger Kopelman, Kimberly Green, Samuel Wambugu, Nana Fosua Clement, Peter Wondergem, and Jennifer Beard. 2019. "Love, Power, Resilience and Vulnerability: Relationship Dynamics between Female Sex Workers in Ghana and Their Intimate Partners." *Culture, Health and Sexuality* 21 (1): 31–45.

Ortner, Sherry B. 2016. "Dark Anthropology and Its Others: Theory since the Eighties." *HAU: Journal of Ethnographic Theory* 6 (1): 47–73.

Padilla, Mark. 2007. "Tourism and Tigueraje: The Structures of Love and Silence among Dominican Male Sex Workers." In Padilla et al. 2007, 38–69.

Padilla, Mark, Daniel Castellanos, Vincent Guilamo-Ramos, Armando Matiz Reyes, Leonardo E. Sánchez Marte, and Martha Arredondo Soriano. 2008. "Stigma, Social Inequality, and HIV Risk Disclosure among Dominican Male Sex Workers." *Social Science and Medicine* 67 (3): 380–88.

Padilla, Mark B., Jennifer S. Hirsch, Miguel Muñoz-Laboy, Robert E. Sember, and Richard G. Parker, eds. 2007. *Love and Globalization: Transformations of Intimacy in the Contemporary World.* Nashville: Vanderbilt University Press.

Page, J. Bryan. 1990. "Shooting Scenarios and Risk of HIV-1 Infection." *American Behavioral Scientist* 33 (4): 478–90.

Page, J. Bryan, and Merrill Singer. 2010. *Comprehending Drug Use: Ethnographic Research at the Social Margins.* New Brunswick, NJ: Rutgers University Press.

Paquette, Catherine E., Jennifer L. Syvertsen, and Robin A. Pollini. 2018. "Stigma at Every Turn: Health Services Experiences among People Who Inject Drugs." *International Journal of Drug Policy* 57:104–10.

Patterson, Thomas L., Brent Mausbach, Remedios Lozada, Hugo Staines-Orozco, Shirley J. Semple, Miguel Fraga-Vallejo, Prisci Orozovich, Daniela Abramovitz, Adela De la Torre, and Hortensia Amaro. 2008. "Efficacy of a Brief Behavioral Intervention to Promote Condom Use among Female Sex Workers in Tijuana and Ciudad Juarez, Mexico." *American Journal of Public Health* 98 (11): 2051–57.

Patterson, Thomas L., Shirley J. Semple, Miguel Fraga, Jesus Bucardo, Adela De la Torre, Juan Salazar-Reyna, Prisci Orozovich, Hugo Salvador Staines Orozco, Hortensia Amaro, and Carlos Magis-Rodríguez. 2006. "A Sexual Risk Reduction Intervention for Female Sex Workers in Mexico: Design and Baseline Characteristics." *Journal of HIV/AIDS and Social Services* 5 (2): 115–37.

Pinedo, Miguel, José Luis Burgos, María Luisa Zúñiga, Ramona Perez, Caroline A. Macera, and Victoria D. Ojeda. 2018. "Deportation and Mental Health among Migrants Who Inject Drugs along the US-Mexico Border." *Global Public Health* 13 (2): 211–26.

Pines, Heather A., Thomas L. Patterson, Gudelia Rangel, Gustavo Martinez, Angela R. Bazzi, Monica D. Ulibarri, Jennifer L. Syvertsen, Natasha K. Martin, and Steffanie A. Strathdee. 2015. "STI/HIV Test Result Disclosure between Female Sex Workers and Their Primary, Non-commercial Male Partners in Two Mexico-US Border Cities: A Prospective Study." *Sexually Transmitted Infections* 91 (3): 207–13.

Poellot, Erica. 2020. *Spirit of Harm Reduction: A Toolkit for Communities of Faith Facing Overdose.* New York: Faith in Harm Reduction/National Harm Reduction Coaltion.

Pollini, Robin A., Remedios Lozada, Manuel Gallardo, Perth Rosen, Alicia Vera, Armando Macias, Lawrence A. Palinkas, and Steffanie A. Strathdee. 2010. "Barriers to

Pharmacy-Based Syringe Purchase among Injection Drug Users in Tijuana, Mexico: A Mixed Methods Study." *AIDS and Behavior* 14 (3): 679–87.

Pollini, Robin A., Perth C. Rosen, Manuel Gallardo, Brenda Robles, Kimberly C. Brouwer, Grace E. Macalino, and Remedios Lozada. 2011. "Not Sold Here: Limited Access to Legally Available Syringes at Pharmacies in Tijuana, Mexico." *Harm Reduction Journal* 8:1.

PubMed. n.d. Bethesda (MD): National Library of Medicine (US), National Center for Biotechnology Information. Accessed May 14, 2022. https://pubmed.ncbi.nlm.nih.gov/.

Rafful, Claudia, María Elena Medina-Mora, Patricia González-Zúñiga, Janis H. Jenkins, M. Gudelia Rangel, Steffanie A. Strathdee, and Peter J. Davidson. 2020. "'Somebody Is Gonna Be Hurt': Involuntary Drug Treatment in Mexico." *Medical Anthropology* 39 (2): 139–52.

Rafful, Claudia, Karla D. Wagner, Dan Werb, Patricia E. González-Zúñiga, Silvia Verdugo, Gudelia Rangel, and Steffanie A. Strathdee. 2015. "Prevalence and Correlates of Neck Injection among People Who Inject Drugs in Tijuana, Mexico." *Drug and Alcohol Review* 34 (6): 630–36.

Rance, Jake, Tim Rhodes, Suzanne Fraser, Joanne Bryant, and Carla Treloar. 2018. "Practices of Partnership: Negotiated Safety among Couples Who Inject Drugs." *Health* 22 (1): 3–19.

Rance, Jake, Carla Treloar, Suzanne Fraser, Joanne Bryant, and Tim Rhodes. 2017. "'Don't Think I'm Going to Leave You over It': Accounts of Changing Hepatitis C Status among Couples Who Inject Drugs." *Drug and Alcohol Dependence* 173:78–84.

Ratliff, Eric A. 1999. "Women as 'Sex Workers,' Men as 'Boyfriends': Shifting Identities in Philippine Go-Go Bars and Their Significance in STD/AIDS Control." *Anthropology and Medicine* 6 (1): 79–101.

Rebhun, Linda-Anne. 1999. *The Heart Is Unknown Country: Love in the Changing Economy of Northeast Brazil*. Stanford: Stanford University Press.

Reck, Gregory G. (1995) 2006. "Out of the Cold, into the Darkness: Shadows of Friendship in Mexico." In *Bridges to Humanity: Narratives on Anthropology and Friendship*, edited by Bruce T. Grindal and Frank A. Salamone, 33–45. Long Grove, IL: Waveland.

Rhodes, Tim. 2009. "Risk Environments and Drug Harms: A Social Science for Harm Reduction Approach." *International Journal of Drug Policy* 20 (3): 193–201.

Rhodes, Tim, and Linda Cusick. 2000. "Love and Intimacy in Relationship Risk Management: HIV Positive People and Their Sexual Partners." *Sociology of Health and Illness* 22 (1): 1–26.

Rhodes, Tim, and Alan Quirk. 1998. "Drug Users' Sexual Relationships and the Social Organisation of Risk: The Sexual Relationship as a Site of Risk Management." *Social Science and Medicine* 46 (2): 157–69.

Rhodes, Tim, Jake Rance, Suzanne Fraser, and Carla Treloar. 2017. "The Intimate Relationship as a Site of Social Protection: Partnerships between People Who Inject Drugs." *Social Science and Medicine* 180:125–34.

Rhodes, Tim, and Carla Treloar. 2008. "The Social Production of Hepatitis C Risk among Injecting Drug Users: A Qualitative Synthesis." *Addiction* 103 (10): 1593–603.

Rhodes, Tim, Karla D. Wagner, Steffanie A. Strathdee, Kate Shannon, Peter Davidson, and Philippe Bourgois. 2011. "Structural Violence and Structural Vulnerability within the

Risk Environment: Theoretical and Methodological Perspectives for a Social Epidemiology of HIV Risk among Injection Drug Users and Sex Workers." In *Rethinking Social Epidemiology: Towards a Science of Change*, edited by P.O. Campo and J.R. Dunn, 205–30. Paris: Springer.

Robbins, Joel. 2013. "Beyond the Suffering Subject: Toward an Anthropology of the Good." *Journal of the Royal Anthropological Institute* 19 (3): 447–62.

Roberts, Dorothy. 2022. *Torn Apart: How the Child Welfare System Destroys Black Families— and How Abolition Can Build a Safer World*. New York: Basic Books.

Roberts, Sarah T., Jessica Haberer, Connie Celum, Nelly Mugo, Norma C. Ware, Craig R. Cohen, Jordan W. Tappero, James Kiarie, Allan Ronald, Andrew Mujugira, Elioda Tumwesigye, Edwin Were, Elizabeth Irungu, Jared M. Baeten, and Partners PrEP Study Team. 2016. "Intimate Partner Violence and Adherence to HIV Pre-exposure Prophylaxis (PrEP) in African Women in HIV Serodiscordant Relationships: A Prospective Cohort Study." *Journal of Acquired Immune Deficiency Syndromes* 73 (3): 313–22.

Robertson, Angela M., Richard S. Garfein, Karla D. Wagner, Sanjay R. Mehta, Carlos Magis-Rodriguez, Jazmine Cuevas-Mota, Patricia González Moreno-Zúñiga, and Steffanie A. Strathdee. 2014a. "Evaluating the Impact of Mexico's Drug Policy Reforms on People Who Inject Drugs in Tijuana, BC, Mexico, and San Diego, CA, United States: A Binational Mixed Methods Research Agenda." *Harm Reduction Journal* 11:1.

Robertson, Angela M., Remedios Lozada, Alicia Vera, Lawrence A. Palinkas, José Luis Burgos, Carlos Magis-Rodriguez, Gudelia Rangel, and Victoria D. Ojeda. 2012. "Deportation Experiences of Women Who Inject Drugs in Tijuana, Mexico." *Qualitative Health Research* 22 (4): 499–510.

Robertson, Angela M., Jennifer L. Syvertsen, Hortensia Amaro, Gustavo Martinez, M. Gudelia Rangel, Thomas L. Patterson, and Steffanie A. Strathdee. 2014b. "Can't Buy My Love: A Typology of Female Sex Workers' Commercial Relationships in the Mexico-US Border Region." *Journal of Sex Research* 51 (6): 711–20.

Robertson, Angela M., Jennifer L. Syvertsen, Gustavo Martinez, M. Gudelia Rangel, Lawrence A. Palinkas, Jamila K. Stockman, Monica D. Ulibarri, and Steffanie A. Strathdee. 2013a. "Acceptability of Vaginal Microbicides among Female Sex Workers and Their Intimate Male Partners in Two Mexico-US Border Cities: A Mixed Methods Analysis." *Global Public Health* 8 (5): 619–33.

Robertson, Angela M., Jennifer L. Syvertsen, M. Gudelia Rangel, Hugo S. Staines, Martina Morris, Thomas L. Patterson, Monica D. Ulibarri, and Steffanie A. Strathdee. 2013b. "Concurrent Sexual Partnerships among Female Sex Workers and Their Non-commercial Male Partners in Tijuana and Ciudad Juarez, Mexico." *Sexually Transmitted Infections* 89 (4): 330–32.

Robertson, Angela M., Jennifer L. Syvertsen, Monica D. Ulibarri, M. Gudelia Rangel, Gustavo Martinez, and Steffanie A. Strathdee. 2014c. "Prevalence and Correlates of HIV and Sexually Transmitted Infections among Female Sex Workers and Their Non-commercial Male Partners in Two Mexico-USA Border Cities." *Journal of Urban Health* 91 (4): 752–67.

Rolon, María Luisa, Jennifer L. Syvertsen, Angela M. Robertson, M. Gudelia Rangel, Gustavo Martinez, Monica D. Ulibarri, Argentina Servin, and Steffanie A. Strathdee. 2013. "The Influence of Having Children on HIV-Related Risk Behaviors of Female Sex Workers and Their Intimate Male Partners in Two Mexico-US Border Cities." *Journal of Tropical Pediatrics* 59 (3): 214–19.

Romero-Daza, Nancy, Margaret Weeks, and Merrill Singer. 2003. "'Nobody Gives a Damn If I Live or Die': Violence, Drugs, and Street-Level Prostitution in Inner-City Hartford, Connecticut." *Medical Anthropology* 22 (3): 233–59.

Salas-Espinoza, Kristian Jesús, Rufino Menchaca-Diaz, Thomas L. Patterson, Lianne A. Urada, Davey Smith, Steffanie A. Strathdee, and Eileen V. Pitpitan. 2017. "HIV Prevalence and Risk Behaviors in Male to Female (MTF) Transgender Persons in Tijuana, Mexico." *AIDS and Behavior* 21 (12): 3271–78.

Sanders, Teela. 2002. "The Condom as Psychological Barrier: Female Sex Workers and Emotional Management." *Feminism and Psychology* 12 (4): 561–66.

———. 2004. "A Continuum of Risk? The Management of Health, Physical and Emotional Risks by Female Sex Workers." *Sociology of Health and Illness* 26 (5): 557–74.

Sandoval, Chela. 2000. *Methodology of the Oppressed*. Minneapolis: University of Minnesota Press.

Schensul, Stephen L., Jean J. Schensul, Merrill Singer, Margaret Weeks, and Marie Brault. 2014. "Participatory Methods and Community-Based Collaborations." In *Handbook of Methods in Cultural Anthropology*, edited by H. Russell Bernard and Clarence C. Gravlee, 185–212. Lanham, MD: Rowman and Littlefield.

Scheper-Hughes, Nancy, and Margaret M. Lock. 1987. "The Mindful Body: A Prolegomenon to Future Work in Medical Anthropology." *Medical Anthropology Quarterly* 1 (1): 6–41.

Segovia, Jimena Silva, and Estefany Castillo Ravanal. 2021 "Estudio de las emociones mercantilizadas que circulan entre trabajadoras sexuales, hombres mineros y sus parejas, en la cultura minera de Antofagasta, Chile." *Revista Latinoamericana de Estudios sobre Cuerpos, Emociones y Sociedad* 13 (36): 44–57.

Shannon, Kate, Anna-Louise Crago, Stefan D. Baral, Linda-Gail Bekker, Deanna Kerrigan, Michele R. Decker, Tonia Poteat, Andrea L. Wirtz, Brian Weir, and Marie-Claude Boily. 2018. "The Global Response and Unmet Actions for HIV and Sex Workers." *Lancet* 392 (10148): 698–710.

Shannon, Kate, Steffanie A. Strathdee, Shira M. Goldenberg, Putu Duff, Peninah Mwangi, Maia Rusakova, Sushena Reza-Paul, Joseph Lau, Kathleen Deering, Michael R. Pickles, and Marie-Claude Boily. 2015. "Global Epidemiology of HIV among Female Sex Workers: Influence of Structural Determinants." *Lancet* 385 (9962): 55–71.

Simmons, Janie, and Merrill Singer. 2006. "I Love You . . . and Heroin: Care and Collusion among Drug-Using Couples." *Substance Abuse Treatment, Prevention, and Policy* 1:7.

Singer, Merrill, and Hans Baer. 2018. *Critical Medical Anthropology*. London: Routledge.

Sirotin, Nicole, Steffanie A. Strathdee, Remedios Lozada, Lucie Nguyen, Manual Gallardo, Alicia Vera, and Thomas L. Patterson. 2010a. "A Comparison of Registered and Unregistered Female Sex Workers in Tijuana, Mexico." Supplement, *Public Health Reports* 125 (S4): S101–9.

Sirotin, Nicole, Steffanie A. Strathdee, Remedios Lozada, Daniela Abramovitz, Shirley J. Semple, Jesús Bucardo, and Thomas L. Patterson. 2010b. "Effects of Government Registration on Unprotected Sex amongst Female Sex Workers in Tijuana; Mexico." *International Journal of Drug Policy* 21 (6): 466–70.

Smith, Daniel Jordan. 2008. "Intimacy, Infidelity, and Masculinity in Southeastern Nigeria." In Jankowiak 2008, 224–44.

Sobo, Elisa Janine. 1995. *Choosing Unsafe Sex: AIDS-Risk Denial among Disadvantaged Women*. Philadelphia: University of Pennsylvania Press.

Sonke, Jill, Tasha Golden, Samantha Francois, Jamie Hand, Anita Chandra, Lydia Clemmons, David Fakunle, Maria Rosario Jackson, Susan Magsamen, Victor Rubin, Kelley Sams, and Stacey Springs. 2019. *Creating Healthy Communities through Cross-Sector Collaboration.* White paper. Gainesville: University of Florida Center for Arts in Medicine.

Speed, Shannon. 2006. "At the Crossroads of Human Rights and Anthropology: Toward a Critically Engaged Activist Research." *American Anthropologist* 108 (1): 66–76.

Sterk, Claire. 1999. *Fast Lives: Women Who Use Crack Cocaine.* Philadelphia: Temple University Press.

———. 2000. *Tricking and Tripping: Prostitution in the Era of AIDS.* Putnam Valley, NY: Social Change Press.

Stoebenau, Kirsten, Michelle J. Hindin, Constance A. Nathanson, Paul Ghislain Rakotoarison, and Violette Razafintsalama. 2009. "'But Then He Became My Sipa': The Implications of Relationship Fluidity for Condom Use among Women Sex Workers in Antananarivo, Madagascar." *American Journal of Public Health* 99 (5): 811–19.

Strathdee, S.A., Daniela Abramovitz, Remedios Lozada, Gustavo Martinez, Maria Gudelia Rangel, Alicia Vera, Hugo Staines, Carlos Magis-Rodriguez, and Thomas L. Patterson. 2013. "Reductions in HIV/STI Incidence and Sharing of Injection Equipment among Female Sex Workers Who Inject Drugs: Results from a Randomized Controlled Trial." *PLOS One* 8 (6): e65812.

Strathdee, Steffanie A., Jaime Arredondo, Teresita Rocha, Daniela Abramovitz, María Luisa Rolon, Efrain Patiño Mandujano, Maria Gudelia Rangel, Horcasitas Omar Olivarria, Tommi Gaines, and Thomas L. Patterson. 2015. "A Police Education Programme to Integrate Occupational Safety and HIV Prevention: Protocol for a Modified Stepped-Wedge Study Design with Parallel Prospective Cohorts to Assess Behavioural Outcomes." *BMJ Open* 5 (8): e008958.

Strathdee, Steffanie A., Leo Beletsky, and Thomas Kerr. 2015. "HIV, Drugs and the Legal Environment." Supplement, *International Journal of Drug Policy* 26 (S1): S27–32.

Strathdee, S.A., R. Lozada, R.A. Pollini, K.C. Brouwer, A. Mantsios, D.A. Abramovitz, T. Rhodes, C.A. Latkin, O. Loza, and J. Alvelais. 2008a. "Individual, Social, and Environmental Influences Associated with HIV Infection among Injection Drug Users in Tijuana, Mexico." *Journal of Acquired Immune Deficiency Syndromes* 47 (3): 369–76.

Strathdee Steffanie A., Brent Mausbach, Remedios Lozada, Hugo Staines-Orozco, Shirley J. Semple, Daniela Abramovitz, Miguel Fraga-Vallejo, Adela de la Torre, Hortensia Amaro, Gustavo Martinez-Mendizabal, Carlos Magis-Rodriguez, and Thomas L Patterson. 2009. "Predictors of Sexual Risk Reduction among Mexican Female Sex Workers Enrolled in a Behavioral Intervention Study." Supplement, *Journal of Acquired Immunodeficiency Syndrome* 51 (S1): S42–46.

Strathdee, Steffanie A., Morgan M. Philbin, Shirley J. Semple, Minya Pu, Prisci Orozovich, Gustavo Martinez, Remedios Lozada, Miguel Fraga, Adela de la Torre, Hugo Staines, Carlos Magis-Rodriguez, and Thomas L. Patterson. 2008b. "Correlates of Injection Drug Use among Female Sex Workers in Two Mexico-US Border Cities." *Drug and Alcohol Dependence* 92 (1–3): 132–40.

Strega, Susan, and Leslie Brown, eds. 2015. *Research as Resistance: Revisiting Critical, Indigenous, and Anti-oppressive Approaches.* 2nd ed. Toronto: Canadian Scholars' Press.

Structural Competency Working Group. 2020. "Structural Competency Working Group." Accessed May 5, 2022. www.structcomp.org.

Syvertsen, Jennifer L. 2012. "Sex Work, Heroin Injection, and Love in Tijuana: A Case Study." Invited Panel, "Steps toward an Anthropology of Affect." Annual Meetings of the American Anthropological Association, San Francisco, CA, November 15, 2012.

———. 2019. "Death Poems for Cindy." *Medicine Anthropology Theory: An Open-Access Journal in the Anthropology of Health, Illness, and Medicine* 6 (2): 120–32.

Syvertsen, Jennifer L., and Angela M. Robertson Bazzi. 2015. "Sex Work, Heroin Injection, and HIV Risk in Tijuana: A Love Story." In "The Ethnography of Affect." Special issue, *Anthropology of Consciousness* 26 (2): 191–206.

Syvertsen, Jennifer L., Angela Robertson Bazzi, and María Luisa Mittal. 2017. "Hope amidst Horror: Documenting the Effects of the 'War on Drugs' among Female Sex Workers and Their Intimate Partners in Tijuana, Mexico." In "Crafting Synergies between Medical and Visual Anthropologies." Special issue, *Medical Anthropology* 36 (6): 566–83.

Syvertsen, Jennifer L., Angela M. Robertson Bazzi, Andrew Scheibe, Sylvia Adebajo, Steffanie A. Strathdee, and Wendee M. Wechsberg. 2014. "The Promise and Peril of Pre-exposure Prophylaxis (PrEP): Using Social Science to Inform PrEP Interventions among Female Sex Workers." *African Journal of Reproductive Health* 18 (3): 74–83.

Syvertsen, Jennifer, Robin A. Pollini, Remedios Lozada, Alicia Vera, Gudelia Rangel, and Steffanie A. Strathdee. 2010. "Managing la Malilla: Exploring Drug Treatment Experiences among Injection Drug Users in Tijuana, Mexico, and Their Implications for Drug Law Reform." *International Journal of Drug Policy* 21 (6): 459–65.

Syvertsen, Jennifer L., Angela M. Robertson, Lawrence A. Palinkas, Gudelia M. Rangel, Gustavo Martinez, and Steffanie A. Strathdee. 2013. "Where Sex Ends and Emotions Begin: Love and HIV Risk among Female Sex Workers and Their Non-commercial Partners along the Mexico-U.S. Border." *Culture, Health and Sexuality* 15 (5): 540–54.

Syvertsen, Jennifer L., Hannah Toneff, Heather Howard, Christine Spadola, Danielle Madden, and John Clapp. 2021. "Conceptualizing Stigma in Contexts of Pregnancy and Opioid Misuse: A Qualitative Study with Women and Healthcare Providers in Ohio." *Drug and Alcohol Dependence* 222:108677.

Tsapelas, Irene, Helen E. Fisher, and Arthur Aron. 2010. "Infidelity: When, Where, Why." In *The Dark Side of Close Relationships II*, edited by William R. Cupach and Brian H. Spitzberg, 195–216. New York: Routledge.

Ulibarri, Monica D., Marissa Salazar, Jennifer L. Syvertsen, Angela R. Bazzi, M. Gudelia Rangel, Hugo Staines Orozco, and Steffanie A. Strathdee. 2019. "Intimate Partner Violence among Female Sex Workers and Their Noncommercial Male Partners in Mexico: A Mixed-Methods Study." *Violence against Women* 25 (5): 549–71.

Ulibarri, Monica D., Steffanie A. Strathdee, Remedios Lozada, Hugo S. Staines-Orozco, Daniela Abramovitz, Shirley J. Semple, Gustavo Martinez, and Thomas L. Patterson. 2012. "Condom Use among Female Sex Workers and Their Non-commercial Partners: Effects of a Sexual Risk Intervention in Two Mexican Cities." *International Journal of STD and AIDS* 23 (4): 229–34.

Urada, Lianne A., Andrés Gaeta-Rivera, Jessica Kim, Patricia E. González-Zúñiga, and Kimberly C. Brouwer. 2021. "Mujeres Unidas: Addressing Substance Use, Violence, and HIV Risk through Asset-Based Community Development for Women in the Sex Trade." *International Journal of Environmental Research and Public Health* 18:3884.

US Department of Homeland Security. 2012. *Yearbook of Immigration Statistics: 2011.* Washington, DC: Office of Immigration Statistics, US Department of Homeland Security.

US Department of State. 2021. *U.S. Relations with Mexico: Bilateral Relations Fact Sheet.* Accessed May 14, 2022. www.state.gov/u-s-relations-with-mexico/.

US Department of Transportation. 2011. "Border Crossing/Entry Data: Annual Data." Bureau of Transportation Statistics. Accessed May 18, 2022. https://explore.dot.gov /views/BorderCrossingData/Annual?%3Aembed=y&%3AisGuestRedirectFrom Vizportal=y.

———. n.d. "Border Crossing/Entry Data." Bureau of Transportation Statistics. Accessed May 18, 2022. www.bts.gov/browse-statistical-products-and-data/border-crossing-data /border-crossingentry-data.

Valdez, Avelardo, Charles D. Kaplan, and Alice Cepeda. 2000. "The Process of Paradoxical Autonomy and Survival in the Heroin Careers of Mexican American Women." *Contemporary Drug Problems* 27 (1): 189–212.

Van Boekel, Leonieke C., Evelien P.M. Brouwers, Jaap Van Weeghel, and Henk F.L. Garretsen. 2013. "Stigma among Health Professionals towards Patients with Substance Use Disorders and Its Consequences for Healthcare Delivery: Systematic Review." *Drug and Alcohol Dependence* 131 (1): 23–35.

Van der Straten, Ariane, Jonathan Stadler, Elizabeth Montgomery, Miriam Hartmann, Busiswe Magazi, Florence Mathebula, Katie Schwartz, Nicole Laborde, and Lydia Soto-Torres. 2014. "Women's Experiences with Oral and Vaginal Pre-exposure Prophylaxis: The VOICE-C Qualitative Study in Johannesburg, South Africa." *PLOS One* 9 (2): e89118.

Vanderwood, Paul J. 2009. *Satan's Playground: Mobsters and Movie Stars at America's Greatest Gaming Resort.* Durham, NC: Duke University Press.

VANDU (Vancouver Area Network of Drug Users). n.d. "Research and Drug User Liberation and Research and the Drug War." Accessed May 14, 2022. https://vandureplace .wordpress.com/research/.

Vargas, João H. Costa. 2008. "Activist Scholarship: Limits and Possibilities in Times of Black Genocide." In Hale 2008, 164–82.

Vera, Alicia, Daniela Abramovitz, Remedios Lozada, Gustavo Martinez, M. Gudelia Rangel, Hugo Staines, Thomas L. Patterson, and Steffanie A. Strathdee. 2012. "Mujer Mas Segura (Safer Women): A Combination Prevention Intervention to Reduce Sexual and Injection Risks among Female Sex Workers Who Inject Drugs." *BMC Public Health* 12:653.

Wagner, Karla D., Jennifer L. Syvertsen, Silvia R. Verdugo, Jose Luis Molina, and Steffanie A. Strathdee. 2018. "A Mixed Methods Study of the Social Networks of Female Sex Workers and Their Primary Non-commercial Male Partners in Tijuana, Mexico." *Journal of Mixed Methods Research* 12 (4): 437–57.

Wallerstein, Nina, and Bonnie Duran. 2010. "Community-Based Participatory Research Contributions to Intervention Research: The Intersection of Science and Practice to Improve Health Equity." Supplement, *American Journal of Public Health* 100 (S1): S40–46.

Wallerstein, Nina, Bonnie Duran, John G. Oetzel, and Meredith Minkler. 2017. *Community-Based Participatory Research for Health: Advancing Social and Health Equity.* San Francisco: Wiley and Sons.

Wang, Caroline, Wu Kun Yi, Zhan Wen Tao, and Kathryn Carovano. 1998. "Photovoice as a Participatory Health Promotion Strategy." *Health Promotion International* 13 (1): 75–86.

Wanyenze, Rhoda K., Geofrey Musinguzi, Juliet Kiguli, Fred Nuwaha, Geoffrey Mujisha, Joshua Musinguzi, Jim Arinaitwe, and Joseph K.B. Matovu. 2017. "'When They Know

That You Are a Sex Worker, You Will Be the Last Person to Be Treated': Perceptions and Experiences of Female Sex Workers in Accessing HIV Services in Uganda." *BMC International Health and Human Rights* 17:11.

Warr, Deborah J., and Priscilla M. Pyett. 1999. "Difficult Relations: Sex, Work, Love and Intimacy." *Sociology of Health and Illness* 21 (3): 290–309.

Wechsberg, Wendee M., Nabila El-Bassel, Tara Carney, Felicia A. Browne, Bronwyn Myers, and William A. Zule. 2015. "Adapting an Evidence-Based HIV Behavioral Intervention for South African Couples." *Substance Abuse Treatment, Prevention, and Policy* 10:6.

Werb, Dan, Greg Rowell, Gordon Guyatt, Thomas Kerr, Julio Montaner, and Evan Wood. 2011. "Effect of Drug Law Enforcement on Drug Market Violence: A Systematic Review." *International Journal of Drug Policy* 22 (2): 87–94.

West, Brooke S., Brandy F. Henry, Niloufar Agah, Alicia Vera, Leo Beletsky, M. Gudelia Rangel, Hugo Staines, Thomas L. Patterson, and Steffanie A. Strathdee. 2020. "Typologies and Correlates of Police Violence against Female Sex Workers Who Inject Drugs at the México–United States Border: Limits of De Jure Decriminalization in Advancing Health and Human Rights." *Journal of Interpersonal Violence* 1–28.

Williams, Erica Lorraine. 2013. *Sex Tourism in Bahia. Ambiguous Entanglements*. Urbana: University of Illinois Press.

Zedillo, Ernesto, Catalina Perez-Correa, Alejandro Madrazo, and Fernanda Alonso. 2019. "Drug Policy in Mexico: The Cause of a National Tragedy; A Radical but Indispensable Proposal to Fix It." *University of Pennsylvania Journal of International Law* 41 (1): 107–76.

Zelizer, Viviana. 2005. *The Purchase of Intimacy*. Princeton: Princeton University Press.

Zigon, Jarrett. 2013. "On Love: Remaking Moral Subjectivity in Postrehabilitation Russia." *American Ethnologist* 40 (1): 201–15.

Zuberi, Tukufu, and Eduardo Bonilla-Silva. 2008. *White Logic, White Methods: Racism and Methodology*. Lanham, MD: Rowman and Littlefield.